MEETING GOD AND THE TOOTH FAIRY

ON THE ROAD TO THE GRAVE

JOHN HUNT

I would like to dedicate every word and syllable of this book to my Lord and Savior, Jesus Christ, whose incredible and astonishing mercy and forgiveness can never be fully comprehended or appreciated.

Acknowledgments

I would like to acknowledge Lori Cripe and her daughters, Valerie and Natelli, with my deepest gratitude and heartfelt thanks for both typing and editing this second volume of a three-part trilogy dealing with various biblical insights. In addition, I am sincerely grateful to Terry Jo Bates for her beautiful and penetrating cover design.

I am extremely grateful for the moral support I have received from my wife, Gail; my son, Caleb, and his wife, Christina; my daughter, Rachel, and her husband, Alex; my father, Vern; my brothers, Greg, Tom, Pat, and Tim; and my sisters, Theresa and Florence.

I also very much appreciate the constant encouragement and inspiration I have received over these many years from all of my brothers and sisters who have attended my Bible study classes. Thank you!

A Note on Quotations

All Scripture quotations are from the New American Standard Bible unless otherwise indicated. The following abbreviations are used for other versions:

KJV   The King James Version

NIV   The New International Version

All italics within quotations were added by the author.

CONTENTS

Preface

I am not a writer, and perhaps most people would agree with this statement. My first attempt at writing anything was in grade school when I was required to write an essay about some personal adventure. I made up a whopping big-fish story about catching a huge fish in Clear Lake, California. I told of how this giant fish pulled both me and my man-made raft all around the lake in its herculean efforts to break loose of me and my fishing pole, but in the end, I managed to land this gigantic black bass onto my floating platform of wooden planks and logs.

I was truly proud of what I had written and thought for sure that I would earn a good grade for all my efforts. Instead, my teacher thought my story was so ridiculous that she read it out loud to the whole class and made sure to make fun of all my misspellings and incorrect grammar and misplaced punctuation marks. She managed to get the entire class laughing at me and making fun of how stupid my story was and how pathetically pitiful my writing happened to be. I was so embarrassed and humiliated by that experience that I never wanted to write again for as long as I lived.

However, when I became a Christian, I felt God was telling me to write for Him, so I followed His nudging to express my thoughts on paper. When manuscript after manuscript and book after book were rejected by one publisher after another, I concluded that God wasn't telling me to write after all. Therefore, I once again put down my pen and pushed aside my writing tablet with another sense of failure and defeat.

Years later, after experiencing a crushing and terrifying attack of the devil, I just started writing without planning to do so and without even praying about it. Instead, the words just started flowing from my heart onto the paper in front of me. I clearly felt God's Spirit urging me to write again, in spite of not being a writer (especially not a good one).

My first published book was titled, "Hopscotching to Hell, Sleepwalking to Heaven," and it was intended to be the first book

1

in a three-part series dealing with many different Scripture verses and the profound insights and personal applications they contain. Well, as I said, I am not a writer, nor am I a good speller or an excellent typist. The truth is, I am one of the least likely candidates that God could call to write on His behalf. However, if these words of mine are truly from Him, then all I can do is believe what He said through his apostle Paul:

> For consider your calling, brethren, that there were not many wise according to the flesh, not many mighty, not many noble; but God has chosen the foolish things of the world to shame the wise, and God has chosen the weak things of the world to shame the things which are strong, and the base things of the world and the despised God has chosen, the things that are not, so that He may nullify the things that are, so that no man may boast before God. (1 Corinthians 1:26-29)

Meeting God and the Tooth Fairy

It is the most natural thing in the world for a child to believe in God because God has put the knowledge of Himself in each and every human being's heart. However, the fool, the ignoramus, and the God hater will sneer at such a reality, saying: "Of course children will believe in God if you tell them that such a Divine Being exists, because a child is just a naïve and gullible simpleton who will also believe in Santa Claus, the Easter Bunny, and the Tooth Fairy if you say they are real." But what these cynics do not realize is that when you tell a child a fanciful story, you are merely speaking to his or her budding imagination and the wonders of something exciting and amazing in their minds. In short, you are only speaking to a child's intellect and not to his God-given spirit—a spirit which has a built-in God consciousness regardless of how others may distort the true image of one's Creator.

Consequently, there is a vast difference between stimulating a child's mind with colorful fantasies and speaking to them about that which is "evident within them; for God has made it evident to them" (Romans 1:19). In addition, it was the wisest of wise men, King Solomon, who wrote:

> Rejoice, young man, during your childhood, and let your heart be pleasant during the days of young manhood. And follow the impulses of your heart and the desires of your eyes. Yet know that God will bring you to judgment for all these things. So, remove grief and anger from your heart and put away pain from your body, because childhood and the prime of life are fleeting.
>
> Remember also your Creator in the days of your youth, before the evil days come and the years draw near when you will say, "I have no delight in them." (Ecclesiastes 11:9-10; 12:1)

These words of the enlightened sage emphasize the truth of a child's capacity to believe and trust in God. However, he reflectively warns that the passage of time and the difficulties of life are bound to make men neglect or forget God if they do not make Him a priority in their lives when they are young. In other words, he cautions young people by declaring that pain, heartbreak, disillusionment, sin, and growing old are destined to destroy or greatly diminish their faith if they fail to cultivate this God gene which is infused within them at their conception.

Furthermore, it was Jesus Christ who said: "Truly I say to you, unless you are converted and become like children, you will not enter the kingdom of heaven"; and when dealing with the arrogant and self-righteous grown-ups of His day, Jesus said: "I thank thee, O Father, Lord of heaven and earth, because thou hast hid these things [God's truths] from the wise and prudent, and has revealed them unto babes." When children were shouting with excitement in the temple over Christ's presence and declaring, "Hosanna to the Son of David," the religious adults cynically asked Jesus, "Do You hear what these children are saying?" To this, Jesus responded, "Yes; have you never read, 'Out of the mouth of infants and nursing babies You have prepared praise for Yourself'?" (Matthew 18:3; 11:25, KJV; 21:15-16).

Lastly, just a surface check of God's Word reveals dozens of times where God addresses all those who honor and obey Him as His "children" — regardless of their age. Those who declare that a child's faith in God is as ridiculous as believing in tooth fairies are blinded by their smug sophistication, and God mocks their "intelligence" with the very wisdom of the children whose faith they ridicule.

The Road to the Grave

A man was strolling along a beach one morning and he happened to find a golden lantern which had washed upon the seashore. Out of curiosity, the fellow picked it up and read the inscription on its side which promised that whoever rubs this enchanted lamp would be granted any wish. The skeptical individual hesitantly rubbed the shining object and, lo and behold, a genie appeared! The ghostly specter then said he would grant the man whatever his heart desired. However, he could only have one request and one request only.

The man was beside himself with excitement when he exclaimed to the genie, "Really?! Well, today is my 60th birthday, and the 60-year-old bag that I am married to is just not what she used to be! So what I would like is a wife that is 30 years younger than myself!" The genie then smiled and said, "Your request is granted" — and instantly the genie transformed the guy into a 90-year-old man!

Well, it doesn't take a genie to turn a person into an "old person." An insightful poem declares:

> When I was young, I laughed and I wept,
> And time crept.
> When I was a youth, I dreamed and I talked,
> And time walked.
> When I became a full-grown man,
> Then time ran.
> When older still, as I daily grew,
> Then time flew.
> Soon I will quickly see that as I travel on,
> My time is gone.

There is a frightful tale about two teenagers who were speeding down the highway in a car one night as they were drinking and laughing and whooping it up, when suddenly the driver lost control of the vehicle, careened off the road, and slammed into a giant oak tree. The impact instantly killed his best friend who was sitting in the passenger's seat. Shortly after the collision, the driver regained consciousness just in time to see the Grim Reaper dragging his companion's soul into the darkness. He watched in horror as his friend screamed and kicked in a desperate attempt to free himself from the icy grip of the Rider of Death. Unable to help his buddy, the survivor of that fatal crash cried out to the Grim Reaper: "Rider of Death, Rider of Death! Wait, wait one minute! I have a request to ask of you." The Grim Reaper paused, slowly turned his head and gazed at him with an icy stare, and inquired, "What is it that you want of me?" The injured young man replied, "I want you to warn me of your coming before I am about to die, so I can prepare myself for you ahead of time." He continued by promising the Grim Reaper if he would but warn him of his arrival, he would go with him into eternity without any protest, unlike his deceased friend. The ghastly apparition considered the young man's proposal and responded with his slow and menacing voice, "Your request is granted!" and then he vanished, pulling the spirit of his friend into the blackness of that night.

Well, the young man eventually recovered from all of his injuries and continued to live a life of wanton pleasure, selfishness, and greed. As the weeks and months and years passed, the man thought nothing of his soul or of his eternal destiny. Decades later, he was sitting at his desk one night and evaluating all of his wealth. Suddenly, the Grim Reaper appeared before him and reached his freezing hand into the man's chest and violently clutched his heart with his bony fingers. The old man then began to suffer from a massive heart attack and cried out, "Wait a minute, wait a minute! You were supposed to warn me of your coming—We had an agreement!"

The Rider of Death peered into the dying man's eyes and proclaimed, "Oh, but I did warn you! I warned you over and over again that I was coming: With every missing hair on your head and every gray hair in your beard, I warned you. With each new wrinkle on your face, I warned you. With your diminishing health, loss of memory, and declining strength, I warned you. Repeatedly, I let you know I was on my way, getting closer and closer to overtaking you. But you didn't listen! You didn't heed! You fool, tonight your soul is required of you and you have done absolutely nothing to prepare for my arrival. Now I will drag your lost soul into eternal judgment." As the old man's spirit left his dying body, he went kicking and screaming into the darkness exactly like his friend did so many years before.

Most people don't realize this story is actually written in their Bible. It is a tale told by the wisest of wise men in Ecclesiastes Chapter 12, which can be referred to, in short, as "the road to dilapidation" or "the road to the grave." Everyone is on this road whether they care to believe it or not, and the Grim Reaper is under no obligation to warn anyone of his coming. Nevertheless, he often does announce his silent and steady pursuit with death's warning signs that, the older one gets, can be seen and heard more frequently. A wise person can read his signs and discern his voice. Solomon wrote:

> Remember also your Creator in the days of your youth, before the evil days come and the years draw near when you will say, "I have no delight in them"; before the sun and the light, the moon and the stars are darkened (no bright days lie ahead), and clouds return after the rain (nothing to look forward to); in the day that the watchmen of the house (our hands, our body) tremble (from old age), and mighty men (our legs) stoop, the grinding ones (our teeth) stand idle because they are few, and those who look through windows grow dim (our eyes fail); and the doors on the street (our mouths) are shut as the sound of the grinding mill is low (the loss of our hearing) and one will arise at the sound of the bird (don't sleep well and arise early), and all the daughters of song will sing softly (unable to loudly project one's voice). Furthermore,

men are afraid of a high place (afraid to climb) and of terrors on the road (always walk cautiously); the almond tree blossoms (hair turns white), the grasshopper drags himself along (walks slowly with canes or walkers), and the caperberry (aphrodisiac or Viagra) is ineffective. For man goes to his eternal home (dies) while mourners go about in the street (life goes on without them). Remember Him before the silver cord (one's nervous system) is broken and the golden bowl (one's mind or memory) is crushed, the pitcher by the well (one's circulatory system) is shattered and the wheel at the cistern (one's heart) is crushed; then the dust will return to the earth as it was, and the spirit will return to God who gave it. … The conclusion, when all has been heard, is: fear God and keep His commandments, because this applies to every person. For God will bring every act to judgment, everything which is hidden, whether it is good or evil. (Ecclesiastes 12:1-7, 13-14)

Yes, "it is appointed for men to die once and after this comes judgment" (Hebrews 9:27). It doesn't take a genie to quickly turn someone into an old person. The elderly can attest that the years fly by and then, before we know it, we find ourselves face to face with the Grim Reaper. He has been known to slay infants, and to cut down the young, and to kill the strong without warning; but he most often will signal his approach many times, in numerous ways, before he swings the final blow with his sickle of death. The road to the cemetery may seem like it will go on forever, but even those who manage to live the longest will always claim that their earthly pilgrimage was very, very short when they come face to face with the rider on the ashen horse whose name is "Death" (Revelation 6:8). Consequently, it is only the wise and the discerning person who can interpret death's warning signs and diligently prepare and direct one's final steps on this very short and very quick road to the grave.

A Tale Told by an Idiot

New research by the British Medical Journal (BMJ) has scientifically tested and verified what is referred to as the "Male Idiot Theory."[1] In essence, the BMJ's fact-finding research proclaims that men really are "idiots" who are driven to take ridiculous risks despite the clear and obvious prospects for self-harm or self-destruction, and that the incredible gambles men take with their lives are almost always done for no defensible reason. The researchers noted an astonishingly lopsided gender difference when it came to handing out the "Darwin Awards"; many more men than women were the recipients.

Simply put, the Darwin Awards are a tongue-in-cheek honor bestowed upon people who do the most foolish things imaginable which are almost guaranteed to result in serious injury or even death. Nearly all of these awards are conferred upon someone who has been killed in the process of engaging in utterly asinine behavior. Therefore, since women can seldom compete with the stupidity of men when it comes to ludicrous conduct, they are rarely endowed with such a distinguished citation as the Darwin Award.

However, anyone who survives a moronic death-defying feat can only be honored with the award if he or she agrees to be sterilized. The entire purpose behind the Darwin Award is to honor the idiotic individuals because they have done all of humanity a great service by eliminating themselves from the human gene pool and thereby assuring the survival of mankind. Their sterilization or death puts an end to the frightful possibility of them having any offspring who are sure to carry the same DNA of imbecility.

Yet there is a form of foolishness and lunacy that far exceeds anything for which the honorees of the Darwin Award are adorned. This is the recognition of being a "fool" that is so preoccupied with this present world that he or she neglects the very reason for their existence. It is a distinction granted to all those who do not put God at the center of their lives by repenting of their sins and committing themselves to the Lord Jesus Christ. These are the ones that the Bible refers to as fools who end up putting their eternal lives, not merely their physical well-being, in danger. No amount of foolish behavior in this world can compare with the risks and perils which people take when it comes to endangering their souls. Over and over again, God's Word refers to such individuals as "fools," and there is not a lost soul in hell today who would not fully agree with this assessment.

Consider Christ's words, "[W]hat does it profit a man to gain the whole world, and forfeit his soul" and "Do not fear those who kill the body but are unable to kill the soul; but rather fear Him who is able to destroy both soul and body in hell." He also asked, "[W]hat will a man give in exchange for his soul?" To the wealthy individual who was totally focused on this world and assumed he had many years remaining in this life, God said, "You fool! This very night your soul is required of you." And, as Jesus explained, "So is the man who stores up treasure for himself, and is not rich towards God" (Mark 8:36; Matthew 10:28; 16:26; Luke 12:20-21).

Shakespeare summed up this kind of life without eternal purpose best when he wrote in his play titled *Macbeth* (Act V, scene 5): "Life is but a walking shadow, a poor player that struts and frets his hour upon the stage and then is heard of no more." He said, "Life is merely a tale told by an idiot — full of sound and fury and signifying nothing." This is exactly — *exactly* — what life becomes without God at the center of our lives and without Jesus Christ as the anchor of our souls! It is "vanity of vanities…All is vanity" (Ecclesiastes 1:2). Remember, there is a type of foolishness that far exceeds the idiotic behavior honored by the Darwin trophy, and it is a recognition that is granted to both men and women alike, to both genders equally throughout all ages — and that is the title of "fool" — an eternal fool.

The Bucket List of a Fool

A bucket list is simply described as a "to-do list" that someone wants to carry out before they die. In other words, it is a checklist of things that people are determined to experience before their lives come to a close, and the lists that people compile can be as varied as the human race itself—from becoming famous to traveling, and from skydiving or bungee-cord jumping to losing weight or accumulating riches.

The Bible talks about a man who had a bucket list that failed to include the most important thing of all. In the eyes of the world, this man's to-do list may have appeared very worthwhile, but in the eyes of heaven his goals were extremely foolish because his plans did not include God or the afterlife. Jesus Christ described this short-sighted man in the 12th chapter of Luke:

> The land of a rich man was very productive. And he began reasoning to himself, saying, "What shall I do, since I have no place to store my crops?" Then he said, "This is what I will do: I will tear down my barns and build larger ones, and there I will store all my grain and my goods. And I will say to my soul, 'Soul, you have many goods laid up for many years to come; take your ease, eat, drink and be merry.'" But God said to him, "You fool! This very night your soul is required of you; and now who will own what you have prepared?" So is the man who stores up treasure for himself, and is not rich toward God. (vv. 16-21)

On another occasion, Christ also questioned the crowds, saying:

> For what does it profit a man to gain the whole world, and forfeit his soul? For what will a man give in exchange for his soul? For whoever is

ashamed of Me and My words in this adulterous and sinful generation, the Son of Man will also be ashamed of him when He comes in the glory of His Father with the holy angels. (Mark 8:36-38)

These words of Jesus strike at the very heart of every bucket list of man, declaring that there is only one agenda that truly matters in the end, and that failure to put this essential on the top of everyone's checklist is the most foolish thing anyone could possibly do. In short, the most important bucket list of all can be summed up in the closing words of the very last book in the Bible:

"Behold, I [Jesus] am coming quickly, and My reward is with Me, to render to every man according to what he has done. I am the Alpha and the Omega, the first and the last, the beginning and the end. Blessed are those who wash their robes, so that they may have the right to the tree of life, and may enter by the gates into the city. Outside are the dogs and the sorcerers and the immoral persons and the murderers and the idolaters, and everyone who loves and practices lying. ..." The Spirit and the bride say, "Come." And let the one who hears say, "Come." And let the one who is thirsty come; let the one who wishes take the water of life without cost. (Revelation 22:12-15, 17)

To wash one's clothing (or spiritual "robe") and make it white in the blood of the lamb is the only action that ultimately matters in this life, and any bucket list that does not include this as the number-one priority becomes just the agenda of a shortsighted fool.

In conclusion, the bucket list of most people is something that can be checked off at some future date that does not involve any sense of urgency. However, God's bucket list for the life of every person says, "'At the acceptable time I listened to you, and on the day of salvation I helped you.' Behold, now is 'the acceptable time,' behold, now is 'the day of salvation'" (2 Corinthians 6:2). And God warns through His prophet Jeremiah that if we continue to procrastinate in getting right with God, our eternal epitaph will someday read: "Harvest is past, summer is ended, and we are not saved" (Jeremiah 8:20).

The Bliss of Being Known in Hell

Imagine standing outside of any Christian church on any given Sunday and asking each person coming out of the worship service, "Would you like to be known in heaven?" Chances are virtually everyone will not hesitate to say, "Of course I want to be known in heaven! Doesn't everyone?" Now suppose you asked everyone coming out of church this question instead: "Would you like to be known in hell?" There is a very good likelihood that most people would look at you with bewilderment or indignation and respond with, "What kind of question is that? Of course I don't want to be known in hell! Who in their right mind would?"

However, if someone were to ask me whether or not I wanted to be known in hell, my reply would be, "I definitely want to be known in hell—because if I am not known in hell, then I am not known in heaven either!" This is because in the 19th chapter of the book of Acts, Luke records a very interesting episode in the missionary experiences of the apostle Paul. He writes:

> God was performing extraordinary miracles by the hands of Paul, so that handkerchiefs or aprons were even carried from his body to the sick, and the diseases left them and the evil spirits went out. But also some of the Jewish exorcists, who went from place to place, attempted to name over those who had the evil spirits the name of the Lord Jesus, saying, "I adjure you by Jesus whom Paul preaches." Seven sons of one Sceva, a Jewish chief priest, were doing this. And the evil spirit answered and said to them, *"I recognize Jesus, and I know about Paul, but who are you?"* And the man, in whom was the evil spirit, leaped on them and subdued all of them and overpowered them, so that they fled out of that house naked and wounded.
>
> This became known to all, both Jews and Greeks, who lived in Ephesus; and fear fell upon

them all and the name of the Lord Jesus was being magnified. Many also of those who had believed kept coming, confessing and disclosing their practices. And many of those who practiced magic brought their books together and began burning them in the sight of everyone; and they counted up the price of them and found it fifty thousand pieces of silver. So the word of the Lord was growing mightily and prevailing. (Acts 19:11-20)

Did you notice what this powerful demon said to these seven "religious" exorcists, these sons of a chief priest? Before viciously attacking them, the evil spirit cried out, "I recognize Jesus, and I know about Paul, but who are you?" Since these seven brothers only heard about Jesus and did not have a personal relationship with him, they were not under God's divine protection and, therefore, were easy targets for the very demons they were trying to confront. In other words, they were not known in hell.

The apostle Paul, on the other hand, was so well known in hell that he undoubtedly had a huge bounty on his head for any evil spirit that could bring him down. Even though Paul was always in Satan's crosshairs, all the powers of hell could not touch him directly. While Paul suffered much at the hands of men who were demonically influenced, as did Christ and the prophets and the rest of the apostles, devils are divinely restricted from physically harming believers — except in very rare circumstances, like in the case of Job or in the instance of the immoral man in the Corinthian church (see Job 2:4-7; 1 Corinthians 5:1-5).

Paul said to Timothy, "Indeed, all who desire to live godly in Christ Jesus will be persecuted. But evil men and impostors will proceed from bad to worse, deceiving and being deceived" (2 Timothy 3:12-13). And it was Jesus who said:

> Blessed are those who have been persecuted for the sake of righteousness, for theirs is the kingdom of heaven. Blessed are you when people insult you

and persecute you, and falsely say all kinds of evil against you because of Me. Rejoice and be glad, for your reward in heaven is great; for in the same way they persecuted the prophets who were before you. (Matthew 5:10-12)

The true followers of Christ are bound to suffer demonically driven persecution. However, it is truly a dangerous thing to enter into the territory of Satan without being a genuine follower of Christ, as demonstrated by the seven sons of Sceva. They were not known in the realm of the damned, and therefore they were not known in the kingdom of heaven either.

So the profound question we all need to ask ourselves is, "Am I known by devils in hell?" Because if not, then neither am I known by Christ and his angels in heaven, and in the end He will say to us, "I never knew you; depart from Me, you who practice lawlessness" (7:23).

A Pig with Two Tails

The peacock may very well be the vainest of all birds, but what beast could be prouder than a pig with two tails; that is, if such a swine actually existed? In the kingdom of animals, a creature with two tails would be considered a mutant or a freak of nature; and even though some rare species of fish actually have two tails, the only other creature to possess such appendages is man.

He or she is the modern-day atheist that walks upright on two legs but struts and swaggers with all the grandeur of a pompous peacock in heat. In essence, atheists are just fairy-tale mutants that don't really exist because, although God could easily create a sow with two curly, wagging tails on the rear of its anatomy, He cannot create an atheist. For God has loudly declared, "The fool has said in his heart, 'There is no God'" (Psalm 14:1).

Nevertheless, the so-called atheist loves to strut back and forth before God and man as he looks back with extreme pride and admiration at his twin tails: "science" and "reason." Oh how he loves his sense of intellectual superiority as he never ceases to proclaim his belief in unbelief. He relishes insulting the God of heaven and reviling His Son, Jesus Christ, and denigrating the Bible, and constantly mocking the faith of Christians. However, he is as foolhardy and brash as the emperor wearing no clothes who had convinced himself and others that his magnificent attire could only be seen by the most intellectually elite and highly sophisticated within his kingdom. Just as this buck-naked emperor had his gullible champions, so too, the modern-day pig with two tails has his enthusiastic fan club as well. His bamboozled cheerleaders are found in great numbers in the media, within the world of entertainment, and around the portals of academia. He is the darling of the cultural elite and the hero of free-thinkers the world over, and anyone who dares to expose this two-tailed boar as an absolute fraud is shouted down by all those who proclaim that the pig's delusions are backed by science and human reason.

In the same way it took a little child to see through the scam of the king wearing no clothes, so at times it takes a child to see through the charade of the atheist with two tails. As Jesus said, "I thank thee, O Father ... because thou hast hid these things from the wise and prudent, and hast revealed them unto babes" (Matthew 11:25, KJV).

The apostle Paul also zeroed in on the delusions of pigs with two tails when he wrote:

> For the time will come when they will not endure sound doctrine; but wanting to have their ears tickled, they will accumulate for themselves teachers in accordance to their own desires, and will turn away their ears from the truth and will turn aside to myths. (2 Timothy 4:3-4)

Men know instinctively that there is a God because God Himself has put this knowledge in the very heart of every man, and He has demonstrated and proven His existence through all that He has made (see Romans 1:18-32).

So the next time you hear the rantings of an atheist or are forced to listen to the diatribe of a godless professor, just look behind the dribble of his empty words and see if you don't notice two wagging tails simply producing a lot of wind and hot air.

Is Cupid Stupid?

Cupid is the god of love in both Greek and Roman mythology. In short, he is the deity of erotic love and beauty who shoots arrows at both men and women alike in order to make them fall in love. Throughout ancient mythological writings, there appears to be two sides to this figure of a winged archer. In the Roman version, he was the son of Venus (the goddess of love) and Mars (the god of War). With two opposite parents, he becomes a basket case with a mixed bag of arrows. His quiver is full of projectiles dipped in both:

love	and	hate
delight	and	disgust
devotion	and	repulsion
yearning	and	loathing
rapture	and	animosity
fondness	and	hostility

Thus goes the list of paradoxes, ad infinitum, ad nauseam. Is it any wonder then that this naked infant boy would not only be lacking in good judgment but that his very age and gender would incline him to be playfully annoying?

As far as Roman and Greek mythology are concerned, Cupid seems to be the culprit behind the longest-fought war in human history: the battle of the sexes. This contention has gone on for thousands of years and is being fought every moment of every day somewhere around the globe, and is destined to be an intense brawl right up to the closing minutes of this present age. So is Cupid stupid or what?! Is he really just a half-wit whose bizarre behavior and kooky intentions lie at the root of so much confusion and misunderstanding between men and women?

Actually, the Romans and the Greeks have misspelled Cupid's name from the beginning. His correct name also begins with c-u and is five letters long, but it is "Curse" — not "Cupid"; and he is not the by-product of Mars and Venus; rather, the offspring of

Satan and sin. The very first love-struck man and woman on Earth were in a constant state of romantic bliss, passionate desire, and downright fascination with one another. They enjoyed a leaderless coexistence in an environment that can only be described as paradise, and the highlight of every day was to walk in wonderful fellowship with their creator as they watched the sun set in the distance.

Now enters "Cupid" (or "Curse") who was conceived in a lie and born out of disobedience. As a result of the devil's deception and the revolt of the first Romeo and Juliet, the curse is given wings and takes flight with his poisoned arrows. Pain, thorns, thistles, sweat, and death now become the order of the day. As for the starry-eyed lovers (Adam and Eve), the curse of Cupid begins with God saying to the woman, "[Y]our desire will be for your husband, and he will rule over you" (Genesis 3:16).

God was referring to neither a sexual nor a romantic desire in this curse; instead, the woman would now desire to control the man, and the man in turn would now rule over the woman. The word "desire" that God used when speaking to Eve, He also said to Cain before he killed his brother, Abel. The Lord said that "sin is crouching at the door; and its *desire* is for you, but you must master it" (4:7).

What a curse! What an incredible curse! The woman is now going to desire controlling a man who is destined to rule over her. Is that not a formula for disaster and a surefire ingredient for conflict, misunderstanding, and frustration? This genie is now out of the bottle and there is no chance of getting him back in. He is now free to roam the earth and fly through the sky unleashing his bottomless quiver of arrows in every direction. However, God has provided an antidote for his poisoned projectiles and an antitoxin for the ongoing conflicts instigated by this curse. The cure is found in the following formula given in Scripture:

> Wives, be subject to your own husbands, as to the
> Lord. For the husband is the head of the wife, as
> Christ also is the head of the church, He Himself

being the Savior of the body. But as the church is subject to Christ, so also the wives ought to be to their husbands in everything.

Husbands, love your wives, just as Christ also loved the church and gave Himself up for her, so that He might sanctify her, having cleansed her by the washing of water with the word, that He might present to Himself the church in all her glory, having no spot or wrinkle or any such thing; but that she would be holy and blameless. So husbands ought also to love their own wives as their own bodies. He who loves his own wife loves himself; for no one ever hated his own flesh, but nourishes and cherishes it, just as Christ also does the church, because we are members of His body. For this reason a man shall leave his father and mother and shall be joined to his wife, and the two shall become one flesh. This mystery is great; but I am speaking with reference to Christ and the church. Nevertheless, each individual among you also is to love his own wife even as himself, and the wife must see to it that she respects her husband. (Ephesians 5:22-33)

Unlike Greek and Roman mythology, God's words are powerfully true and His commands are not imaginary, nor are his mandates for husbands and wives fabricated myths. They are the stinging arrows of truth, and they are words that are "living and active and sharper than any two-edged sword, and piercing as far as the division of soul and spirit, of both joints and marrow, and able to judge the thoughts and intentions of the heart" (Hebrews 4:12).

Conflicts between men and women are not due to the shenanigans of an infant born of an imaginary god named Mars and a fictional goddess named Venus. On the contrary, they are spawned out of a curse named "Cupid" or a cupid spelled "curse." Either

22

way, it's not Cupid who is stupid, it is all the men and women who disregard what God has to say to them when it comes to the battle of the sexes.

The Naked Truth Behind the Fig Leaf

For thousands of years, the fashion business has been booming. Today, it has become a trillion-dollar industry the world over, producing myriads of styles, ranging anywhere from the extremely practical to the utterly ridiculous, in a wide variety of sizes and colors. Why all the outfits, costumes, and garments—especially since no other creature on Earth has need of them? Why do only humans require a wardrobe, particularly since we are already born with a suit—a birthday suit? Even if climate were not a factor, men and women would have the urge to conceal at least the bare minimum of their anatomy. But why? Why the constant obsession to cover up? Why the compulsion to put something on, even if all we own is something dirty, ugly, or uncomfortable?

These are questions that merit an answer, even though so few people bother to ponder the amazing phenomenon of clothing, and in spite of the fact that there was actually a time in human history where clothing didn't exist and where a man and a woman "were both naked and were not ashamed" (Genesis 2:25). The answer is anything but skin deep—it is profoundly deep! If men understood the spiritual significance of clothing, they would genuinely prefer to be publicly stripped of every shred of physical apparel rather than have their souls exposed to the trauma of being truly seen and known by others.

Clothes symbolize the absolute need to conceal our offenses against a holy and righteous God. No sooner did the first naked couple on Earth disobey their Creator then the sense of shame entered the picture and a desperate desire to hide materialized. However, Adam and Eve's foolish and futile attempts to hide from God and to cover up with fig leaves proved to be both ridiculous and bankrupt. Instead, God Himself "made garments of skin for Adam and his wife, and clothed them" (3:21). Notice that making clothes out of animal skins meant that a creature totally innocent of any wrongdoing had to die and shed its life's blood. The Scriptures declare that "according to the Law, one may almost say, all things are cleansed with blood, and without shedding of blood there is no forgiveness" (Hebrews 9:22).

Consequently, when nudists strut up and down the streets of San Francisco or recline on public beaches, uninhibited and unashamed of their bodies, what they are asserting (without even realizing it) is that there is no such thing as sin and thus, no need for a covering. Jesus Christ put His finger on the need to cover up nonetheless, when He said:

> That which proceeds out of the man, that is what defiles the man. For from within, out of the heart of men, proceed the evil thoughts, fornications, thefts, murders, adulteries, deeds of coveting and wickedness, as well as deceit, sensuality, envy, slander, pride and foolishness. All these evil things proceed from within and defile the man. (Mark 7:20-23)

Furthermore, God proclaimed through the prophet Jeremiah that "the heart is more deceitful than all else and is desperately sick; who can understand it? I, the Lord, search the heart, I test the mind, even to give to each man according to his ways, according to the results of his deeds" (Jeremiah 17:9-10). In other words, human nakedness manifests a profound spiritual truth—a truth that goes much deeper than man's epidermis. Nakedness points to the innate embarrassment of having all of one's secret sins revealed to the world—all of one's impure thoughts, desires and deeds; all of one's hateful and uncharitable thinking; and all of one's greed, envy, malice, and pride exposed to the world for everyone to gawk at.

In light of this, most men and women would rather be stripped of their clothing than have their secret sins laid bare for all to observe. This is the naked truth that lies behind the fig leaf; it is the profound symbolism that is manifested in clothing and divulged in the desperate desire to put garments on before wandering out in public.

In the end, clothes will be the determining factor of whether a person goes to heaven or to hell. If men do not put on the righteousness of Jesus Christ, or clothe themselves in His spotless garments, then both the prophet Daniel and the apostle John predict that they will be destined to stand before the all-consuming holiness of an eternal God, and in His presence they will have resurrected bodies without a stitch of clothing to cover them (see Daniel 7:9-10; Revelations 20:11-15; 3:18).

Your Call is Important to Us (as Long as You Don't Call!)

Let's face it, genuine customer service is something out of ancient history. It has gone the way of the rotary phone and has suffered the same fate as the Edsel automobile. This very unpleasant reality was once again driven home to me as I tried desperately to talk to a human being in order to update my auto insurance policy.

I had owned a clunker of a car with almost 200,000 miles on it, and it was totally on life support with absolutely no hope of ever being resuscitated (outside of a first-class miracle from heaven or a massive infusion of money from an eccentric millionaire). It burned oil, failed its smog test, and the driver's seat was so worn out that it took planks of plywood just to keep it propped up. So with a total sense of fatalism, I finally "bit the bullet" and traded in that pathetically dying vehicle for a shiny new mode of transportation.

Consequently, I called my "friendly" insurance company in order to add my handsome new car to my auto policy and drop that suffocating bucket of bolts in the final grips of its death rattle. What should have been a quick and easy transaction over the phone turned into another hopeless experience of total frustration. I was communicating with one impersonal recording after another as the emotionally detached and automated speech droned on and on: "If you want English, push this button…If you want another language, push that button…If you want something else, push some other button, etc." Ultimately, the robotic voice on the other end of the line put me on hold indefinitely while another mechanically indifferent recording assured me every 30 seconds that "my call is very important to them" and that "someone will be with me shortly." The recording then repeated this mantra so many times that my eyes begin to gloss over.

Eventually, when someone with actual blood coursing through their veins finally answered the phone, their totally disinterested voice suggested they didn't even want to be bothered giving me the time of day, let alone be truly helpful in addressing my needs.

Ultimately, as if all the bureaucratic red tape and meaningless runaround weren't enough to ruin my day, my call got disconnected and I had to start this agonizing process all over again!

There ought to be a special place in hell...Oops...Sorry...I was just thinking out loud! However, let's be honest, every automated phone message that forces us to jump through one annoying hoop after another simply shouts: "You really don't matter to us! Listening to you is a waste of our time! Your money is all that is important, so unless you are sending more of it, don't call us, we'll call you!"

Although genuine customer service has become nothing more than smoke and mirrors today, there is nonetheless a God in heaven who will never ignore us or pretend to care. He is a God who waits anxiously for our call and looks forward to hearing from us each and every day. His is actually more concerned for our well-being and our future than we are ourselves. He pleads with us, and even commands us, to call on Him continuously.

Many people can relate to the frustration (and perhaps even the panic) one senses when in an emergency situation and they have a dead cell phone or a disconnected landline. The ability to communicate can mean life or death. Similarly, communicating with God through our prayers is even more important to our physical and spiritual well-being than most people realize.

Paul tells us to "pray without ceasing" (1 Thessalonians 5:17). He says, "I want the men in every place to pray, lifting up holy hands, without wrath and dissension (1 Timothy 2:8). Jesus commanded us to "keep on the alert at all times, praying" (Luke 21:36). Prayer is man's only hope. It is as important to our souls as breathing and sleeping is to our bodies. A man or woman's prayer life will not only determine the course of their lives, but it will most certainly determine their ultimate destiny in the afterlife.

That is why God will never, ever, say to us when we call, "If you want this language, push this button, or if you want something else, push another button." He will never force us to jump through one ridiculous hoop after another before listening to what we have to say. And He will certainly never tell us that "our call is important to Him" and then put us on hold until our hair turns gray.

The shortest prayer in the Bible can be found in Matthew 14:30 when Peter, in the middle of the night and in the midst of a storm, got out of a boat to walk towards Jesus on the water. Once Peter realized there was no physical means of holding him up, he glanced at the threatening waves (taking his focus off of Christ), and felt the force of the howling wind and began to sink like a stone into a watery grave. In total desperation and with all of his heart he cried out, "Lord, save me!"

The Lord didn't then say to Peter, "Your call is very important to Me" or "if you want Hebrew push this button" or "if you want Greek push that button." He didn't put Peter on hold with double-talk and then ignore him. Instead, the Bible says, "Immediately Jesus stretched out His hand and took hold of him, and said to him, 'You of little faith, why did you doubt?' When they got into the boat, the wind stopped. And those who were in the boat worshiped Him, saying, 'You are certainly God's Son!'" (Matthew 14:31-33).

Prayer can make all the difference in the world for individuals, churches, and even nations. James tells us, "The effective prayer of a righteous man can accomplish much" (James 5:16). Indeed, God says, "[I]f my people, who are called by my name, will humble themselves and pray and seek my face and turn from their wicked ways, then will I hear from heaven and will forgive their sin and will heal their land" (2 Chronicles 7:14, NIV). Prayer coupled with a right relationship with God can stop the rotation of the earth, moon, and sun (Joshua 10:12-14). Prayer can even raise the dead (1 Kings 7-23; 2 Kings 4:18-37; Luke 7:11-16; John 11:38-44; Acts 9:36-41; 20:7-12). Prayer has even turned back time (2 Kings 20:5-11), defeated overwhelming armies (Joshua 9-12), and produced water from a rock (Exodus 17:5-6).

In short, with God there is no hold time, no runaround, no disconnect—just an immediate audience with the King of kings, the Lord of lords, and the God of gods. As a matter of fact, there is coming a day during Christ's millennial reign "that before [we] call, [He] will answer; and while [we] are still speaking, [He] will hear" (Isaiah 65:24). Now that's how important we are to Him in comparison to the monotonous recordings that pretend to care as their disingenuous words echo over and over again ad infinitum, ad nauseam, that "Your call is important to us."

The Land of Duuuh

The word "duh" is defined as the dash character in Morse code, echoic (resembling an echo) of the sound of this character as produced by an old-fashioned telegraph. The word "duh" has also evolved into a slang expression that can mean two different things, depending on the context: (1) a sarcastic assertion used when the answer to a question is so obvious that virtually any child would know it and (2) an expression while contemplating a thought in an attempt to come up with the correct answer. For example:

> Question: "Is the sun hot?"
> Answer: "Duh!" (meaning "who doesn't know the answer to that?!")
> Question: "How hot is the sun?"
> Answer: "Duuuh?" (meaning "let me think about the question a moment before I respond).

The informal expression of "duh" revolves around knowledge. Either we readily know without investigation that something is a fact, or we are uncertain as to the truth of the matter. Therefore, it is interesting to note that according to the Bible, knowledge is predicted to increase greatly just prior to the return of Jesus Christ at the end of this age. The prophet Daniel describes the end times and foretells the following:

> [A]t that time [just before the end of the world] Michael, the great prince who stands guard over the sons of your people, will arise. And there will be a time of distress such as never occurred since there was a nation until that time; and at that time your people, everyone who is found written in the book, will be rescued. Many of those who sleep in the dust of the ground will awake, these to everlasting

life, but the others to disgrace and everlasting contempt. Those who have insight will shine brightly like the brightness of the expanse of heaven, and those who lead the many to righteousness, like the stars forever and ever. But as for you, Daniel, conceal these words and seal up the book until the end of time; many will go back and forth, and knowledge will increase. (Daniel 12:1-4)

A cursory look at history demonstrates a virtual explosion of knowledge within a relatively short period of time. Consider the discoveries and inventions made in the span of only one century: telephones, electricity, automobiles, airplanes, and rockets, to name a few. For all the previous centuries, modes of transportation and communication remained essentially the same. Today, however, no one can possibly keep up with the incredible influx of information and travel. Nevertheless, the apostle Paul warns that in spite of people's increasing knowledge, their godlessness will blind them from the certainty of truth. He said,

[R]ealize this, that in the last days difficult times will come. For men will be lovers of self, lovers of money, boastful, arrogant, revilers, disobedient to parents, ungrateful, unholy, unloving, irreconcilable, malicious gossips, without self-control, brutal, haters of good, treacherous, reckless, conceited, lovers of pleasure rather than lovers of God, holding to a form of godliness, although they have denied its power; avoid such men as these. For among them are those who ... [are] always learning and never able to come to the knowledge of the truth. (2 Timothy 3:1-7)

Anyone with spiritual insight (and not merely head knowledge) should not be shocked as they witness our modern-day tidal wave of knowledge submerging the truth about God and drowning out His still, small voice of understanding. Consequently, the closer that mankind draws toward the end of this age, the more the world will begin to resemble the land of "duuuh." In the very epicenter of our information explosion, the earth is becoming a growing symphony of conflicting views and a modern-day tower of Babel where confusion and ignorance reign supreme, and "where envying and strife is, there is confusion and every evil work" (James 3:16, KJV). In short, there are sinister forces of wickedness that are hell-bent on destroying all of mankind out of their infernal malice towards God and their satanic hatred against the men and women who are created in His image and likeness (see Ephesians 6:10-17).

Therefore, the more that mankind rejects the truth of God's Word, and the more men neglect or refuse to commit to His Son Jesus Christ, the more men's knowledge will lead them deeper and deeper into a frightful no-man's-land of satanic confusion and division—and the more obvious the answer to this question will become: "Does God's Word really tell men the absolute truth in the midst of our world's ocean of confusion?"—Duh! There is no one in heaven or hell who does not know the answer to this question. It is only here on Earth, the land of "duuuh," where men can possess great knowledge, yet live in great ignorance of the truth.

Angel in the Fog

Angels are mentioned over 270 times in Scripture, and they are described as ministering spirits or divine messengers possessing super-human powers and intelligence. They are not only majestic, but they are also very holy and can be extremely intimidating in the sight of men. As a matter of fact, the prophet Daniel encountered angels on two different occasions that sapped him of all his strength and vitality to the point where he could barely even speak (see Daniel 8-9). However, there are other times that angels appear in human form to men, and their presence seems so ordinary that individuals are totally unaware they are in the very presence of a God-sent ministering spirit. As the author of Hebrews says: "Do not neglect to show hospitality to strangers, for by this some have entertained angels without knowing it" (Hebrews 13:2).

There are volumes of books, testimonies, and articles written by people who have experienced encounters with angelic beings. These occurrences are so numerous and so varied that even if half of these recorded manifestations were dismissed as delusional or fabricated, the remaining records could not, in all honesty, be discarded as deliberate deceptions or sheer hallucinations. Having said all of this, I feel hesitantly compelled to recount a personal experience that has left me seriously wondering if what happened to me was a genuine encounter with a messenger of God, or if it was a mere mortal whom God used to speak to me during my time of need. My prayer is that in relating the following incident, it may be an encouragement to others (whether saved or lost) in need of divine encouragement or spiritual assurance.

My encounter took place on a New Year's Day, which happened to be on a Sunday. Almost without exception, the dawning of a new year is somewhat depressing for me, and this particular morning was especially disheartening because all I could think about was the inevitable struggles of another year in front of me. I realize that for most people (especially Christians), such a negative state of mind runs contrary to the many Scripture verses that speak of joy, hope and blessing. However, I felt mentally, emotionally, physically and spiritually spent, and I dreaded the thought of going through one more spiritual battle in my Christian walk.

Feeling very discouraged and wanting to be alone, I told my wife, Gail, to go to church without me and I would catch up with her after I finished taking down our Christmas tree. She obliged me, and once the Christmas tree was out of the living room, I slowly walked to my car and drove to church in a complete fog. It was actually a warm, sunny day without a cloud in the sky, but my mind was in a total haze, like a thick mist. I had no more energy or desire to attend even one more church service. However, I did everything I could to shake off this feeling of defeat as I kept repeating to myself what the apostle Paul said to Timothy: "Suffer hardship with me, as a good soldier of Christ Jesus" (2 Timothy 2:3), but in spite of my efforts, I kept thinking:

> *Another year: Another year of running my guts out for God and going nowhere; of pouring myself out with sweat and tears with virtually nothing to show for it; of countless battles and so few victories; and of teaching Bible studies, writing books, witnessing and serving the Lord while accomplishing little or nothing.*

In spite of all these negative thoughts suffocating my mind, I earnestly tried not to let the devil drag me into the "slough of despondence" or pull me into the "mud of self-pity," but all I could see and feel in the midst of this sunny morning was the thick fog and numbing dampness. As I got out of my car and walked up to the entrance of the church, I felt my spirit dragging my carcass through the front doors and saying, "Suck it up! Just suck it up and quit wallowing in this depression!" Yet I honestly felt that I had no more strength left in me.

However, as soon as I crossed the threshold of the lobby, I was suddenly approached by a man I had never seen before. He came towards me so quickly that I didn't even have time to take off my sunglasses, and I instinctively tensed up as I thought he was going to accost me for money. Instead, he urgently grabbed my hand and said, "I want to pray with you, Brother!" He then began praying earnestly for me as I stood there in my mental fog and confusion. All I could think of was, *"This guy is just wasting my time,"* because what he was saying in his prayer was not what I needed to hear.

When he finished praying, I politely thanked him and turned to go into the main sanctuary, but as I began to walk away, he called to me and said, "By the way, Brother, what's your name?" I replied, "John," and he responded with, "Well, that's my name too!" (Had his name been different than mine, I'm sure I would not have remembered it, due to the haziness of my mind.) I also thought how he seemed strangely out of place: He appeared to be of Indian descent and was dressed in some form of garb worn in India, and he had somewhat long black hair and a short dark beard, but I don't recall him having an accent.

I then entered the sanctuary where about 2,000 people were seated and where the lights were all off, except for the spotlight shining on the pastor preaching his sermon. Because I was so late for the service, I simply stood all alone in the back, in the dark, as the preacher was winding down the topic on John the Baptist. He concluded his remarks by saying, "I want you to know three things here this morning:

1. You are doing better than you think you are;
2. (This spiritual warfare) is not all about you; and
3. Jesus had great things to say about John, yet John never heard them!"

These closing words of the preacher's sermon pierced my heart and spoke to my mind so powerfully that an infusion of God's spirit overwhelmed me and I began to weep convulsively, albeit silently, in the darkness. Through my tears, I asked myself, *"What just happened here? Who was that guy who prayed with me in the lobby and where did he come from? Who was he?"*

I rushed out of the sanctuary to see if I could find him, but he was gone. I went to the restroom to blow my nose and to wipe away my tears, and when I came out of the men's room, I searched for him again but was unable to locate his whereabouts. I met up with family members and friends and immediately inquired if any of them had seen the man whom I tried to describe. No one had ever noticed anyone fitting the description I gave. I was so frustrated at myself: *"Why hadn't I paid more attention? Why wasn't I more focused when he was praying?"* I realize I was in such a mental stupor that the whole experience seemed surreal or like a disorienting dream. For weeks and months subsequent to this encounter, I had searched for him at every church service but without success.

To this day, I cannot be absolutely certain whether I came face to face with an angel or if God simply communicated to me through a fellow human being. One thing I do know with total conviction is that he was sent to me by the Lord Himself. The fact that my name, John, was also that of the stranger who approached me and that the sermon happened to be about John the Baptist, tells me my whole experience was orchestrated by God. Another thing I know without question is that if I had not forced myself to go to church in spite of my discouragement, I would have missed an unexpected blessing from God. The writer of Hebrews tells us:

> Let us hold fast the confession of our hope without wavering, for He who promised is faithful; and let us consider how to stimulate one another to love and good deeds, *not forsaking our own assembling together*, as is the habit of some, but encouraging one another; and all the more as you see the day drawing near. (Hebrews 10:23-25)

In conclusion, the Bible makes it abundantly clear that angels and demons are locked in an eternal war of good vs. evil, the souls of men are at the very epicenter of this battle, and what lies in the balance is heaven and hell and the saved and the lost.

Nevertheless, in the midst of this spiritual conflict and in the confusion of the haze of war, when we least expect it, God may manifest Himself in the time of our greatest need through an angel in the fog.

The Village Idiot

"Simpleton," "buffoon," "fool," "lunatic," "moron," "dolt," and "imbecile" are just a few of the litany of descriptive synonyms for "idiot." There is no shortage of insults when it comes to describing an idiot. This is especially true of a "village idiot," a fool who is well known within his community and is thus often ridiculed and scorned by many for his bizarre beliefs and his deranged behavior. Now would you ever think of Jesus as being the village idiot? How about the apostle Paul as the town imbecile, or the prophets Isaiah and Jeremiah as demented lunatics? Well, this is exactly how they were viewed by their contemporaries and precisely how they were treated by the people of their day. In fact, they were loathed by many of the religious leaders and "spiritual" laity as well.

When Jesus spoke in the synagogue of His own hometown, His neighbors became so enraged with Him that they tried to throw Him off a cliff, His fellow Jews wanted to stone Him, the Pharisees despised Him, the governmental authorities sought to kill Him, the masses demanded to crucify Him, and the powers that be had Him murdered (Luke 4:14-30; John 11:8, 47-53; Luke 13:31-32; John 19:15; Luke 23:24-25). Talk about the village idiot! No human soul was more despised and more abused than the only begotten Son of Almighty God Himself. The world viewed Jesus Christ as being little more than a raving lunatic and despised him as being nothing less than a pathetic fool.

And how about the apostle Paul? He was another village idiot whom his fellow citizens could not tolerate. He tells us that he was imprisoned, beaten, and often in danger of death. He continues:

> Five times I received from the Jews thirty-nine lash-
> es. Three times I was beaten with rods, once I was
> stoned, three times I was shipwrecked, a night and
> a day I have spent in the deep. I have been on
> frequent journeys, in dangers from rivers, dangers
> from robbers, dangers from my countrymen,

dangers from the Gentiles, dangers in the city, dangers in the wilderness, dangers on the sea, dangers among false brethren; I have been in labor and hardship, through many sleepless nights, in hunger and thirst, often without food, in cold and exposure. Apart from such external things, there is the daily pressure on me of concern for all the churches. (2 Corinthians 11:24-28)

Paul also tells us in his first letter to the Corinthian church:

God has exhibited us apostles last of all, as men condemned to death; because we have become a spectacle to the world, both to angels and to men. We are fools for Christ's sake, but you are prudent in Christ; we are weak, but you are strong; you are distinguished, but we are without honor. To this present hour we are both hungry and thirsty, and are poorly clothed, and are roughly treated, and are homeless; and we toil, working with our own hands; when we are reviled, we bless; when we are persecuted, we endure; when we are slandered, we try to conciliate; we have become as the scum of the world, the dregs of all things, even until now. (1 Corinthians 4:9-13)

Legend tells us that Isaiah was so despised that the people of his day put him into a hollowed-out log and sawed him in two (Hebrews 11:37). Consider what the prophet Jeremiah claimed:

I have become a laughingstock all day long; everyone mocks me ... for me the word of the Lord has resulted in reproach and derision all day long. ... For I have heard the whispering of many, "Terror on every side! Denounce him; yes, let us denounce him!" All my trusted friends, watching for my fall, say: "Perhaps he will be deceived, so that we may prevail against him and take our revenge on him." ... Cursed be the day when I was born; let the day not be blessed when my mother bore me! Cursed be the man who brought the news to my father, saying, "A baby boy has been born to you!" and made him very happy. But let that man be like the cities which the Lord overthrew without relenting, and let him hear an outcry in the morning and a shout of alarm at noon; because he did not kill me before birth, so that my mother would have been my grave, and her womb ever pregnant. Why did I ever come forth from the womb to look on trouble and sorrow, so that my days have been spent in shame? (Jeremiah 20:7-8, 10, 14-18)

Jeremiah's contemporaries plotted to murder him, they imprisoned him, and he was thrown into a cistern (Jeremiah 26:11-15; 32:2; 38:6-7). Jewish tradition tells us that he was eventually murdered by his own countrymen after they forced him to flee to Egypt with them.

Jesus accused the religious leaders of killing the prophets and warned, "Woe to you when all men speak well of you, for their fathers used to treat the false prophets in the same way" (Matthew 23:29-39; Luke 6:26). The Son of God explained:

If the world hates you, you know that it has hated Me before it hated you. If you were of the world, the world would love its own; but because you are not of the world, but I chose you out of the world, because of this the world hates you. Remember the word that I said to you, "A slave is not greater than his master." If they persecuted Me, they will also persecute you; if they kept My word, they will keep yours also. But all these things they will do to you for My name's sake, because they do not know the

One who sent Me. (John 15:18-21) (Also see
Matthew 10:22; 24:9; Mark 13:13; Luke 19:14; 21:17;
and John 7:7.)

In light of what the Bible has to say about its prophets and
about Jesus and His true followers, is it any wonder that "the more
things change, the more things remain the same"? The village
idiots today are viewed as being intolerant, hateful, dangerous,
homophobic, narrow-minded, and ignorant. Creationists are
scorned, pro-lifers are despised, those who oppose gay marriage
are held in contempt, and the promoters of biblical morality are
ridiculed and labeled as being heartless and mean-spirited. The
media, the entertainment industry, academia, and a sizeable
number of Americans today view the committed followers of Jesus
Christ as little more than village idiots who need to be silenced one
way or another.

However, since the prophets, the disciples, and even the Son of
God were viewed as village idiots during their day, then perhaps
the greatest privilege for a modern-day follower of Christ is to be
viewed as the proverbial village lunatic in the eyes of the world.
Because in the eyes of heaven, such an outcast is truly enlightened,
such a fool is truly a person of understanding, and such a
simpleton is truly the wisest of wise men.

The Headless Wonder

Birthdays are nice, but too many of them will kill you! Regardless of how old a person may become, he will never be able to escape the fact that the death rate is still one per person, for "it is appointed for men to die once and after this comes judgment" (Hebrews 9:27).

A man by the name of Methuselah lived longer than any other human being in recorded history. In Genesis 5:25, we are told he inhaled the breath of life for an astounding 969 years! Nevertheless, there seems to be a strange twist of irony in his incredible longevity, and that is the sad fact that his multitude of birthdays is all we know about him. Apparently his accomplishments and achievements were nil or not worth noting.

If there were an inscription on his headstone, I'd be very curious to know what it stated. Perhaps it read, "Here lies Methuselah, the composer of many years and the author of nothing." Or maybe, "Here lies the lucky man that almost lived 1,000 years even though he had nothing to show for it." I don't mean to sound uncharitable about a man I never met, but it is as if he did little more than eat, drink, and sleep like an unthinking cow ceaselessly chewing its cud and staring blankly into space for centuries.

Well, several thousand years have come and gone since the old man died, yet his spirit of longevity still exists in our world today—especially in America. No other nation on Earth strives as hard as ours to discover the fountain of youth or to find the holy grail of immortality. Billions of dollars are spent annually in man's exhaustive attempts to look young and to prolong his years. Cosmetics, medications, diets, surgeries, exercise programs, and countless snake oils proclaiming to be miracle drugs are but a few of the many things in which people invest so heavily, in order to look young, become energetic, and live long. This is not to suggest that any of these actions or pursuits are wrong in and of themselves. After all, valuing one's life is good, caring for one's health is wise, grooming one's appearance is proper, applying cosmetics is enhancing, and dieting and exercising are praiseworthy — all of which improve one's capacity to get the most out of living.

Nevertheless, we need to resign ourselves to the fact that our days are numbered and that the quality, not the quantity, of life is what's most important: "As for the days of our life, they contain seventy years, or if due to strength, eighty years, yet their pride [the best of years] is but labor and sorrow; for soon it is gone and we fly away" (Psalm 90:10). What is interesting about this claim of Moses' is the fact that in spite of all of man's technological advances and his disciplines to stay young, the average lifespan in the most industrialized nations still hovers between 70 and 80 years[2]. In short, the celebration of too many birthdays will always take its toll because the aging process can only be delayed but never terminated.

Yet some men and women have so revolted at this grim reality that man has now engineered an ingenious concept, hoping to prolong one's days indefinitely, and it is a horrifying experiment that seems to be taken right out of the pages of the legendary tale of Frankenstein. It is the field of "cryonics" — an area of medical science which freezes entire bodies or severed heads in liquid nitrogen, essentially for the purpose of adding more birthdays to one's yearly existence. If a person has a terminal disease (and a lot of money), he can have himself frozen in a type of suspended state of animation or frigid buoyancy; and if his body has been too ravaged by sickness, age, or deformity, he can simply have his head removed and put on ice. Of course the idea behind all of this frostbite is that sometime in the future, science might come up with a cure or a donated body, and then they can resurrect this frozen mummy or frigid head to become whole again and live longer.

Is cryonics really the answer to death, or is it the brainstorm of a world gone mad? Is deep freezing a headless body or a bodiless head the answer to living, or is it the epitome of ignorance? In the fictional story of the *Legend of Sleepy Hollow* by Washington Irving, the headless horseman is always pursuing Ichabod Crane, in search of his head. But in today's real world, it is a head in search of another's body.

However, it is in Christ that "we live and move and have our being" (Acts 17:28, NIV), not in the miracle of liquid nitrogen or in man's foolish attempts to resurrect himself. Jesus said, "I am the resurrection and the life; he who believes in Me will live even if he dies, and everyone who lives and believes in Me will never die" (John 11:25-26). Christ also declared:

> Truly, truly, I say to you, an hour is coming and now is, when the dead will hear the voice of the Son of God, and those who hear will live. ... Do not marvel at this; for an hour is coming, in which all who are in the tombs will hear His voice, and will come forth; those who did the good deeds to a resurrection of life, those who committed the evil deeds to a resurrection of judgment. (5:25, 28-29)

In addition, the prophet Daniel foretells of the coming day where:

> Many of those who sleep in the dust of the ground will awake, these to everlasting life, but the others to disgrace and everlasting contempt. Those who have insight will shine brightly like the brightness of the expanse of heaven, and those who lead the many to righteousness, like the stars forever and ever. (Daniel 12:2-3)

Lastly, Isaiah proclaimed, "Your dead will live; their corpses will rise. You who lie in the dust, awake and shout for joy, for your dew is as the dew of the dawn, and the earth will give birth to the departed spirits" (Isaiah 26:19).

Clearly, the resurrection of our bodies at the Lord's command is inevitable. However, man's ridiculous attempt to resurrect people after attaching a person's head to someone else's headless

body begs the question, "Who really is the headless wonder here —
the frozen mummy or the senseless scientist who wants to play
God?" It is truly the ultimate act of vanity and foolhardiness to
play God in such a way. We should instead take to heart the words
of the psalmist:

> Lord, make me to know my end and what is the extent of
> my days; let me know how transient I am. Behold, You
> have made my days as handbreadths, and my lifetime as
> nothing in Your sight; surely every man at his best is a
> mere breath. Surely every man walks about as a phantom;
> surely they make an uproar for nothing; he amasses riches
> and does not know who will gather them. And now, Lord,
> for what do I wait? My hope is in You. Deliver me from all
> my transgressions; make me not the reproach of the foolish.
> (Psalm 39:4-8)

Let's Hear it for Mr. Puddleglum, Gloomy Gus, Sour Sam, and Grumpy Cat

I have a confession to make (and anyone who knows me would wholeheartedly agree): I am a hard-boiled pessimist. As a matter of fact, if Murphy had not already written his famous laws, I am sure that I would have been the first to do so. Like Murphy, I believe "if there are two or more ways to do something, and one of those ways can result in a catastrophe, then someone will do it." This is Murphy's original Law, which has morphed over time into, "anything that can go wrong, will." I also agree with Murphy's conclusions which include: "If everything seems to be going well, you have obviously overlooked something," and "left to themselves, things tend to go from bad to worse," and finally, "smile ... tomorrow will be worse." Plus, I'll throw in three quotes that Murphy didn't think of: "Exercise daily, eat wisely, and die anyway," "life is hard and then you die," and "the light at the end of the tunnel is actually an oncoming train."

In light of this, most people would consider me as being anything but a person of faith, a Bible believer, or someone seriously committed to Jesus Christ. Although I am not a preacher (nor am I the son of a preacher), I have often been referred to as "the pastor of disaster," "the prophet of gloom," "the shepherd of negativity," or "the minister of doom." As a matter of fact, if I were a preacher, my congregation would no doubt be referred to as "the Church of the Melancholy Muchachos" (and of course I would be its only member, so it would be called "the Church of the Uno Melancholy Muchacho").

Frankly, people both inside and outside the Church question my Christian faith due to my lack of being upbeat and optimistic. Instead, I am regularly viewed as a heretic that goes by the name of "Gloomy Gus" or "Mr. Puddleglum." My daughter, Rachel, bought me a book and calendar of "Grumpy Cat" for Christmas. This famous sourpuss always has a serious frown on its face which coincides with its negative and pessimistic thoughts being expressed in bitter one-liners or snide captions. So if even my own daughter views me as a killjoy, then there must be a seed of truth to it.

Nevertheless, I honestly think that God could use a few more cynical and negative people like me today (as long as they are sober and not sour, and as long as they are serious and not bitter) in the midst of so much religious fluff, positive thinking, and optimistic assumptions. Preachers and church members everywhere (especially in America) have managed to replace the gospel of repentance from sin and of obedience to Christ with a social gospel that says, "I'm okay, you're okay"; "God wants you to be healthy and wealthy"; "Jesus wants to bless us in whatever lifestyle we choose"; "think positive and positive things will happen"; and "just name it and claim it — and the Lord will grant it to you." They assert there is no final Judgment Day, nor eternal hell nor divine commandments that are set in stone, and that all paths lead to heaven so, therefore, all religions and beliefs are equally valid. They profess that God is not really an all-consuming fire of holiness who demands that we turn from our sins; rather, He is just a cuddly mascot who wants to bless us in whatever we choose to believe. He is merely a senile, benevolent old granddaddy that desires to pat us on the head and encourage us to do whatever makes us happy.

Well, amidst all our religious optimism, hopeful conjectures, and sloppy sentimentality, sometimes it takes a Gloomy Gus, a Mr. Puddleglum, a Grumpy Cat, or a Sour Sam to balance out the truth and to give the full counsel of God — in other words, someone who is not afraid to "tell it like it is" or to declare (as the late radio host, Paul Harvey, used to say), "and now you know the rest of the story."

Indeed, the Bible tells us to "rejoice before the Lord," "rejoice in [the Lord's] salvation," "rejoice and be glad," "rejoic[e] in hope," and "[r]ejoice in the Lord always; again I will say rejoice!" (Leviticus 23:40; 1 Samuel 2:1; Psalm 118:24, Romans 12:12; Philippians 4:4), along with handfuls of other Scriptures that encourage us to be joyful and expectant. However, if we flippantly say that "all things work together for good" (Romans 8:28, KJV), then we are living in a fool's paradise that fails to see and understand how we are in a spiritual war with the powers of darkness—powers that are hell-bent on damning as many souls as they possibly can, to spite the God of heaven and to lead men (who are created in God's image) to eternal damnation—separated from their Creator in the same manner as the demons.

The Bible clearly states that we are living in a world under siege, both physically and spiritually, where many are the wounded and the slain. Since the creation of the world, mankind has cried an ocean of tears and is destined to sob a sea of tears more before Christ returns and before that glorious day when:

> "Behold, the tabernacle of God is among men, and He will dwell among them, and they shall be His people, and God Himself will be among them, and He will wipe away every tear from their eyes; and there will no longer be any death; there will no longer be any mourning, or crying, or pain; the first things have passed away." And He who sits on the throne said, "Behold, I am making all things new." And He said, "Write, for these words are faithful and true." (Revelation 21:3-5)

Consequently, until that day comes:

> Cursed is the ground because of you [Adam]; in toil you will eat of it all the days of your life. Both thorns and thistles it shall grow for you; and you will eat the plants of the field; by the sweat of your face you will eat bread, till you return to the ground, because from it you were taken; for you are dust, and to dust you shall return. (Genesis 3:17-19)

In other words, "Life is hard and then you die." Regardless of all our gushing optimism and positive assurances, we are admonished to "weep with those who weep." The Bible reveals to us that the Son of God Himself wept and in the Sermon on the Mount, Jesus declared, "Blessed are those who mourn, for they shall be comforted" (Romans 12:15; Luke 19:41; John 11:35; Matthew 5:4). King Solomon wrote:

> It is better to go to a house of mourning than to go to a house of feasting, because that is the end of every man, and the living [spiritually alive person] takes it to heart. Sorrow is better than laughter, for when a face is sad a heart may be happy. The mind of the wise is in the house of mourning, while the mind of fools is in the house of pleasure. (Ecclesiastes 7:2-4)

Thus, there may very well be times when it takes a Gloomy Gus or a Mr. Puddleglum or a Grumpy Cat or a Sour Sam to set the record straight. At the same time, we can be assured that in the center of all the world's pain, suffering, and dying, God is too good to be unkind and too wise to make mistakes. We need to know that although God will not always deliver us from our struggles when and where and how we want Him to, He tells us:

> Do not fear, for I have redeemed you; I have called you by name; you are Mine! When you pass through the waters [difficulties], I will be with you; and through the rivers, they will not overflow you. When you walk through the fire [trials], you will not be scorched, nor will the flame burn you. For I am the Lord your God, the Holy One of Israel, your Savior. (Isaiah 43:1-3)

Jesus has ensured to men and women everywhere that He came to give them truly fulfilling and abundant lives, in spite of the trials and disappointments we experience (John 10:10).

So let's hear it for the Puddleglums, the Gloomy Guses, and the Grumpy Cats of the world today, because these Sour Sams can enable us to keep our feet firmly planted in Christ, while others have their feet firmly planted in midair.

The Mindless Joy of Groupthink

Rugged individualism, independent thinkers, and people with backbones of steel are becoming nonexistent in our day and age. If ever there were an endangered species today, it is the men and women who dare to stand against the growing mass of humanity that prides itself as being part of "the group."

This is especially true on our university and college campuses across America. Groupthink in our nation is orchestrated by the media, required in the entertainment world, demanded within academia, and insisted upon by those in the realm of politics. Unfortunately, this appeal to go along with the group has even crept into many religious institutions of our day. Any failure to conform with the group is met with contempt from these very groups that demand tolerance and inclusiveness within their vast ranks.

If "the group" had a national anthem or a fight song today, it would probably go something like this:

> Groupthink! Groupthink!
> The marvelous wonders of groupthink—
> Where no one really has to think!
> Just regurgitate, regurgitate, how fun it is to regurgitate,
> And how easy it is to regurgitate and never have to investigate!
>
> Groupthink! Groupthink!
> Oh, the marvelous wonders of groupthink!
> We'll tell you how to think, when to think, and what to think!
> So you'll always know the joys and wonders of groupthink—
> Which never requires anyone to think!

Don't have an opinion, don't have a belief, don't have a conviction.

Just regurgitate what the group thinks!

Don't dare even think to think, because the thought police and the thinking police will tell you what you have to think!

All other think is hateful think! All other think is intolerant think!

All other think is racist, dangerous, and ignorant think!

So always remember: Don't think—regurgitate.

Just regurgitate what the group thinks!

Oh, the mindless joys of groupthink!

And the political correctness of groupthink!

Oh, the sophisticated bliss of groupthink!

Don't ever think differently from what the group thinks,

Because it frees us from ever having to truly think!

So never forget never to think,

Unless, of course, it's what the group thinks!

In short, the phenomenon and power of groupthink are most often driven by a fear of men, rather than a fear of God. What man demands has now replaced what God commands. However, the Bible repeatedly warns men that the fear of man brings a snare, while the fear of God is the beginning of wisdom. The psalmist declared:

> Do not trust in princes, in mortal man, in whom there is no salvation. His spirit departs, he returns to the earth; in that very day his thoughts perish. How blessed is he whose help is the God of Jacob, whose hope is in the Lord his God, who made heaven and earth, the sea and all that is in them; who keeps faith forever. (Psalm 146:3-6)

In conclusion, the majority is seldom trustworthy and "the group" rarely speaks for God. Therefore, we should always ask ourselves if our thinking and our convictions line up with the Word of God, or are our beliefs just a regurgitation of what the group thinks?

Swine and the Thought Police

"O'er the land of the free and the home of the brave" are some of the famous words of "The Star-Spangled Banner" written by Francis Scott Key. He penned these words after watching the bombarding of American forces at Fort McHenry during the Battle of Baltimore on the night of September 13, 1814. He was confined onboard the British ship *Minden* as he tried to negotiate the release of an American prisoner. While under virtual house arrest, he watched the exploding rockets and the bursting shells; and as the glimmering radiance from detonating bombs illuminated the tattered American flag, Francis was truly moved by America's desperate struggle for freedom.

He was so stirred by the determination and sacrificial efforts of people yearning to breathe free that he composed his immortal hymn depicting the intense labor pains of the birth of a nation, and the hardships that gave life to liberty and breath to freedom — freedoms the world had never seen before — freedom of religion, speech, and the press; the right to bear arms; freedom to assemble; and a number of other protections and prohibitions guaranteeing the liberties of one people under God. The authors of America's Declaration of Independence summed these freedoms up as the right to "life, liberty, and the pursuit of happiness"; and although slavery was still a sad reality during its signing, the Founding Fathers nevertheless planted the seeds of freedom so deep that their dreams of liberty eventually became a reality for every citizen within America's borders.

However, the freedoms that God bestowed upon this nation were never free. They were purchased with the blood of many patriots, and they have only endured because of the bloodletting of many others after them. Yet in spite of the enormous cost of lives and treasure to secure America's liberties, the United States today is losing more and more of its independence with each passing year and with the beginning of each new decade — not by invading armies or foreign powers, but by an insidious gnawing within the entrails and around the foundations of our nation's

Constitution. The dismantling of the Constitution and the Bill of Rights—the very documents that guaranteed the liberties which our nation has enjoyed for more than 200 years—has resulted in this slow erosion of America's freedoms.

Now, "the land of the free and the home of the brave" is beginning to resemble George Orwell's famous satire, *Animal Farm*. In his book, Orwell describes how the animals on a farm overthrow a cruel and oppressive owner named Mr. Jones; and after the successful revolution, the beasts of the farm draw up a constitution that stated, "all animals are created equal" and any creatures that walked on two legs were enemies. (To spare the fowl on the farm, the wings of the chickens and the birds on the estate were counted as legs.)

In essence, the pigs on the newly established "animal farm" slowly and cunningly began to monopolize all authority and control over the farm until they established total domination over the rest of the four-legged creatures. A pig by the name of Napoleon emerged as the supreme leader, and he skillfully consolidated all of his power by using the dogs as his thought police, his policy enforcers, and his personal bodyguards. Furthermore, the sheep became the gullible, mindless followers who believed and reiterated all the lies and doublespeak of Napoleon and his fellow swine. Time and time again, the hard-working farm animals were exploited, brutalized, and marginalized by the pigs and the dogs while repeatedly being reassured that every act of oppression was a necessary precaution to prevent Mr. Jones from ever again gaining control of the farm.

George Orwell's insightful words became a sarcastic and powerful condemnation of the Communist Revolution and the wickedness of Joseph Stalin and his brutal secret police. Well, if ever there were an example of history repeating itself, it's the satire of *Animal Farm* recurring in America today. The animals were constantly led to believe that they were all equal and free while in actuality, they were being more and more intimidated, exploited, and subjugated. Gradually, the animals became oppressed until they awoke one day to discover that their enslavement under the pigs and the dogs was far worse than anything they had experienced under Mr. Jones. They discovered too late that their original constitution which declared "all animals are created equal" had been changed to read "all animals are created equal, but some animals are more equal than others."

The U.S. Constitution that once declared "all men are created equal and are endowed with certain inalienable rights" has been shredded by godless judges and Christ-dishonoring attorneys and politicians in their attempts to undo what the Founding Fathers worked so hard to create. With the aid of many political lawmakers and progressive thinkers, the Constitution and the Bill of Rights have been modified to declare "all Americans are equal, but some are more equal than others."

With the new "hate crime laws" and other shortsighted legalization, we now see that a crime committed against one class of people does not receive the same punishment as the exact same crime committed against a different group of people. In addition to the equal but unequal doublespeak, the thought police are out in force to make sure the God of the Bible is no longer mentioned anywhere in the public forum where He was once greatly honored and respected. Prayer and the reading of the Bible are outlawed in the halls of education, and the very mention of intelligent design is ridiculed and prohibited in the corridors of academia and in the face of evolutionary "theories." The God of the Bible has been expelled from virtually everywhere, except from behind the closed doors of a church or the private gathering in a home. There is even an all-out attempt by the ACLU and others to remove God's name from our dollar bills, from the Pledge of Allegiance, and from every government building. Many of these same people also want to eliminate every cross and every Christian symbol within America's national cemeteries and parks.

Through some convoluted legislation called the "fairness doctrine," the freedoms to convey one's religious or political views through the airways, on television, or over the internet are now in danger. Essentially, the fairness doctrine states that there must be an opposing viewpoint to any religious or political commentary;

otherwise, such programming must be taken off the airways or shut down completely. For this reason, the Bible is now in danger of being labeled a "hate book" because it condemns homosexuality and proclaims that there is only one true faith and only one way to get to heaven.

In addition, the one public forum where an individual would expect to have the purest freedoms of expressions is where the thought police are concentrated most: in our colleges and universities. They have become hotbeds of thought control and intimidation, where the exchange of ideas and open debate are not permitted when it comes to Christianity, the Bible, and conservative points of view. Within the halls of academia, Islam can be promoted while Christianity must be denounced, liberalism is exalted while biblical views are condemned, alternative lifestyles are defended and encouraged while traditional values are labeled as hateful and intolerant, and the murder of the unborn has become a sacred right while the defense of such helpless human beings has been condemned as imposing upon one's freedom of choice.

Anything that does not toe the line of liberal ideology is attacked by modern-day Napoleons and today's thought police. Government and political correctness have been put in the place of God and His Word. As a result, Lord help anyone whom the thought police accuse of violating their interpretation of the separation of church and state. "Freedom of religion" has now been twisted to mean "freedom from religion," and the public acknowledgment of Jesus Christ, an intolerable offense.

Yes, *Animal Farm* is truly alive and well today: The mindless sheep on the farm have ensured their own enslavement; the naïveté and apathy of the masses have enthroned the God-haters, or—as George Orwell described them—"the pigs"; and the gullible and foolhardy have empowered the thought police, or—as *Animal Farm* portrays them—"the dogs." Perhaps it is no mere coincidence that the Son of God Himself said, "Do not give what is holy to dogs, and do not throw your pearls before swine, or they will trample them under their feet, and turn and tear you to pieces" (Matthew 7:6). It is really the pigs and the dogs that are trampling underfoot the pearls of liberty and attacking the ones who attempt to exercise their guaranteed freedom of religion.

However, the Bible speaks of a special judgment in store for the modern-day Napoleons and thought police when it says:

> Why are the nations in an uproar and the peoples devising a vain thing? The kings of the earth take their stand and the rulers take counsel together against the Lord and against His Anointed, saying, "Let us tear their fetters apart and cast away their cords from us!" He who sits in the heavens laughs, the Lord scoffs at them. Then He will speak to them in His anger and terrify them in His fury. (Psalm 2:1-5)

Yes, the modern-day thought police and their masters are truly enjoying their day in the sun, and they will soon succeed in stamping out any vestige of God in every public forum and will even prevail in outlawing the Bible as a "hate book." Eventually, even home Bible studies will be outlawed and only state-run churches and state-approved religious doctrines will be allowed.

As a result, "the land of the free and the home of the brave" is rapidly becoming the land of the sheep and the home of the enslaved. Man's hatred and indifference towards God is slowly becoming his undoing. Every attempt to create Utopia on Earth without Christ is gradually fulfilling the prophetic words of William Penn as he declared, "Those who refuse to be governed by God are destined to be ruled by tyrants." To paraphrase his immortal words, "Those who will not submit to the God of heaven are doomed to be controlled by intimidating thought police and by pigheaded oppressors."

The Crippled and the Lame

Over 20 years ago, the United States enacted legislation titled the "Americans with Disabilities Act." The ADA was designed to integrate people with disabilities fully into the mainstream of American life. However, like so many well-meaning administrative programs, the ADA spawned another bloated government bureaucracy with a "one-size-fits-all" mentality. Because of this, a number of greedy and unethical attorneys used the ADA as a springboard to sue small businesses and to attack struggling companies for their inability to comply with so many of these new government regulations. From expensive walkways to modified restrooms and from required parking spaces to a host of other accommodations, the pressure to eliminate every suggestion of discrimination against the disabled has become almost fanatical.

Don't misunderstand me; discrimination against the disabled needs to be eradicated, using every reasonable form of consideration. However, I can't help but wonder what the watchdogs of the ADA would do if they were around during the time of Moses. What I mean is that when it came to the employment of priests, God was extremely discriminatory. He said,

> Speak to Aaron, saying, "No man of your offspring throughout their generations who has a defect shall approach to offer the food of his God. For no one who has a defect shall approach: a blind man, or a lame man, or he who has a disfigured face, or any deformed limb, or a man who has a broken foot or broken hand, or a hunchback or a dwarf, or one who has a defect in his eye or eczema or scabs or crushed testicles. No man among the descendants of Aaron the priest who has a defect is to come near to offer the Lord's offerings by fire; since he has a defect, he shall not come near to offer the food of his God. He may eat the food of his God, both of the most holy and of the holy, only he shall not go in to

the veil or come near the altar because he has a defect, so that he will not profane My sanctuaries. For I am the Lord who sanctifies them." (Leviticus 21:17-23)

Whoa! Talk about discrimination against the disabled! Lawyers today would be salivating for a chance to sue God and Moses and Aaron's priesthood for such insensitivity and blatant prejudice against the handicapped. However, the apostle Paul clearly tells us in his letter to the Galatians that the Old Testament law (including the laws against disabled priests) is our tutor. He said,

[B]efore faith came, we were kept in custody under the law, being shut up to the faith which was later to be revealed. Therefore the Law has become our tutor to lead us to Christ, so that we may be justified by faith. But now that faith has come, we are no longer under a tutor. (Galatians 3:23-25)

Simply stated, many of the ceremonial laws set forth by Moses were fulfilled in Christ and are therefore no longer in effect. From the dietary laws to the requirements of the Sabbath, their legalistic demands are no longer applicable. However, we always need to ask ourselves what these obsolete regulations were trying to tell us. Rather than accusing God of being mean-spirited when it comes to the disabled, we humbly need to look at God's physical demands and understand what He is saying to us spiritually.

A priest was in the position of spiritual leadership; therefore, if he were physically blind, his impaired vision pointed to spiritual blindness. This is exactly what Jesus accused the priests of His day as being. He declared no less than 10 times in the gospels that the religious leaders were blind, and James tells us that spiritual leaders will incur a much stricter judgment before God (James 3:1). Therefore, it is absolutely crucial that pastors, ministers, priests, and teachers see clearly, or they must be disqualified from leadership roles among God's people.

A "lame man" spiritually would point to someone whose walk is characterized by a constant up-and-down motion; his inconsistent walk would disqualify him from spiritual leadership.

A man with a "disfigured face" would point to someone who is two-faced or hypocritical. If his nose was deformed it would suggest a lack of spiritual discernment. Consequently, he could not lead others properly in the ways of God.

If he had a broken hand, it would point to broken fellowship with others. And it was Jesus who said that if your brother has something against you, you must reconcile with him before offering sacrifices to God (Matthew 5:23-24). A broken foot would manifest a crippled walk before the Lord and therefore an inability to "walk the walk."

A hunchback would point to a spiritual leader who does not walk upright or with integrity; a "dwarf" would point to one whose spiritual growth is stunted; a "defect in the eye" points to a lack of clarity in regards to the things of God; "eczema" would allude to sinful conditions; scabs suggest spiritual wounds that are not completely healed before God; and lastly, "crushed testicles" would point to someone who is unable to impart spiritual life to others.

The fact that God allowed priests with these physical defects to eat the priestly bread would suggest that they may be spiritually saved, or part of God's people, but they are prohibited from being in leadership positions because of their defects.

God has absolutely nothing against the crippled and the lame. As a matter of fact, in Jesus' parable about a man giving a big dinner, he says it is like God commanding his servants to go out at once into the streets and lanes and into the highways and hedges and bring into His kingdom "the poor and crippled and blind and lame" (see Luke 14:16-24). God is always calling into His kingdom the spiritually disabled; He just does not want such spiritually handicapped people occupying positions of leadership among His people.

Seeing someone with a physical deformity can be a reminder to us of the words of our tutor (the Old Testament law) and an opportunity to recall God's wisdom in His requirements and His love in His inclusiveness. We need to realize that God is not mean-spirited and that the "Americans with Disabilities Act" cannot be applied when it comes to God's spiritual principles. Pastors, ministers, and priests today can serve the Lord regardless of any physical handicap; however, if they are blind, lame, crippled, impotent, diseased, or sick *spiritually*, they may eat of God's food — His Word — but they are in no position to feed God's people with His Word.

Consequently, any lawyer or army of attorneys who desires to sue God for discrimination is going to find their profit-driven lawsuits utterly fruitless; because none of their threats or intimidations will be able to get God to change the moral demands that He places upon his spiritual leaders — not even the all-powerful government legislation called the "Americans with Disabilities Act."

The Devil's Treadmill

In most places throughout the world, the use of treadmills in factories and mills is a thing of the past. At one time, workmen and/or animals would walk in place on wide, flexible straps in order to generate power by the transfer of motion. Their feet and body weight would propel gears or machinery for grinding wheat, crushing rocks, turning axles, or doing any number of work-related tasks. Even prisoners were once forced to work off their sentences by monotonously walking on treadmills.

Today, countless multitudes spend their lives on treadmills (not the kind in gyms, either). They are the devil's treadmills, used by Satan to keep men and women in a perpetual state of mindless motion in order to keep them from seeking rest in God. He drives people with monotonous labor, wearisome routines, and unending rounds of deadlines and pressing schedules. Like Pharaoh of Egypt, Satan enslaves much of mankind with tedious and burdensome responsibilities to the point where their lives seem like endless marathons of getting up and going to work, getting up and going to work, getting up and going to work.

Life basically becomes a revolving door of leaving for work and coming home to sleep. What little time remains between working and sleeping is consumed by other brainless routines such as social media or by just collapsing and vegetating in front of the television set before repeating the same humdrum of another tiresome day. Well, there is an old adage that says, "the more things change, the more things remain the same." When Moses and Aaron came to Pharaoh, they said,

> "Thus says the Lord, the God of Israel, 'Let My people go that they may celebrate a feast to Me in the wilderness.'" But Pharaoh said, "Who is the Lord that I should obey His voice to let Israel go? I do not know the Lord, and besides, I will not let Israel go." Then they said, "The God of the Hebrews has met with us. Please, let us go a three

days' journey into the wilderness that we may sacrifice to the Lord our God, otherwise He will fall upon us with pestilence or with the sword." But the king of Egypt said to them, "Moses and Aaron, why do you draw the people away from their work? Get back to your labors!" Again Pharaoh said, "Look, the people of the land are now many, and you would have them cease from their labors!" So the same day Pharaoh commanded the taskmasters over the people and their foremen, saying, "You are no longer to give the people straw to make brick as previously; let them go and gather straw for themselves. But the quota of bricks which they were making previously, you shall impose on them; you are not to reduce any of it. Because they are lazy, therefore they cry out, 'Let us go and sacrifice to our God.' Let the labor be heavier on the men, and let them work at it so that they will pay no attention to false words." (Exodus 5:1-9)

We see from the writings of Moses that God wants men to drop what they are doing and "go out into the wilderness" to meet with Him. He wants them to get away from their dull and backbreaking activities and to be still before Him. But, like Pharaoh of old, the devil becomes enraged and demands that men be given more and more to do with less and less time to do it. Especially in the midst of today's economic hardships, people everywhere are forced to work harder and longer just to try to make ends meet.

Ceaseless work and constant activity constitute Satan's master plan to keep men from connecting "in the wilderness" (or in a quiet place in one's surroundings) with the Lord of heaven. People claim they can't go to church, a Bible study, or a prayer meeting, and cannot seek God in undisturbed communion because they are too exhausted or because their work schedules interfere with their relationship with God, but somehow they manage to find enough spare time to spend hours on the internet or to leisurely play games on cell phones.

Talk about a vicious treadmill! The devil knows full well that God dwells in quiet places and in calm vicinities, so he goads men with endless labors and fills their lives with constant noise and commotion. The Bible tells us to "[b]e still, and know that I am God" (Psalm 46:10, NIV), but the devil yells, "Keep moving, don't stop! Turn up the volume! Watch another program! Have a party! Call somebody! And if you even think about praying, put it off until tomorrow because there is just too much to do today."

Work! Work! Work! Distract! Distract! Distract! That is Satan's motto. And if you finish working, he screams, "Do something else to keep busy or to waste more time!" But whatever you do, don't be still and don't be silent, or you might hear the beckoning whispers of God's gentle and quiet spirit. Even dedicated followers of Christ can be unwittingly goaded by Satan to get on the treadmill of religious activities and the Ferris wheel of social activism in order to keep them from connecting with God.

The Gospel of Luke tells of an occasion involving two sisters. While Martha was totally preoccupied with working, Mary chose to "go into the wilderness" and sit at the feet of Jesus. Mary sat motionless before the Son of God and was transformed by every word He spoke to her. She was truly at rest and at peace, while Martha was entangled in a flurry of busyness which only made her anxious and irritable (Luke 10:38-42). Notice how this infernal Pharaoh managed to work Martha into such a frenzy of activity in serving Christ that she became overwhelmed to the point of resentment. She despised her sister, Mary, for not getting on the treadmill with her when it came to preparing the meal, setting the table, and providing for their guests.

Martha wasn't the only believer whom Jesus had to reprove for being more preoccupied with activity than with Him. Christ rebuked the church of Ephesus because the devil so managed to goad them with "religious" works that they "left [their] first love" (Revelation 2:4). Satan doesn't mind if people do a lot of work for God as long as they are not consumed with God. The devil knows that unless God's people get alone with their Creator "in the wilderness," virtually none of their labors will be anointed of Him. Religious activity without God's anointing just becomes a bunch of busywork that is "full of sound and fury and signifying nothing" (Shakespeare's *Macbeth*, Act V, scene 5).

Not putting God first because of work is a tactic of the Pharaoh from hell demanding that we keep moving on his infernal treadmills. God says to "be still," while Satan says to "keep moving!" The choice is ours and, like Mary of old, if we choose the better part, we will not be denied it.

"The Big One" Has Two Brothers

Seismology is a branch of geology that studies earthquakes and attempts to measure and predict the vibrations of the earth's interior. It is an earth science that is becoming more and more relevant as earthquakes around the globe continue to increase in both numbers and magnitude.

Back in the 1990s there were almost 200,000 earthquakes that claimed over 112,000 lives (averaging 9,333 per month).[3] From the year 2000 to 2009, there were nearly 262,000 quakes killing approximately 520,000 people (averaging 43,333 per month).[4] Then in less than two months into the next decade, over 125,000 people had been killed (averaging 62,500 per month) by more tremors measuring 7.0 to 9.0 on the Richter scale. Today, earthquakes continue to grow exponentially in number and intensity.[5]

However, seismologists keep telling us that we haven't seen anything yet. They continue to predict "the big one" is coming to California because of the San Andreas fault. "The big one" is the name scientists have given to the expected quake that will be triggered when the tectonic plates of the Pacific slide against the North American plates along the fault line of the San Andreas Valley. These experts tell us that when (not "if") this quake hits, it will unleash one of the most destructive forces ever witnessed by mankind.

Well, Jesus Christ was not a certified seismologist and neither were the rest of the biblical prophets, but what they have predicted concerning earthquakes would make even the most pessimistic seismologist and the most doomsday geologist seem upbeat and optimistic in comparison. Jesus and the prophets predict that "the big one" has two giant brothers and that the last brother to arrive will make all of the combined earthquakes in recorded history look absolutely tame in comparison.

These two massive brothers will act as two huge bookends enclosing volumes of death and carnage within a seven-year period known as the "great tribulation." This seven years of mass destruction will begin with a combined war and an asteroid, and it will end with a gigantic quake that will be triggered by the sun itself.

Ezekiel the prophet tells us this seven years of hell on Earth will begin with Israel being invaded by "the land of Magog" (Russia) along with a number of Islamic nations (see Ezekiel 38-39). However, the prophet John tells us that just when these invading armies are about to strike, an angelic being in heaven will throw a censer filled with fire to the earth "and there followed peals of thunder and sounds and flashes of lightning and an earthquake" (Revelation 8:5). John goes on to say that there comes "hail and fire, mixed with blood" as "a great mountain burning with fire" destroys a third of the ships at sea and kills a third of the creatures in the oceans and that a third of these waters become like the blood of a dead man (vv. 7-9). As a result of this asteroid colliding with the earth, God says through His prophet Ezekiel,

> In My zeal and in My blazing wrath I declare that on that day there will surely be a great earthquake in the land of Israel. The fish of the sea, the birds of the heavens, the beasts of the field, all the creeping things that creep on the earth, and all the men who are on the face of the earth will shake at My presence; the mountains also will be thrown down, the steep pathways will collapse and every wall will fall to the ground. (Ezekiel 38:19-20)

This war and this asteroid will cause every insect, every bird, every fish, every beast, and every man on Earth to shake at God's presence. The firestorms ignited by this war and by this blazing mountain will choke the earth with smoke thick enough to diminish the light of the sun, moon, and stars by a third (see Revelation 8:7-12). A quarter of mankind is going to be destroyed in this global holocaust and its resulting earthquake, but this worldwide quake is actually the "big one's" bigger brother. Their biggest brother will arrive seven years after this initial shaking of the continents.

The last big brother will appear because of the sun. From the prophet Isaiah to the prophet Habakkuk, and from the apostle John to the Son of God Himself, the Bible predicts over 20 different times that our sun is going to go out like a lightbulb and the earth is going to be plunged into total darkness. It appears from the predictions that the sun will someday explode and, after scorching men with intense heat, it will become "as black as sackcloth" (see Joel 2:2, 10, 31; 3:15; Amos 8:9; Micah 3:6; Habakkuk 3:11; Job 5:14; Isaiah 5:30; 8:20, 22; 13:10; 24:23; 30:26; 59:9-10; Jeremiah 6:4; 15:9; Matthew 24:29; Mark 13:24; Luke 21:25; Acts 2:20; Revelation 6:12).

John tells us that an angelic being pours out a bowl upon the sun and it causes the temperatures of the earth to rise dramatically. Then another angel pours out his bowl upon the world and it becomes darkened (Revelation 16:8-9). What is described here is what appears to be a type of nova that quickly becomes a black hole. There may be some other interpretation to explain how our sun and moon will become "seven times brighter" (Isaiah 30:26). However, this is exactly what takes place when a massive star has too little fuel left to maintain its temperature. It expands dramatically and then experiences a gravitational collapse. As our sun caves in on itself, all of the atoms and molecules that make up the 900,000-mile diameter of the sun will be compacted into a dense ball no bigger than 15 miles across. Its corresponding gravitational pull will become so intense that not even light will escape its magnetic force. It will, as the prophets predict, become as "black as sackcloth," or something very similar to what scientists describe as a black hole.

Consequently, this catastrophic phenomenon will have a massive effect upon the crust of the earth. Our planet is kept in its orbital path by the gravitational pull of the sun. The world is spinning on its axis at 1,000 miles per hour and is traveling through space at 67,000 miles an hour. With this in mind, consider what Isaiah the prophet predicts is going to happen to the world:

Behold, the Lord lays the earth waste, devastates it, distorts its surface and scatters its inhabitants. ... the foundations of the earth shake ... The earth is split through, the earth is shaken violently. The earth reels to and fro like a drunkard and it totters like a shack. (24:1, 18-20)

The prophet John says, "He [Christ] broke the sixth seal, and there was a great earthquake; and the sun became black as sackcloth made of hair ... and every mountain and island were moved out of their places" (Revelation 6:12, 14). Talk about "big brother"! This guy is colossal! Everything is coming down when he shows up. From the Sears Tower to the Eiffel Tower, and from the Golden Gate Bridge to the pyramids of Egypt, everything is going to collapse like the sudden destruction of the twin towers on 9/11. Nothing is going to be left standing—nothing! Mountains are going to be moved, islands are going to disappear, and every man-made structure is going to crumble into dust.

So the next time seismologists talk about "the big one," know for sure that the "big one" they have in mind will be nothing but a faint tremor in comparison to its "bigger" and "biggest" brothers. These two earthquakes will mark the beginning and the end of the world as we know it. The predictions of the true geophysicists and the real geoscientists (the prophets, the apostles, and the Son of God) make the predictions of today's geologists seem like child's play in comparison. The "big one" has two massive siblings that seismologists can't even begin to imagine without knowing the prophecies of God's true earthquake prognosticators.

A Little Man Finds a Big Way

I happen to be one of those hardheaded individuals who believe "where there is a will, there is a way." It's true; people who really desire to do something in life can usually find a way to accomplish it, regardless of the difficulties and the costs involved. Yet how often do people say they can't go to church or attend a Bible study or get alone with God in prayer because of their work schedule, or because of the kids, or because of being tired, or because of the weather? Or because, because, because!

Well, if there were one man in the Bible who could have given an excuse for not trying to seek God, it would have been a very short and very despised man by the name of Zaccheus. The Gospel of Luke tells us that he was a chief tax collector who wanted to see Jesus, but because of his little stature he could not peer over the heads of the crowds. Not only was he limited because of his size, but being a tax collector, he was ostracized from society and despised within the Jewish community. And being a chief tax collector made him even more contemptible. He no doubt bribed a Roman official for his job and greatly enriched himself by taxing his countrymen more than was required. It is likely that Zaccheus could only view Jesus from a distance and no doubt had to strain to hear him speak, because his social status made him such an outsider. Yet he was totally mesmerized by this carpenter from Galilee and made up his mind to find a way to get close to him.

Luke's account tells us of this determined little man when he wrote:

> Zaccheus was trying to see who Jesus was, and was unable because of the crowd, for he was small in stature. So he ran on ahead and climbed up into a sycamore tree in order to see Him, for He was about to pass through that way. When Jesus came to the place, He looked up and said to him, "Zaccheus, hurry and come down, for today I must stay at your house." And he hurried and came down and

received Him gladly. When [the crowds] saw it, they all began to grumble, saying, "He has gone to be the guest of a man who is a sinner." Zaccheus stopped and said to the Lord, "Behold, Lord, half of my possessions I will give to the poor, and if I have defrauded anyone of anything, I will give back four times as much." And Jesus said to him, "Today salvation has come to this house, because he, too, is a son of Abraham. For the Son of Man has come to seek and to save that which was lost." (Luke 19:3-10)

The writer of Hebrews tells us that God "is a rewarder of those who [diligently, KJV] seek Him" (Hebrews 11:6), and the epistle of James admonishes us to "[d]raw near to God and He will draw near to [us]" (James 4:8). That is the divine order. God does not impose Himself on anyone, but He is always looking for people who are looking for Him.

In 2 Chronicles we learn about a king of Judah named Asa. God said to him and his people:

[T]he Lord is with you when you are with Him. And if you seek Him, He will let you find Him; but if you forsake Him, He will forsake you. For many days Israel was without the true God and without a teaching priest and without law. But in their distress they turned to the Lord God of Israel, and they sought Him, and He let them find Him. (2 Chronicles 15:2-4)

God also said to this Judean king that "the eyes of the Lord move to and fro throughout the earth that He may strongly support those whose heart is completely His" (2 Chronicles 16:9).

If someone says they "can't find God," it is because they are not looking for God. If people merely make up excuses for not going to church or not studying the Bible, it is because they have little or no appetite for the things of God. Therefore, they simply rationalize and justify their lack of interest in heavenly things by making excuses. However, the apostle Paul tells us if men would but seek for God, if they would grope for Him, that He is not far from anyone, and that in Him we live and move and exist (Acts 17:27-28). In other words, God is closer to us than our next breath. Consequently, any pretexts that are manufactured when it comes to sincerely connecting with God are just that: a masquerade of endless excuses. He can be seen, if only we are determined to see Him.

Like all men, Zaccheus was a born sinner. But unlike most men, Zaccheus was a true seeker. He found a way around his short-comings and discovered a solution to his predicament, because he was absolutely determined to see the Son of God in spite of his disadvantages. The diligence of this little man who found a big way is a mute testimony to the rest of us that "where there is a will, there is a way" and that "God is a rewarder of those who diligently seek Him."

Fire in the Belly

Exactly what is "fire in the belly"? To the Chinese, it means being angry, and to others it may mean heartburn or indigestion. But to most people in the Western Hemisphere, it simply means being driven or consumed with an inner drive or ambition to achieve a goal or to accomplish a task. In short, fire in the belly is zeal. It is characterized as a passion and enthusiasm for what is really important to a person, which can be a gamut of things, depending upon each individual's priorities.

As such, individuals can be seen in subzero temperatures with their shirts off and their faces painted, screaming themselves hoarse as they root for their favorite football team; others devote almost every waking hour to train for an Olympic medal; still others throw their heart and soul into a profession. People can even be zealous when it comes to engaging in a number of criminal activities or get-rich-quick schemes. One can be driven by greed to do almost anything, but the fire in the belly that I am talking about is to be driven by purpose—to be motivated to push one's self against all hardships and in the face of all setbacks in order to give one's life meaning.

Thomas Edison was unquestionably a man with fire in the belly. He was driven by a passion to discover and a zeal to invent. Regardless of how many disappointments he would experience, he would say, "I have not failed. I have just found 10,000 ways that don't work." Virtually his entire life was devoted to harnessing energy and converting various materials into a number of marvelous innovations and labor-saving devices.

But how is it that certain people become driven by a passion that ignites their life's objective while so many others have little or no energy in regards to a purpose-driven life? We can always suggest that temperament or environment and genetics are what make some people ambitious and other people lethargic. However, if we seriously reflect upon what God has made each individual for, then it becomes clear that every human being has a

God-given purpose and is designed to have "fire in the belly" when it comes to the things of God.

When someone once asked Christ which was the greatest commandment, Jesus responded by quoting from the book of Deuteronomy: "You shall love the Lord your God with all your heart, and with all your soul, and with all your strength, and with all your mind" (Luke 10:27; see also Deuteronomy 6:5). Apart from God, there is no everlasting purpose, regardless of how passionate a person becomes in his life's pursuits.

At the same time, it is very possible to have a zeal for God yet be totally out of the will of God and completely miss God's intention for one's life. The apostle Paul had a zeal for God that outshone all of his contemporaries. However, the Bible tells us that Paul was at war with Jesus as he impetuously persecuted the true followers of God's Son. Today, many Muslims are so driven by religious zeal that they are willing to kill themselves in their fanatical attempts to please their god and their fellow believers. The Pharisees and religious leaders of Jesus' day were extremely zealous in regards to their theological traditions, but Christ called them hypocrites, whitewashed tombs, and blind guides who strained out gnats and who swallowed camels (Matthew 23:13-28).

"Fire in the belly" apart from a personal relationship with Christ becomes a mindless fanaticism, which is far worse (and in some cases, far more dangerous) than being apathetic and indifferent to the things of God. Religious fanatics can be found by the millions in cults, false religions, and a host of metaphysical beliefs and practices. From voodoo loyalists to UFO enthusiasts, people may manifest a passion and a zeal, but their fire in the belly is destined to self-destruct because God is not in it, despite the fact that they may claim He is. When speaking of the religious Jews of his day, the apostle Paul declared:

> For I testify about them that they have a zeal for God, but not in accordance with knowledge. For not knowing about God's righteousness and seeking to establish their own, they did not subject themselves

to the righteousness of God. For Christ is the end of the law for righteousness to everyone who believes. (Romans 10:2-4)

Paul says that these religious people had a zeal for God, but their fire in the belly only made their religious commitments all the more tragic. Conversely, he said in his letter to Titus,

> For the grace of God has appeared, bringing salvation to all men, instructing us to deny ungodliness and worldly desires and to live sensibly, righteously and godly in the present age, looking for the blessed hope and the appearing of the glory of our great God and Savior, Christ Jesus, who gave Himself for us to redeem us from every lawless deed, and to purify for Himself a people for His own possession, zealous for good deeds. (Titus 2:11-14)

God wants us to be zealous for good works in the name of Jesus Christ, not driven by psychotic self-interests or demented fanaticism. The God of heaven wants men to be focused, to be driven in the right direction, and—equally important—to be consistent.

At the beginning of Jesus' public ministry, he was outraged at the wickedness and the dishonesty of the money changers in the temple. He made a whip and drove out these hypocritical thieves and angrily turned over their money tables while saying to them, "It is written, 'My house shall be called a house of prayer'; but you are making it a robbers' den" (Matthew 21:13). At the very end of Christ's public ministry, He did the exact-same thing because the corrupt money changers had returned with all of their thievish and covetous practices.

Concerning these two incidents, His disciples remembered that it was written of Jesus saying, "Zeal for Your house will consume me" (John 2:17). From start to finish in Jesus' public ministry, He demonstrated unwavering zeal. He was not a blind fanatic but rather a purpose-driven man of God who manifested clearly what it means to have "fire in the belly."

The Gospel of John tells us of an occasion in Jesus' ministry when his disciples went into a village to purchase some food, and while they were gone, Christ initiated a conversation with a woman drawing water from a well. He spent the entire time witnessing to this lost and sinful woman and He led her to salvation. When the disciples returned, they encouraged Jesus to eat lunch with them. However, Christ responded by saying:

> "I have food to eat that you do not know about." So the disciples were saying to one another, "No one brought Him anything to eat, did he?" Jesus said to them, "My food is to do the will of Him who sent Me and to accomplish His work." (4:32-34)

Jesus made it very clear that a man must have much more than meat or vegetables if he is to have true meaning in life, and an eternal significance does not exist apart from a proper relationship with God. A person may find fulfillment in a job or in a career, but it is not their God-given meaning. By trade, the Apostles were fishermen; Paul was a tentmaker; Jesus, a carpenter; Luke, a physician; Matthew, a tax collector; and David, a king. But these were only their temporary professions, not their eternal purpose for living.

Only a proper connection with God can give a person everlasting purpose. And only a Christ-centered fire in the belly can generate a zeal that is truly quest-motivated. In the book of Acts, we read of a woman named Tabitha who had one talent: She could sew like the wind. That was her passion, and she used her divinely given gift with all of her heart to glorify God. She had a fire in the belly to serve Christ with her abilities, and in turn, God glorified Tabitha by selecting her to be the only grown woman in the Bible to be raised from the dead (Acts 9:36-42).

To the world, a sewing needle and a thread may not appear to have much significance, but this woman found her passion and used it for God's glory. Her love for God ignited a fire in the belly that drove her to serve Him with all of her heart, mind, soul, and strength. In contrast, Jesus severely rebuked the church of Laodicea for their halfheartedness when it came to their divinely ordained purpose, and He strongly reproved the church of Sardis for their incomplete deeds and for letting their passion for Him die out. He reproached the church of Ephesus for losing their first love, and He condemned the churches of Pergamum and Thyatira for compromising with evil and with false doctrine. However, He highly commended the weak and struggling church of Philadelphia for their steadfast commitment to Him and to His Word. He also encouraged the persecuted church of Smyrna and told them that their steadfastness towards Him made them rich in the eyes of God (Revelations 2 and 3).

Only two of the seven churches of Asia maintained their fire in the belly for Christ, and therefore they were highly praised. To the other churches, Jesus emphasized that He will not tolerate compromise or a lack of passion in their relationship with Him. To Him, it is like being in a passionless marriage where His spouse has little desire to please Him and little admiration for Him. She simply does the bare minimum to maintain a marriage that is on life support.

Instead, He demands a fulfilling and enriching relationship that is built not on perfection, but passion. Our human mistakes He understands, but our lack of devotion and intensity He will not tolerate. He made us to know Him, love Him, and serve Him with all of our entity. Failure to connect with Him in this way is to miss why we were made in the first place (regardless of how much passion and drive we may exhibit for the fleeting things in this world).

Hence, with the things that really matter from an eternal perspective, to demonstrate a "fire in the belly" as exuberant as the passion of a sport's fanatic would be a worthy ambition for each of us.

Friends that Bend

The type of people with whom we associate says a lot about us. Wise King Solomon noted, "As in water face reflects face, so the heart of man reflects man" (Proverbs 27:19). In other words, our friends reflect us. They are mirrors projecting our own image. As the old adage says, "Show me the company that you keep, and I will show you what kind of person you are."

In addition to acting as a reflection, friendships are bonds that bend, similar to how refraction is the bending of light rays. Our friends direct us with their likes and dislikes, they influence us with their values and activities, and they can motivate and inspire as well as support and sympathize. A friend's character can go a long way in shaping our own character. Good friends can be reliable, trustworthy, and dependable, while others can be superficial, parasitical, and draining. However, regardless of what they are like, the bottom line is that we are the ones that choose them.

They can motivate us to obtain a college degree or influence us to become addicted to drugs, they can lead us to prison or steer us to prosperity, and they can bring us to heaven or drag us to hell. Friendships are so powerful that not only can they determine the course of our lives, but they can be extremely instrumental in determining our eternal destiny. Unquestionably, there are a multitude of saints in the kingdom of Christ who are eternally grateful to those whose company brought them to God, and there are countless souls in the abode of the damned who are cursing the ones whose influence brought them to such a horrible place.

It was the apostle Paul who said to the Corinthians, "Do not be deceived: 'Bad company corrupts good morals'" (1 Corinthians 15:33). In short, if we associate with thieves, we will likely become a thief; if we hang around with drug addicts, odds are that we will turn into a drug addict; if we keep company with criminals, we will end up behind bars; and if we pal around with gossips, we will develop a habit of slandering as well.

The opposite is also true: If we spend quality time and daily time with God in prayer and in reading His Word, we will inevitably become godlier; and if we constantly keep company with those who follow and obey God, we will become as they are. This is the primary reason why God tells His people to "not forsak[e] our own assembling together, as is the habit of some, but encourag[e] one another; and all the more as you see the day [of Christ's return] drawing near" (Hebrews 10:25). The importance of assembling together in Jesus' name with like-minded people cannot be overemphasized.

Consider these wise words from Solomon:

> Two are better than one because they have a good return for their labor. For if either of them falls, the one will lift up his companion. But woe to the one who falls when there is not another to lift him up. Furthermore, if two lie down together they keep warm, but how can one be warm alone? And if one can overpower him who is alone, two can resist him. A cord of three strands is not quickly torn apart. (Ecclesiastes 4:9-12)

Oftentimes, when Christians least feel like gathering together with other believers is the time they especially need to do so. When followers of Christ are struggling most with temptations and with discouragement is when they earnestly need to seek out other followers of the Lord. In the book of Malachi, we read of how a number of God's people became so discouraged in their walk with Him that they began to feel like their commitment to the Lord was pointless. But God said,

> "Your words have been arrogant against Me ... Yet you say, 'What have we spoken against You?' You have said, 'It is vain to serve God; and what profit is it that we have kept His charge, and that we have walked in mourning before the Lord of hosts? So

now we call the arrogant blessed; not only are the doers of wickedness built up but they also test God and escape.'" Then those who feared the Lord spoke to one another, and the Lord gave attention and heard it, and a book of remembrance was written before Him for those who fear the Lord and who esteem His name. "They will be Mine," says the Lord of hosts, "on the day that I prepare My own possession, and I will spare them as a man spares his own son who serves him." So you will again distinguish between the righteous and the wicked, between one who serves God and one who does not serve Him. (3:13-18)

Malachi tells us that when the believers of his day felt most discouraged and least like serving God they "spoke to one another." In other words, they encouraged each other to continue serving the Lord in spite of their circumstances and disillusionments; and God took note of it. Indeed, Jesus said, "For where two or three are gathered together in my name, there am I in the midst of them" (Matthew 18:20, KJV). This is why the powers of darkness will always do everything they can to keep Christians from gathering together in the name of Jesus Christ. They know full well the potency of fellowships, and they understand completely how vulnerable believers are when they get out of the habit of assembling together.

Satan will ceaselessly attempt to thwart individuals from convening together for the purpose of reading God's Word or seeking God in prayer. The devil will throw every obstacle and rationalization before men and women to prevent them from becoming a band of godly brothers and sisters. He is fully aware that a single burning ember will quickly become an ice cube in the midst of a damp and frigid environment; whereas the greater the number of flaming coals, the hotter the fire, the brighter the light, and the more warmth and radiance, the more likely it is to attract the religiously lost and the spiritually lukewarm.

In short, friends that continue to encourage one another in the Lord are most likely going to end up on the right side of eternity. However, friendships that encourage us in godless behavior and influence us in evil activities are sure to bring us to ruin, both in this life and the next. Friends bend us one way or another and the closer the friend, the more powerful the bend. If it were possible to interview every person in prison and every soul in hell, asking them what greatest single factor brought them to their deplorable surroundings, the answers would most likely include "the friends they chose and the company that they kept."

God called Abraham His friend (Isaiah 41:8), and Jesus said to His disciples,

> Greater love has no one than this, that one lay down his life for his friends. You are My friends if you do what I command you. No longer do I call you slaves, for the slave does not know what his master is doing; but I have called you friends, for all things that I have heard from My Father I have made known to you. (John 15:13-15)

There is no greater friend to have than God, and there are no better friendships to maintain than those consisting of God's friends. But like all friendships, it must be built on trust, grounded in loyalty, nurtured in fellowship, and cultivated in companionship. And like all friendships, it will be tested and it will be tried, but such trials will inevitably determine just how genuine a friendship truly is.

In conclusion, we would do well to reflect on our own group of friends while asking ourselves two very important questions: "Does this friend draw me closer to God or further away from Him?" and "Am I the type of friend who is bringing this person nearer to the Lord or distancing him or her from the Lord?" In either case, the answer will say a great deal about us, because we are either bending or being bent by truly powerful forces.

Hard-pressed in Hardpan

Virtually nothing can grow in hardpan because of its insoluble materials and minerals which restrict the downward flow of water and nutrients into the soil. To get anything to flourish or produce fruit in such an environment requires a great deal of sweat and back-breaking labor from someone determined and hard-pressed to get something to germinate and develop to maturity under such circumstances.

The apostle Paul addressed being hard-pressed during his service to his Savior when he wrote:

> For to me, to live is Christ and to die is gain. But if I am to live on in the flesh, this will mean fruitful labor for me; and I do not know which to choose. But I am hard-pressed from both directions, having the desire to depart and be with Christ, for that is very much better; yet to remain on in the flesh is more necessary for your sake. Convinced of this, I know that I will remain and continue with you all for your progress and joy in the faith. (Philippians 1:21-25)

Paul said that he was "hard-pressed" in two directions: desiring to die and be with Jesus in heaven, and wanting to live on and help save others for the sake of Christ and to edify believers in their Christian faith. He concluded that to die and be with the Lord was much better, but to live on was necessary for the salvation of souls and for the building up of Christ's Church. Unquestionably, Paul became the greatest of the Apostles in terms of bearing fruit for the Lord. However, his tremendous harvest did not come without tremendous costs. He told the Corinthian church that he served Christ

> in far more labors, in far more imprisonments, beaten times without number, often in danger of

death. Five times I received from the Jews thirty-nine lashes. Three times I was beaten with rods, once I was stoned, three times I was shipwrecked, a night and a day I have spent in the deep. I have been on frequent journeys, in dangers from rivers, dangers from robbers, dangers from my country-men, dangers from the Gentiles, dangers in the city, dangers in the wilderness, dangers on the sea, dangers among false brethren; I have been in labor and hardship, through many sleepless nights, in hunger and thirst, often without food, in cold and exposure. Apart from such external things, there is the daily pressure on me of concern for all the churches. (2 Corinthians 11:23-28)

This beaten, tortured, and imprisoned man goes on to say that he was constantly concerned about those who were weak in their faith and for any believer who fell into sin. He was hard-pressed to save souls for heaven in a world full of hardpan, and no doubt he often experienced discouragement in all his efforts to bear fruit for Christ. Nonetheless, these words spoken by Jesus can be very reassuring:

Truly, truly, I say to you, unless a grain of wheat falls into the earth and dies, it remains alone; but if it dies, it bears much fruit. He who loves his life loses it, and he who hates his life in this world will keep it to life eternal. If anyone serves Me, he must follow Me; and where I am, there My servant will be also; if anyone serves Me, the Father will honor him. (John 12:24-26)

Undoubtedly, as the apostle Paul languished in one prison after another, he must have thought that so much of his labor was in vain. With each new trial and with every new disappointment, he must have felt like he was digging in soil as unyielding as cement and that his repeated attempts to share the gospel of salvation were often futile. He yearned to die and be done with his hardships, loneliness, and pain. He longed to be with Christ and forever be out of the devil's crosshairs.

Nevertheless, due to his love for God, he was hard-pressed to bear fruit for Christ and he became the most spiritually productive man the world had ever seen. This is because he died long before he was dead. He died to the world, to his passions, and to the distractions around him in his hard-pressed efforts to be fruitful for the kingdom of God. Consequently, for the past 2,000 years his hard labor in hardpan continues to bring forth fruit for Christ even today. Almost half of the New Testament was written by him, and only God knows how much spiritual fruit his writings ceaselessly spawn with each new generation.

With this in mind, anytime one's labors for God seem pointless, let the life of this hard-pressed man toiling in hardpan serve as a reminder that if anyone—from Sunday school teachers to worldwide evangelists, and from Christian parents to faithful prayer warriors—is hard-pressed enough, even in a world of hardpan, he or she can bear fruit with the grace of God working through their lives.

Back to the Future

An Assemblyman from Virginia once said, "I know of no way of judging of the future but by the past." Someone else once declared, "We learn from history that we do not learn from history." And lastly, there is a well-worn quote, "Those that fail to learn from history are doomed to repeat it."

It is genuinely uncanny how history continues to repeat itself and how mankind almost seems incapable of learning from its past failures and previous mistakes. The communist revolution reenacted the atheistic and brutal blunders of the French Revolution; Hitler followed Napoleon's folly with his invasion of Russia; America made the same mistakes as the French in Vietnam; the Viet Minh became the forerunners of the Viet Cong as they repeated their guerilla warfare; Afghanistan has become the proverbial revolving door for one nation after another; and ancient Israel continuously imitated the disastrous errors of their rebellious forefathers.

Flavius Josephus, a first-century Jewish historian, recorded many of the recycled failures of God's chosen people, but it took a prophet to foretell future events through the spectacles of Jewish history. Jesus Christ could see thousands of years into the future and (more than any historian) pointed to past recorded chronicles to predict impending judgments and to foretell coming events. For example, Jesus looked back in the past and foretold how homosexual activity and gay marriage would be widespread and promoted just prior to His return. He said,

> It was the same as happened in the days of Lot: they were eating, they were drinking, they were buying, they were selling, they were planting, they were building; but on the day that Lot went out from Sodom it rained fire and brimstone from heaven and destroyed them all. It will be just the same on the day that the Son of Man is revealed. ... Remember Lot's wife. (Luke 17:28-30, 32)

The Scriptures strongly suggest that seven years before the total destruction of the world, Jesus will return in the clouds (when no one sees Him), and will steal away all those who are truly committed to Him (see Matthew 24:40-41; 25:1-13; Luke 21:36; 1 Corinthians 15:51-53; 1 Thessalonians 4:13-18; Revelation 3:10-11). However, two prominent activities will characterize people at the time when Christ raptures His obedient followers: First, they will be preoccupied with material things and by making a living. Secondly, homosexuality will be very prevalent and acceptable, and the present gay lifestyles will become so approved that the prophet Jude predicts these practices will be promoted even within the Church. He said,

> For certain persons have crept in unnoticed, those who were long beforehand marked out for this condemnation, ungodly persons who turn the grace of our God into licentiousness. ... And angels who did not keep their own domain, but abandoned their proper abode, He has kept in eternal bonds ... just as Sodom and Gomorrah and the cities around them, since they in the same way as these indulged in gross immorality and went after strange flesh. (Jude 4, 6-7)

This is why Jesus said, "Remember Lot's wife." Because although she was a lifelong heterosexual, her heart was with those who lived in this preferred sexual practice.

Even the apostle John suggests that the capital city of Israel will promote and legalize the gay agenda (just before Christ's return) when He predicted that Jerusalem will "mystically" be called "Sodom" (Revelation 11:8). Jesus and the prophets clearly saw the world's present sexual behavior by gazing through the looking glass of past events, and past events almost always point to future events—especially when it comes to the end of the age and the second coming of Christ.

There are over 1,000 references to Christ's second coming in the Old Testament, and there are over 300 prophecies concerning Jesus' return in the New Testament.[6] Jesus said if people wanted to get a glimpse of this coming event, they needed to look back at the past. He said,

> And just as it happened in the days of Noah, so it will be also in the days of the Son of Man: they were eating, they were drinking, they were marrying, they were being given in marriage, until the day that Noah entered the ark, and the flood came and destroyed them all. (Luke 17: 26-27)

Exactly what was it like during the days of Noah that Jesus looked back on in order to predict the future? The book of Genesis tells us that "the Lord saw that the wickedness of man was great on the earth, and that every intent of the thoughts of his heart was only evil continually" (Genesis 6:5).

Jesus saw the coming wickedness of mankind by observing the corruption of mankind in the past. Although the critic will argue that the moral conduct of man has remained constant for centuries, the truly honest and informed person can see clearly that mankind's wickedness is increasing exponentially and his present corruption is a definite reflection of a specific time in past history.

Jesus also pointed to His coming resurrection by pointing back to the historical episode of Jonah being entombed in the belly of a huge fish for three days and three nights (Matthew 12:39; Luke 11:29-30). Christ also referred back to David and his famished men when justifying how his own hungry disciples were feeding themselves on a Sabbath day (Mark 2:23-28; Matthew 12:1-8; 1 Samuel 21:1-6). When foretelling of the coming day of judgment, Jesus looked back to the men of Nineveh and to the Queen of the South to predict this awesome judgment of the damned (Matthew 12:41-42). He pointed back to the murder of Cain and to the slaying of Zechariah the prophet to foretell of how severely his own generation was going to be judged for killing God's messengers (Luke 11:48-52).

Yes, it is truly astonishing how often men fail to learn from past events and how history seems to be hopelessly stuck on rewind. The past is just a dead giveaway when it comes to knowing the future. This is one of the reasons why it is so important to understand history. The great historian Arnold Toynbee observed, "Civilizations die from suicide, not by murder."[7] They fall from within as they repeat the behavior and blunders of past generations.

Therefore, it would be wise to remember the words of Jesus and the prophets. We need to look behind us if we really want to see what's in front of us. To know the future clearly, we need to clearly see the past. "Back to the future" — what a concept! Jesus knew this notion very well. That is why He encourages us to intently look into the past if we truly want to see what is ahead of us in the future — and then prepare for what is coming!

The Resurrection of the Damned

The Bible speaks of two very distinct resurrections, and everyone who has ever lived is destined to be in either one or the other. There will be absolutely no exceptions. Young or old, rich or poor, strong or weak, believer or atheist, it doesn't matter; everyone will someday be resurrected from the grave. Everyone! The only question is, "Which resurrection will it be?" It's going to be in either the resurrection of the righteous or the resurrection of the damned.

The Bible refers to the damned as being the spiritually "dead" and the Scriptures foretell exactly how and when they will be resurrected. It will take place at the very end of Christ's 1,000-year reign on Earth. He will begin this millennial reign after returning to a world that has been utterly destroyed with war and natural disasters. He will slay the wicked; imprison Satan and the powers of darkness; recreate the ravaged world, making it new; and set up His rule and dominion for 10 centuries. It's immediately after this 1,000-year reign of Christ's that this incredible and awesome day of judgment takes place. There will be no righteous or saved in this terrifying judgment, only the damned. The apostle John describes this dreadful event:

> Then I saw a great white throne and Him who sat upon it, from whose presence earth and heaven fled away, and no place was found for them. And I saw the dead [the damned], the great and the small, standing before the throne, and books were opened; and another book was opened, which is the book of life; and the dead were judged from the things which were written in the books, according to their deeds. (Revelation 20:11-12)

This is the judgment of the spiritually "dead." Then John goes on to describe their resurrection: "And the sea gave up the dead [the damned] which were in it, and death [the grave] and Hades

[hell] gave up the dead which were in them; and they were judged, every one of them according to their deeds" (20:13).

What John describes here is truly mind-boggling. He says that all the lost souls in hell will be called forth from their place of torment. Then Christ will summon forth their decaying or decomposed corpses from the seas and the graves of the world, and their spirits will be reunited with their resurrected bodies. They will stand trembling before this all-consuming fire of holiness who is seated upon this blazing throne, as described by the prophet Daniel:

> I kept looking until thrones were set up, and the Ancient of Days took His seat; His vesture was like white snow and the hair of His head like pure wool. His throne was ablaze with flames, its wheels were a burning fire. A river of fire was flowing and coming out from before Him; thousands upon thousands were attending Him, and myriads upon myriads were standing before Him; the court sat, and the books were opened. (Daniel 7:9-10)

This throne has wheels on it which suggests that the one who is seated upon it is not constrained by time or space. He can travel anywhere — past, present, or future — and bring all the facts, the deeds, and the motives of each condemned soul into focus.

Jesus Himself spoke of this day when He declared,

> Woe to you, Chorazin! Woe to you, Bethsaida! For if the miracles had occurred in Tyre and Sidon which occurred in you, they would have repented long ago in sackcloth and ashes. Nevertheless I say to you, it will be more tolerable for Tyre and Sidon in the day of judgment than for you. And you, Capernaum, will not be exalted to heaven, will you? You will descend to Hades; for if the miracles had occurred in Sodom which occurred in you, it would

have remained to this day. Nevertheless I say to you that it will be more tolerable for the land of Sodom in the day of judgment, than for you. (Matthew 11:21-24)

Jesus went on to say,

[E]very careless word that people speak, they shall give an accounting for it in the day of judgment. For by your words you will be justified, and by your words you will be condemned. ... The men of Nineveh will stand up with this generation at the judgment, and will condemn it because they repented at the preaching of Jonah ... The Queen of the South will rise up with this generation at the judgment and will condemn it, because she came from the ends of the earth to hear the wisdom of Solomon; and behold, something greater than Solomon is here. (12:36-37, 41-42)

There are none saved in this condemned sea of humanity, and it appears that this judgment will transpire in only one day—"the day of judgment." God, being God, will be able to judge each condemned soul simultaneously, and each soul being judged will be fully aware of every other damned soul's judgment.

This is the final judgment where God and His Word will finally be vindicated. This is the judgment where truth will finally win out, where "every knee will bow" and "every tongue will confess that Jesus Christ is Lord" (Philippians 2:10-11). This is the judgment where every false religion, deceptive teacher, heretic, apostate, and doctrine of demons will be exposed for what they are; where all the lies of Darwinism, UFOs, witchcraft, and every form of demonology will be seen for what it really is; and where the "politically correct" mask of homosexuality, gay marriage, abortion, and "tolerance" will be ripped off and revealed for the wickedness that it truly is. Apart from the damned but also witnessing this judgment will be the saved—all of God's people, His martyrs, and His followers—who will be exalted before all of God's enemies—those who despised, mocked, persecuted, and murdered God's chosen ones.

This is the resurrection of the damned and their final judgment, which must take place so that all of God's creation will witness His justice. Both the saved and the lost will concur with the righteous verdicts that God pronounces upon all the damned that stand silent before Him. Even saved family members will sadly but wholeheartedly agree and support His sentence of eternal fire for their loved ones who continued to spurn God's mercy and reject His salvation, and instead chose to trample underfoot His laws, His commands, and His overtures of love and grace.

The apostle John says that the final destination of the resurrected damned will be in the "lake of fire" which "is the second death. ... And if anyone's name was not found written in the book of life, he was thrown into the lake of fire" (Revelation 20:14-15). In light of this very sober reality, the only remaining question now is, "Exactly what resurrection am I going to be part of—the resurrection of the righteous, or the resurrection of the damned?" There are no other alternatives and the choice is entirely and eternally up to each and every individual.

Firing Squad for Firewood Gatherings

What would you think of a society or a country that executed people for gathering firewood? The slaying is not attributable to some desperate scarcity of fuel, or because the wood is being used for some murderous act. No, it's just that collecting sticks on a certain day of the week is declared to be a capital offense. Would you not conclude that this justification for capital punishment is a complete and total miscarriage of justice?

Now what would you think of a god who demanded the brutal killing of someone for picking up tree branches on a Saturday? Would you not assume that such a deity is as heartless and cruel as a sociopathic killer? Such a being would undoubtedly be viewed as a diabolical personage who is utterly and criminally insane.

Well, the God of the Bible demanded such a punishment for just such a trivial offense. In the book of Numbers, we read:

> Now while the sons of Israel were in the wilderness, they found a man gathering wood on the sabbath day. Those who found him gathering wood brought him to Moses and Aaron and to all the congregation; and they put him in custody because it had not been declared what should be done to him. Then the Lord said to Moses, "The man shall surely be put to death; all the congregation shall stone him with stones outside the camp." So all the congregation brought him outside the camp and stoned him to death with stones, just as the Lord had commanded Moses. (Numbers 15:32-36)

Being stoned to death has got to be a very painful way to die and undergoing such a torturous end for such a frivolous offense would only add tremendous insult to the hapless individual's demise. Consequently, the mystery of such an act of brutality can never be understood with the eyes of the flesh; it can only be comprehended with the eyes of the Spirit. As the apostle Paul put it, "[A] natural man does not accept the things of the Spirit of God, for they are foolishness to him; and he cannot understand them, because they are spiritually appraised" (1 Corinthians 2:14). Furthermore, Paul tells us in his letter to the Galatians:

> Before this faith came, we were held prisoners by the law, locked up until faith should be revealed. So the law [our tutor] was put in charge to lead us to Christ that we might be justified by faith. Now that faith has come, we are no longer under the supervision of the law. You are all sons of God through faith in Christ Jesus. (3:23-26, NIV)

So if the law is our tutor and our natural minds cannot comprehend the things of God, then with prayerful humility, we need to sit before God's law and ask what it is that the teacher is trying to convey to us, rather than turning on our heel and walking away in a self-righteous huff. We will never understand the true meaning of God's laws and His prophetic words unless we allow the Holy Spirit to open our eyes to these spiritual matters.

First of all, we need to ask, "Why was the Sabbath so important that anyone could be executed for profaning it with the slightest bit of work?" Secondly, we need to inquire, "Why, if keeping the Sabbath in the Old Testament was so essential, is it no longer required in the New Testament?"

In short, what our tutor, or the law, is teaching us is this: God created the heavens and the earth in six days and on the seventh day He rested. He therefore required His people to rest in His finished work of creation every Sabbath day (see Genesis 2:1-4; Exodus 20:8-11; Deuteronomy 5:12-14). Jesus Christ referred to Himself as being the Lord of the Sabbath, and when He died on the cross to save men from their sins, one of the last things He said before giving up His spirit with a loud cry was, "It is finished" (Matthew 12:8; John 19:30). In other words, Christ's redemptive work on the cross cannot be improved upon or substituted. It is finished! Ultimately, anyone who tries to get to heaven by their own way or with their own good works will suffer a tortuous and eternal death.

Nevertheless, a multitude of professing Christians today have replaced commitment to Christ and repentance from sin with a social gospel of serving meals, building houses for the needy, prospering the poor, and promoting social justice, gay rights, and environmental responsibility. They have placed their salvation upon their "works" rather than resting in the complete redemptive work of Jesus Christ.

However, we must "rest" in the finished work of the Son of God on the cross the way the Old Testament saints were commanded to rest in God's finished work of creation. The Sabbath pointed to Christ and the Sabbath had its fulfillment in Christ. Consequently, it doesn't matter if we do manual labor on Saturdays in this new dispensation, because the Sabbath is spiritually representing Christ. We are no longer bound by such laws because they were merely our tutor to lead us to God's salvation in His Son Jesus.

This is also true for almost all of God's Old Testament laws that demanded the execution of people who transgressed them. For example, adultery was punishable by death in the writings of Moses. However, when an adulterous woman was brought before Jesus and the religious leaders wanted to stone her to death, Jesus said, "He who is without sin among you, let him be the first to throw a stone at her." Consequently, all of the woman's accusers left her, and Jesus said to the adulterous, "Did no one condemn you? ... I do not condemn you, either. Go. From now on sin no more" (Leviticus 20:10; John 8:7; 10-11).

Jesus did not say that the woman was innocent of a capital offense, rather that the death penalty would no longer be in effect. Nevertheless, the fact that he commanded her to "sin no more" shows us that the consequence of eternal death (hell) is still in effect for unrepentant sinners. The Old Testament law (our tutor) demanded that people be executed for murder, adultery, idolatry, witchcraft, homosexuality, blasphemy, breaking the Sabbath, fornication, kidnapping, and even cursing one's father and mother (see Exodus 21:12; Leviticus 18:20; 20:2-6, 9, 13; 24:16; Numbers 15:32-36; Deuteronomy 22:20-21; 24:7). However, the demand for the execution of those who engage in such behavior has been rescinded in all of these cases, with the possible exception of murder.

On the other hand, the New Testament makes it perfectly clear that apart from Christ's redemption, these same practices will result in everlasting death where the "worm does not die, and the fire is not quenched" (see Mark 9:43-48). As the apostle Paul declared,

> [D]o you not know that the unrighteous will not inherit the kingdom of God? Do not be deceived; neither fornicators, nor idolaters, nor adulterers, nor effeminate, nor homosexuals, nor thieves, nor the covetous, nor drunkards, nor revilers, nor swindlers, will inherit the kingdom of God. (1 Corinthians 6:9-10)

Without the redemptive work of Jesus, we would still be bound by the letter of the law. In light of this fact, God's laws regarding execution are meant to teach us profound spiritual truths, and they are meant to help us understand how completely holy God is and thus comprehend the seriousness of breaking His commands. When we criticize or attack the Bible because of its laws on capital punishment, we are making judgments based upon our natural reasoning and not from God's divine perspective.

Instead, we ought to reflect upon what God's tutor (His law) was trying to teach His people through that very unfortunate and presumptuous man who thought nothing of the profound significance of working on the Sabbath day. His fate is a solemn warning to everyone who refuses to rest in the finished work of Jesus Christ on His cross of redemption. No amount of "social justice" works will ever become a substitute for Christ's "finished" work—as the execution of one Sabbath-breaker profoundly demonstrates.

Santa Claus, Butlers, and Mascots

Few things distort one's view and understanding of God more readily than having a low opinion of Him. Yet from the dawn of human history, men have failed miserably to comprehend the true nature of God and to perceive His profound righteousness. It is a biblical fact that God has made man in His own image and likeness (Genesis 1:26-27). Nevertheless, throughout all the ages since man's fall, he has tried desperately to remake God in his own image and likeness and into an entity around whom he feels most comfortable and who makes little or no demands upon him.

The true knowledge of God has consequently become so fragmented and convoluted that the world is now swimming in a sea of different religious beliefs and an ocean of opposing spiritual convictions. Unfortunately, even within the Christian Church there seems to be a myriad of different opinions regarding His true nature, His inspired Word, and His moral laws. Men are willing to believe many accurate things about God in regards to His loving, merciful, and compassionate nature. Man can even accept the fact that He is omnipresent, omniscient, and omnipotent, as well as righteous and just. But unless we see His holiness, we are bound to cultivate a low opinion of Him.

Before Isaiah became God's chosen prophet, he knew many things about God in the abstract. It was only after he was catapulted into the very presence of God that he came face to face with God's holiness and immediately recognized the depths of his own sinfulness. His opinion of God was transformed in an instant when he saw God's righteous glory filling the temple in heaven and declared,

> "Woe is me, for I am ruined! Because I am a man of unclean lips, and I live among a people of unclean lips; for my eyes have seen the King, the Lord of hosts." Then one of the seraphim flew to me with a burning coal in his hand, which he had taken from the altar with tongs. He touched my mouth with it

and said, "Behold, this has touched your lips; and your iniquity is taken away and your sin is forgiven." (Isaiah 6:5-7)

When men truly see God's holiness (the way that Isaiah did), they instinctively realize how unholy they really are. It is this profound understanding of God that brings us to a clearer comprehension of our Creator's character, His infinite mercy and compassion, and His undeserved bestowal of grace.

However, when men fail to recognize the supreme holiness of God, it is very easy to view Him as some kind of Eternal Santa Claus, Celestial Butler, or Heavenly Mascot that exists to give them what they want, to comply with their every wish, or to comfort them in all their sorrows and cheer them on in their life's ambitions. In short, without a lofty opinion of God, it is very unlikely we will view Him as little more than the Genie in a Bottle or the comforting Teddy Bear that makes us feel warm and secure. He is likely to be reduced in our minds as some kind of senile, benevolent old man who blesses us in our sins and, furthermore, approves of our immoral practices and just wants us to be happy and prosperous without having to obey Him.

We get a genuine glimpse of what God is like by looking at His Son Jesus. To commune with the Father, Jesus would pray to Him. When He taught His disciples to pray, He identified God as being a fatherly person in heaven whose name is hallowed, whose will must be done, and whose kingdom of righteousness will eventually be established on Earth in the same way that it is in heaven. He emphasized the absolute need to be forgiven of our sins and to extend God's forgiveness to those who have wronged us as well. He expressed that we are to be dependent upon God for our daily and temporal needs.

Likewise, the apostle Paul enlightened men on how to approach God in prayer when he wrote,

Be anxious for nothing, but in everything by prayer and supplication with thanksgiving let your requests be made known to God. And the peace of God, which surpasses all comprehension, will guard your hearts and your minds in Christ Jesus. (Philippians 4:6-7)

Instead of viewing God as a jolly Santa Claus or a doting butler or a comforting mascot, our view of Him must be "high and lifted up." A high opinion of God instills in men a sense of reverence, respect, and a realization that He is a loving father who is too good to be unkind and who is too wise to make mistakes. This high opinion of Him transforms our humble requests into an "assurance of things hoped for, the conviction of things not seen" (Hebrews 11:1). It gives us confidence to approach Him as a father and to view Him as a friend, and it inspires us to know Him better and to love him deeper. It motivates us to want to please Him more and to serve Him with greater zeal and thoughtful intensity.

However, a higher opinion of Him is not sloppy sentimentality. We fear His holiness, yet rejoice in His goodness; we aspire to exalt Him rather than bring Him down to our level; we long to be alone with Him instead of feeling obligated to attend religious services; and we yearn to read His Word and to listen to His voice rather than be shackled with "dos and don'ts" and suffocated with commandments and restrictions. Thus, our high opinion of God compels us to more eagerly want Him and to more sincerely love and appreciate Him.

On the other hand, we are diminished when we diminish God. A low opinion of our Creator retards our understanding of Him. He becomes a butler rather than a father, He is mistaken for a magic wand rather than an intimate friend, and He is viewed as a security blanket instead of a comforter. In the end, He is portrayed as a broad-minded deity who blesses men in their sins and encourages their immoral practices rather than a holy God who cannot allow unrepentant sinners to go unpunished.

Now we would do well to ask ourselves, "Do I think of God in sentimental terms, or do I view Him as One who is high and lifted up?" Our honest answer to this question will say a lot about whether we truly exalt Him as God or simply ascribe Him as someone to conform to our every whim.

Famous for Being Famous

Recent headlines and newscasts spoke glowingly of a famous fashion designer who was at the height of his glorious career and whose potential for even greater fame and fortune knew no bounds. He was the darling of the fashion industry and the envy of many clothing designers, yet he decided that his existence was not worth living, so he took his own life. Needless to say, his suicide shocked the fashion world and baffled much of the rest of humanity. Why would someone who seemed to have every reason for living put an end to his being while so many others who are destitute or far less successful find meaning and purpose to their lives?

The answers can be extremely complex. However, beneath all the speculation and all of the hand-wringing, there is a very real possibility that such an individual was simply famous for being famous. In other words, beneath all the glitz and glitter, under all the status and influence, and below all the money and material possessions, there sadly was an empty suit. There was no substance, no essence, and no lasting purpose. Such a life only becomes a black hole of self-centeredness and an empty void of self-gratification, and all the bulging bank accounts, glittering lights, and doting admirers cannot fill the gravitational pull of a collapsed star. Such external things only add to the intensity of a black hole, or an emotional vacuum, which only increases its powerful force with the passing of time.

When people become temporarily famous without possessing heavenly fame, they merely become famous for being famous. Fame, in and of itself, becomes as empty as the wind and as fleeting as the whirlwind. It can shake a lot of leaves in its passing, but once it has blown over, nothing more is seen of it. If anything, its rapid departure usually does more harm than good to those closest to its flurry and to those left behind in its wake.

Apart from a proper relationship with God, life is meaningless and whatever good we may attempt to do apart from Him is pointless. Jesus promised, "He who has found his life will lose it, and he who has lost his life for My sake will find it." He assured us that whoever so much as gives to another "a cup of cold water to drink" (in His name), such an individual would "not lose his reward." He further declared, "I came that [you] may have life, and have it abundantly" and "I am the resurrection and the life; he who believes in Me will live even if he dies, and everyone who lives and believes in Me will never die" (Matthew 10:39, 42; John 10:10; 11:25-26).

It was the Son of God Himself who asked, "For what does it profit a man to gain the whole world, and forfeit his soul? For what will a man give in exchange for his soul?" (Mark 8:36-37). In other words, all the fame and fortune people can achieve and accumulate in this life is void and vain if God is not the epicenter of their lives. As Jesus once said to the rich and famous of His day, "[T]hat which is highly esteemed among men is detestable in the sight of God" (Luke 16:15).

God has nothing against famous people. As a matter of fact, many of his closest friends in the Bible became legendary in their own time and famous for all generations. However, a person who is merely famous for being famous in the eyes of the world (and not in the eyes of the kingdom of God) is just simply famous for being famous—nothing more—and His fame is destined to disappear like fleeting smoke.

So the next time you notice the rich and famous of this world being surrounded by their delirious fans and fawned over by the adoring media, without being judgmental, ask yourself, "Are they truly famous in the eyes of those in heaven, or are they merely famous for being famous in the eyes of men?" I would sincerely hope for the former, because if the latter, they are destined to become infamous and not famous from an eternal perspective.

Warrior in His Birthday Suit

"A young man was following [Jesus], wearing nothing but a linen sheet over his naked body; and [the mob arresting Christ] seized him. But he pulled free of the linen sheet and escaped naked" (Mark 14:51-52). It appears this naked man was none other than John Mark who authored the Gospel of Mark. It was in the upper room of his house that the Last Supper was held, and he appears to be the one who prepared and served the Passover meal to Jesus and His disciples.

Therefore, after Jesus and His Apostles left the Upper Room and went to the garden of Gethsemane, John Mark seems to have gone to bed wearing nothing but his birthday suit. It also appears that Judas and the mob carrying swords and clubs came to Mark's house first in their attempts to find and arrest Jesus. As the crowd pounded on the disciple's front door, John Mark quickly jumped out of bed and in his haste just wrapped himself in his bedsheet. When he informed Judas and his gang that Jesus had already left, Judas knew from experience that Christ could be found at the place called Gethsemane. Once the angry horde left the house, out of alarm and concern for Jesus, Mark followed them. Not having time to even get dressed, he ran after them in a panic.

Well, the rest is history. A naked man trying to follow Christ at a distance, wearing nothing but a linen sheet, ends up running for his life wearing nothing but the suit that he was born in. Now imagine an ancient warrior going into an intense battle, buck naked, and the only thing that he carries is a sword, or a modern-day soldier engaged in a fierce conflict without having a stitch of clothing on, armed only with his rifle. What do you honestly think their chances of survival will be?

Their odds of living through such an ordeal are virtually zero, even if they were extremely skilled in their weapon of choice. Why? Because they have no protection; from their head to their toes, they are completely vulnerable to their surroundings and to the climate around them. From rough terrain to the freezing cold, and from the blistering heat to biting insects, the stark-naked commandos will soon discover their skill with a saber or their competence with a firearm is of little or no value without their full armor.

How often, though, do we find unclothed warriors attempting to do battle within the epicenter of all warfare — "the spiritual war"? Christians have been given the "full armor of God" as described in Ephesians 6:10-18, and regrettably most church members fail to use it — at least in its entirety. Many would be hard-pressed to even name the items listed (with perhaps the exception of the sword which is the Word of God).

However, without putting on the "full armor of God" there is no possibility of overcoming the forces of darkness that are hell-bent on damning as many souls as possible, in order to spite the God of heaven and to prevent men from inheriting the glorious and eternal state that they themselves had previously forfeited. In light of such an intense conflict with such a determined and powerful foe, the apostle Paul admonishes all believers to

> be strong in the Lord and in the strength of His might. Put on the full armor of God, so that you will be able to stand firm against the schemes of the devil. For our struggle is not against flesh and blood, but against the rulers, against the powers, against the world forces of this darkness, against the spiritual forces of wickedness in the heavenly places. Therefore, take up the full armor of God, so that you will be able to resist in the evil day, and having done everything, to stand firm. Stand firm therefore, having girded your loins with truth, and having put on the breastplate of righteousness, and having shod your feet with the preparation of the gospel of peace; in addition to all, taking up the shield of faith with which you will be able to extinguish all the flaming arrows of the evil one. And take the helmet of salvation, and the sword of the Spirit, which is the word of God. With all prayer

and petition pray at all times in the Spirit, and with this in view, be on the alert with all perseverance and petition for all the saints. (Ephesians 6:10-18)

The very first thing that the apostle commands believers to put on is "truth." He says that we must gird our loins with it! In other words, in this spiritual battle, a Christian must be a person of honesty and integrity, filling their mind with the truthfulness of God's Word; otherwise, their bare and exposed behinds will become a huge and easy target for Satan to aim at in his obsession to destroy and eliminate them as any threat to his kingdom.

The next crucial piece of armor is the breastplate of righteousness, which mandates that believers must exemplify lives beyond reproach. For example, if a professing follower of Christ is living an immoral lifestyle, such as engaging in an adulterous affair, then he is without the defense of the breastplate of righteousness. He becomes a conspicuous mark for the evil one to ruin and to destroy his profession of faith.

The third part of a Christian's armor is his shoes, which is the need to share one's faith with others both "in season and out of season" (2 Timothy 4:2). Paul told the believers to "shod your feet with the preparation of the gospel of peace," suggesting that just as horseshoes are nailed onto a horse's hooves in preparation for traveling, so too, followers of Christ need to be prepared to impart the gospel with others when the opportunity presents itself. Jesus said, "[E]veryone who confesses Me before men, I will also confess him before My Father who is in heaven. But whoever denies Me before men, I will also deny him before My Father who is in heaven" (Matthew 10:32-33).

The fourth implement in the full armor of God is the shield of faith which is essential in deflecting the fiery arrows of the evil one that are strategically aimed at discouraging, depressing, and disheartening those in the service of the King of kings. Faith is all important in this spiritual warfare, because "without faith it is impossible to please God" and "it is by grace [we] have been saved, through faith … not by works, so that no one can boast" (Ephesians 2:8-9, NIV; see Hebrews 11:6).

The fifth part of the full armor of God is the helmet of salvation, which in essence emphasizes the extreme importance of knowing exactly what one professes to believe, regarding their faith in Christ. In a world that is flooded and gutted with phony prophets, false religions, cults, godless philosophies, bogus theories, and erroneous doctrines, Christians who don't have a firm understanding of their salvation become easy targets for the powers of darkness. The devils of deceit will always aim their poisoned falsehoods at people's minds just as effectively as Satan did to the very first woman when he convinced her mind that God was lying to her and that she surely would not die when she ate the forbidden fruit, but rather that she would become like God (Genesis 3:4-5). On account of this, Paul cautioned the believers at Corinth, saying:

> I am afraid that, as the serpent deceived Eve by his craftiness, your minds will be led astray from the simplicity and purity of devotion to Christ. For if one comes and preaches another Jesus whom we have not preached, or you receive a different spirit which you have not received, or a different gospel which you have not accepted, you bear this beautifully. (2 Corinthians 11:3-4)

The father of lies will always aim his most powerful weapons at a person's mind because he knows that any direct hit will likely be fatal or at least have a very paralyzing effect upon one's ability to wage war against him.

Finally, the Bible, or the Word of God (which is the "sword of the Spirit"), is the *last* (not the first and only) object itemized in the armor of God. Without the sword of God's Word—and without the will to wield it—the chances of a believer's ability to advance and to defend himself become nil. He is virtually defenseless against these spiritual forces of wickedness, and a believer who only has a Bible under his arm (while not wearing the full armor of God) is as useless and ridiculous-looking as a warrior running around in his birthday suit in the midst of combat.

It is only after a soldier's entire uniform is put on that he picks up his weapon; and in any spiritual conflict, it's only after God's full armor is adorned that one picks up the sword of God's Word. The writer of Hebrews described the power of God's Word as "living and active and sharper than any two-edged sword, and piercing as far as the division of soul and spirit, of both joints and marrow, and able to judge the thoughts and intentions of the heart" (Hebrews 4:12). To be effective with this powerful weapon, one must study it in depth. As the apostle Paul admonished Timothy, "Be diligent to present yourself approved to God as a workman who does not need to be ashamed, accurately handling the word of truth. But avoid worldly and empty chatter, for it will lead to further ungodliness" (2 Timothy 2:15-16).

It was Christ who did battle with Satan in the wilderness by knowing how to handle the sword of God's Word. However, the devil also quoted Scripture in his attempts to bring Christ down (Matthew 4:1-11; Luke 4:1-13). Satan knows the Bible backwards and forwards and in every language on Earth, so unless a Christian is able to divide the Word of God correctly, the devil will use a believer's own sword against him in his endeavor to destroy him.

In conclusion, a supplementary part of the full armor of God is prayer, the bow and arrow. Prayer is absolutely imperative in overcoming a relentless adversary who never sleeps and never takes a day off or rests from his work. Prayer becomes one's most powerful long-range weapon. Without it, God's archenemy is sure to get the best of any believer, regardless of how well he may know his Bible.

> For though we walk in the flesh, we do not war according to the flesh, for the weapons of our warfare are not of the flesh, but divinely powerful for the destruction of fortresses. We are destroying

speculations and every lofty thing raised up against the knowledge of God, and we are taking every thought captive to the obedience of Christ. (2 Corinthians 10:3-5)

Unfortunately, very few people (both inside and outside the Church) really understand what is at stake in this spiritual war against the unseen enemy whose infernal malice towards God and man knows no bounds. In fact, a growing number of pastors, ministers, and priests today reject the notion of a personal devil, an eternal hell, and the infallibility of all Scripture. Consequently, when they quote from the Bible, their use of God's sword becomes very ineffective, and their failure to put on the full armor of God makes them absurdly comical targets to an enemy that is anything but amusing and who is anything but halfhearted in his attempts to eternally damn the human race with his endless arsenal of weapons.

Getting Physically Fit for the Worms

In spite of the fact that America continues to experience an epidemic of obesity and is now bursting with vast health-related problems, as a nation we are doing everything in our power to promote healthy lifestyles. In other words, right smack in the center of our overindulgence and lack of discipline, Americans are becoming obsessed with an insatiable desire to be energetic, physically fit, and attractive. Diet books are almost guaranteed to become bestsellers and weight-loss gimmicks abound, while exercise gurus and fitness programs multiply exponentially. Furthermore, health commercials continue to proliferate with a never-ending drumbeat of miracle cures and vitamin supplements in conjunction with condemning unhealthy choices and bad habits.

Fast food restaurants, vending machines, and cafeterias are scrambling to promote more nutritious menus as legislators and government bureaucrats trip over one another in their endless nanny attempts to outlaw beverages and foods containing sugars and fats (especially in and around academic institutions). What a paradox! In the depths of our country's compulsion to look attractive and become fit, there seems to be no reversing the upward trend towards excess pounds and bulging waist lines. Poor health decisions escalate at the same pace as glamor, muscle, fashion, fitness, and health magazines proliferate.

However, in the center of all these obsessions, contradictions, and preoccupations with the physical body, one thing seems to be completely overlooked or forgotten and that is the worm. Yes, the worm! God says, "[I]t is appointed for men to die once and after this comes judgment" (Hebrews 9:27). Men may continue to exhaust themselves in their efforts to discover the holy grail of immortality and physical attractiveness, but nothing can stop the onslaught of physical decline, the grave, and finally "the worm."

All of man's endeavors to be physically fit and outwardly attractive are pointless in the face of the worm. Worms are destined to reduce every man to zero. Beauty queens, plain Janes, weightlifters, couch potatoes, the rich, the poor, the powerful, the weak, the famous, and the anonymous are all destined to be eaten by worms. Yes, the lowliest creatures on Earth are assigned the task of turning men into dust. The prophet Isaiah proclaimed,

> Listen to Me, you who know righteousness, a people in whose heart is My law; do not fear the reproach of man, nor be dismayed at their revilings. For the moth will eat them like a garment, and the grub will eat them like wool. But My righteousness will be forever, and My salvation to all generations. (Isaiah 51:7-8)

Consider Samson, who was unquestionably the strongest, fastest, and most intimidating man in all of history. He tore up a raging lion with his bare hands, he ran down and captured 300 foxes singlehandedly, he killed 1,000 attacking Philistines with the jawbone of a jackass, and he ripped up a 2-ton city gate from its foundation and ran 20 miles with it on his back—all the way to a mountain opposite Mount Hebron (Judges 14-16). In our day and age, Samson would truly become the poster boy for all marathoners, weightlifters, boxers, wrestlers, and professional athletes (not to mention his success as a "chick magnet" or womanizer). His potential for greatness was unlimited. Yet his shortsightedness and his focus on the things of this world, rather than the things of eternity, left him blind, enslaved, and humiliated in the realms of both heaven and Earth. He ended up under a pile of rocks where the worms and insects and myriads of microbes feasted upon his once-glorious frame. In spite of all his magnificence and all his herculean achievements, his fate was that of all men—to be devoured by the grubs.

Consequently, it is a person's soul and not his physical anatomy that is all important. As the apostle Paul declared, that "bodily discipline is only of little profit, but godliness is profitable for all things, since it holds promise for the present life and also for the life to come" (1 Timothy 4:8). He also said,

I do all things for the sake of the gospel, so that I may become a fellow partaker of it. Do you not know that those who run in a race all run, but only one receives the prize? Run in such a way that you may win. Everyone who competes in the games exercises self-control in all things. They then do it to receive a perishable wreath, but we an imperishable. Therefore I run in such a way, as not without aim; I box in such a way, as not beating the air; but I discipline my body and make it my slave, so that, after I have preached to others, I myself will not be disqualified. (1 Corinthians 9:23-27)

Finally, he wrote,

For I am already being poured out as a drink offering, and the time of my departure has come. I have fought the good fight, I have finished the course, I have kept the faith; in the future there is laid up for me the crown of righteousness, which the Lord, the righteous Judge, will award to me on that day; and not only to me, but also to all who have loved His appearing. (2 Timothy 4:6-8)

The Son of God said:

Truly, truly, I say to you, an hour is coming and now is, when the dead will hear the voice of the Son of God, and those who hear will live. For just as the Father has life in Himself, even so He gave to the Son also to have life in Himself; and He gave Him authority to execute judgment, because He is the Son of Man. Do not marvel at this; for an hour is coming, in which all who are in the tombs will hear His voice, and will come forth; those who did the good deeds to a resurrection of life, those who committed the evil deeds to a resurrection of judgment. (John 5:25-29)

The prophet Daniel also prophesied saying,

Many of those who sleep in the dust of the ground will awake, these to everlasting life, but the others to disgrace and everlasting contempt. Those who have insight will shine brightly like the brightness of the expanse of heaven, and those who lead the many to righteousness, like the stars forever and ever. (Daniel 12:2-3)

Furthermore, Isaiah disclosed, "Your dead will live; their corpses will rise. You who lie in the dust, awake and shout for joy, for your dew is as the dew of the dawn, and the earth will give birth to the departed spirits" (Isaiah 26:19).

Therefore, we must know for certain that no matter how physically fit and attractive we may become in this world, without Christ, our bodies are destined to eternally rot and decompose in an eternal fire where the "worm does not die, and the fire is not quenched" (Mark 9:43-48; Matthew 5:22-30; 10:28). We must also know for certain that the worm will have the final say regarding the fate of all men in this life, and they will have the ultimate say in the next life for all those who become physically fit in the eyes of men but fail to become spiritually fit in the eyes of God.

The Death of Time

The late Carl Sagan often declared that the universe is the only eternal reality. Sagan was a staunch atheist who actually viewed the cosmos as being divine and the architect of all things. To this man of science, the star system and everything it contains is all powerful, beautiful, mysterious, and everlasting.

In his own words, he declared, "THE COSMOS IS ALL THAT IS OR EVER WAS OR EVER WILL BE."[8] The cosmos is supreme and all encompassing. It is COSMOS, with all capitals. He believed that humanity is the product of a long series of biological accidents.[9] Regarding human origins, Sagan emphatically proclaimed, "Evolution is a fact, not a theory" and humans emerged by a "powerful but random process."[10][11] In one of his lectures dealing with the Big Bang and God, Sagan said that if the universe had a beginning from a divine origin, then God Himself had to have had a beginning and therefore "if we say that God has always existed, why not save a step and conclude that the universe has always existed?" Consequently, neither a creator nor a "Big Bang" is needed for the cosmos to exist.

The bottom line to all of this brilliant man's flawed reasoning is that if the cosmos had no beginning and will have no end, then time itself is eternal with no beginning and no end. However, the Bible depicts that there was an interval where time never existed and there is coming a day when time will again cease to exist. In short, time is not eternal. It is merely temporal, and therefore it is destined for the tomb. This is because only God is eternal and eternity is where He dwells: "For thus says the high and exalted One who lives forever, whose name is Holy, 'I dwell on a high and holy place'" (Isaiah 57:15). In other words, God is outside of time; he dwells in eternity and time itself is His creation. He is not imprisoned in time, rather He is the author of time. From nanoseconds to light-years, he is the designer and the begetter of time.

Man, not God, is the one who is held hostage by time. Men are incarcerated, impounded, and confined by seconds, weeks, months, and years, while God exists in a totally different dimension. As the very first words of the Bible declare, "In the beginning God created the heavens and the earth" (Genesis 1:1). In pronouncing the physical universe into existence, God simultaneously created the space-time continuum. According to Einstein, space and time are relative, and (within the vastness of the cosmos) time cannot be separated from space.

Let's further examine the first chapter of Genesis:

> Then God said, "Let there be light"; and there was light. God saw that the light was good; and God separated the light from the darkness. God called the light day, and the darkness He called night. And there was evening and there was morning, one day. (vv. 3-5)

Of note is the common phrase steadfastly proclaimed on each of the six days of creation:

Verse 5:   "[T]here was evening and there was morning, one day" (Day 1 — God separates light from darkness).

Verse 8:   "[T]here was evening and there was morning, a second day" (Day 2 — God separates the waters from the land).

Verse 13:   "There was evening and there was morning, a third day" (Day 3 — God creates the vegetation, plants, and trees).

Verse 19:   "There was evening and there was morning, a fourth day" (Day 4 — God creates the sun, the moon, and the stars).

Verse 23:   "There was evening and there was morning, a fifth day" (Day 5 — God creates the birds, the fish, and all water creatures).

Verse 31:   "[T]here was evening and there was morning, the sixth day" (Day 6 — God creates all the insects, all the animals, and finally — man).

What is truly fascinating is the order of creation. The "sequence" of the formation of the universe is all important when it comes to understanding time and establishing the truth of the "six days" of creation. Notice that on the first day God created light and darkness and separated the light from the darkness. However, it wasn't until the *fourth day* that God created the light bearers — the sun, the moon, and the stars:

> Then God said, "Let there be lights in the expanse of the heavens to separate the day from the night, and let them be for signs and for seasons and for days and years; and let them be for lights in the expanse of the heavens to give light on the earth"; and it was so. God made the two great lights, the greater light to govern the day, and the lesser light to govern the night; He made the stars also. God placed them in the expanse of the heavens to give light on the earth, and to govern the day and the night, and to separate the light from the darkness; and God saw that it was good. There was evening and there was morning, a fourth day. (vv. 14-19)

Unless scientists, astronomers, evolutionists, theologians, and the world of academia understand this, they will forever be bewitched into believing that our universe is much older than it is, currently estimated by the field of science to be between 13½ and 15 billion years old. The light of the farthest stars which can be observed in a galaxy at the very edge of our known universe is approximately 13½ billion light-years away.[12] Since it takes a year for light to travel the distance of one light-year, scientific reasoning deduces our universe must be billions of years old.

However, God filled the entire universe with blinding light in an instant and then separated the existing light with darkness. Light and darkness were in existence before the bearers of light came into being. It is as though God simply walked into a room, turned on a light switch, then reduced the light into light beams or light rays that were divided by darkness. Then he attached the beams of light to objects and hung them in the expanse.

People will understandably mock at such an analogy, because "scientifically" light cannot exist apart from a source, and the source must always come before the light. However, God (who can do anything but sin) created the source of light after the existence of light. God formed the light and the bearers of light in reverse order which not only explains the truth of the six days of creation, but also explains how time itself came into existence and how the space-time continuum was born through this handiwork.

Simply put — very simply put — the space-time continuum (or Einstein's theory of special relativity) says that if a person could stand on the sun and look at Earth from a telescope, the observer would not see what is happening that same moment on Earth, but rather what transpired eight or nine minutes earlier on the planet. This is because Earth is 93 million miles from the sun, and light traveling at 186,000 miles per second would take almost 10 minutes to reach us, therefore space and time become relative to the velocity of light itself. The closest star system to planet Earth (outside of our sun) is the Alpha Centauri which is approximately 4.3 light-years away. As such, to be observing Earth from that distance would mean that the observer would not be witnessing what is being done at that moment, but actually events that transpired over 4 years earlier on our world. So according to the theories of relativity, "the further out in space you go, the farther back in time you go."

Consequently, time began when the universe began, or when "[i]n the beginning, God created the heavens and the earth." And when He stretched out the heavens in an instant, the atomic clock began to tick. And just as surely as time had a beginning, it will also have an end; it will cease to exist. The apostle John foretells the day that days will end:

> Then I saw a great white throne and Him who sat
> upon it, from whose presence earth and heaven fled

away, and no place was found for them. And I saw the dead (the damned), the great and the small, standing before the throne, and books were opened; and another book was opened, which is the book of life; and the dead were judged from the things which were written in the books, according to their deeds. And the sea gave up the dead which were in it, and death and Hades (hell) gave up the dead which were in them; and they were judged, every one of them according to their deeds. Then death and Hades were thrown into the lake of fire. This is the second death, the lake of fire. And if anyone's name was not found written in the book of life, he was thrown into the lake of fire. (Revelation 20:11-15)

This is the day in which the universe disappears from the face of Him who sits upon the throne of judgment and judges all the unsaved souls that ever lived, those whose spirits have come out of hell and are reunited with their resurrected bodies. They stand before this all-consuming fire of holiness, as the prophet Daniel describes,

I kept looking until thrones were set up, and the Ancient of Days took His seat; his vesture was like white snow and the hair of His head like pure wool. His throne was ablaze with flames, its wheels were a burning fire. A river of fire was flowing and coming out from before Him; thousands upon thousands were attending Him, and myriads upon myriads were standing before Him; the court sat, and the books were opened. (Daniel 7:9-10)

The cosmos is not "the only eternal reality." The cosmos is temporary! It is destined to disperse in an instant as it flees from the presence of Him who sits upon the throne. And once the universe vanishes from the face of the One who spoke it into existence, all time will cease with it. The space-time continuum will dissolve with the dematerialization of the physical heavens and Earth.

At this point, eternity will be all there is. No one in heaven or in the lake of fire will be conscious of time, not only because it will cease to exist, but because it becomes irrelevant and inconsequential. Instead, the final book of the Bible declares,

> Then I [the apostle John] saw a new heaven and a new earth; for the first heaven and the first earth passed away, and there is no longer any sea. And I saw the holy city, new Jerusalem, coming down out of heaven from God, made ready as a bride adorned for her husband. And I heard a loud voice from the throne, saying, "Behold, the tabernacle of God is among men, and He will dwell among them, and they shall be His people, and God Himself will be among them, and He will wipe away every tear from their eyes; and there will no longer be any death; there will no longer be any mourning, or crying, or pain; the first things have passed away." And He who sits on the throne said, "Behold, I am making all things new." And He said, "Write, for these words are faithful and true." Then He said to me, "It is done. I [not the universe!] am the Alpha and the Omega, the beginning and the end." (Revelation 21:1-6)

The apostle John goes on to describe,

> There will no longer be any curse; and the throne of God and of the Lamb will be in it, and His bondservants will serve Him; they will see His face, and His name will be on their foreheads. And there will no longer be any night; and they will not have need

of the light of a lamp nor the light of the sun, because the Lord God will illumine them; and they will reign forever and ever [in timeless eternity]. (22:3-5)

What a glorious "time" that will be for everyone who loves the Lord and served Him well while living on this planet from the dawn of time's creation! Night and day will cease and so will time as it dissolves into eternity and the space-time continuum vanishes with the universe that flees before the face of Him who sits upon the throne (20:11).

The Sons of Pinocchio

Perhaps the most well-known and animated liar in all of fiction or cartoon fables is the wooden puppet named Pinocchio. In Carlo Collodi's fairy tale, Pinocchio lies three different times to a kind-hearted fairy, and each time he attempts to deceive her, his nose grows longer and longer until it becomes so long that it prevents him from escaping her presence. Instead, his protruding nose impedes him from even reaching the front door of the pixie's living room. Also in Collodi's colorful allegory, a cricket is portrayed as Pinocchio's conscience (or inner voice) that tells the puppet "only good sons have the chance of becoming real boys"; and yet the wooden figure just can't seem to stay out of trouble. In the end, after proving himself brave, truthful, and unselfish, sacrificing himself while rescuing his creator (Geppetto), Pinocchio is transformed into a real live boy. So it is with all liars and sinners. We need to get right with our Creator if we are to enjoy eternal life with Him.

Well, Pinocchio may be a fictional character, but in reality, misleading others with our words seems to be the order of the day. It's been said that by the age of four, 90% of children have grasped the concept of lying.[13] According to a 2002 study conducted by the University of Massachusetts, 60% of adults can't have a 10-minute conversation without lying at least once.[14]

The research by a psychologist at the University of Virginia, Bella DePaulo, PhD., confirms Nietzche's assertion that the lie is a condition of life. DePaulo and her colleagues had 147 people between the ages of 18 and 71 keep a diary of all falsehoods they told over the course of one week. She found that most people lie once or twice a day and that both men and women lie in approximately a fifth of their social exchanges lasting 10 or more minutes.[15] In her research, an "official" lie is one that actually misleads or deliberately conveys a false impression (not mindless pleasantries or polite cover-ups, such as "I am fine, thanks," or "no trouble at all," or "no, that dress doesn't make you look fat").

According to the Statistic Brain Research Institute, the lying statistics data break down as follows:

12% of adults "admit to telling lies 'sometimes' or 'often.'"

80% of women "admit to occasionally telling harmless half-truths."

31% of people "admit to lying on their resumes."

13% of patients "lie to their doctor."

32% of patients "'stretched the truth' to their doctor."

40% "lied about following a doctors [sic] treatment plan."

30% "lied about their diet and exercise regiments."

60% of people "lie at least once during a 10-minute conversation."

Men tell an average of 6 lies per day to their partner, boss, or colleagues.

Women tell an average of 3 lies per day to their partner, boss, or colleagues.[16]

Surprisingly, in the face of all the research and statistics about lying, it appears that most men and women don't realize just how prone they are to lying to others or attempting to deceive those around them. Take the apostle Peter, for example. If it were possible to go back in time and ask him if he considered himself to be a liar, there is a very good chance he would say (and firmly believe) that he was basically an honest and truthful guy. However, when the pressure was on, as he was warming himself by the fire in the courtyard where Jesus was being questioned on the night of His betrayal, three different times Peter denied knowing Christ, even to the point where he was cursing and swearing that he didn't know Jesus. It was only after the cock crowed twice that Peter remembered the Son of God's prediction about his lying; and it was at that very moment that Peter's eyes met those of Jesus looking into his eyes as if to say, "I told you that you would soon lie about knowing me." Then, and only then, did Peter realize the enormity of his deceitful words, and he went forth and wept bitterly over his lack of courage to tell the truth (Matthew 26:69-75; Mark14:66-72; Luke 22:54-62; John 18:25-27).

The traits of honesty, truthfulness, and integrity do not come naturally to mankind because all of us have a fallen nature and every human "heart is more deceitful than all else and is desperately sick" (Jeremiah 17:9). From infancy to old age, people do not have to be taught how to lie because lying and deceiving can become as natural as breathing and as unconscious as blinking—especially when the pressure to lie becomes the most expedient thing to do at the moment.

Like the famous Pinocchio, mankind's lies can pour forth like water when it comes to gaining an advantage or avoiding embarrassment or negative consequences. Unlike Pinocchio, however, people's noses don't grow every time they falsify the truth; if they did, it's very likely that truthfulness and honesty would become a lot more common than it is today; and for those who continue to lie, plastic surgery for nose reductions would undoubtedly become a revolving-door enterprise.

Pinocchio has many, many sons and daughters today, but they are not actually the offspring of an imaginary doll, but rather, children of "the father of lies"; that is, Satan. Jesus Christ said to the religious leaders of His day, "You are of your father the devil, and you want to do the desires of your father. He was a murderer from the beginning, and does not stand in the truth because there is no truth in him. Whenever he speaks a lie, he speaks from his own nature, for he is a liar and the father of lies" (John 8:44). Ultimately, if we don't want to be affiliated with the devil, we must refrain from speaking his language.

This is why God "desire[s] truth in [our] innermost being" (Psalm 51:6). One of the greatest compliments that Jesus ever gave anyone was when he said of Nathanael, "Behold, an Israelite indeed, in whom there is no deceit!" (John 1:47). It is integrity that is essential in the eyes of God if we are to be called a "true Israelite" (or a true follower of Jesus Christ). We are told in Proverbs:

There are six things which the Lord hates, yes, seven which are an abomination to Him: haughty eyes, a lying tongue, and hands that shed innocent blood, a heart that devises wicked plans, feet that run rapidly to evil, a false witness who utters lies, and one who spreads strife among brothers. (Proverbs 6:16-19)

God addresses the tongue hundreds of times in the book of Proverbs alone, indicating its significance, such as when Solomon maintained, "He who guards his mouth and his tongue, guards his soul from troubles" (21:23). Additionally, James tells us that the tongue is the very world of iniquity and is a fire that is set ablaze by hell itself (James 3:6). Jesus said, "[E]very idle word that men shall speak, they shall give account thereof in the day of judgment" (Matthew 12:36, KJV). The apostle John declared that all unrepentant liars will be eternally lost:

But for the cowardly and unbelieving and abominable and murderers and immoral persons and sorcerers and idolaters and all liars, their part will be in the lake that burns with fire and brimstone, which is the second death. ... Outside are the dogs and the sorcerers and the immoral persons and the murderers and the idolaters, and everyone who loves and practices lying. (Revelation 21:8; 22:15)

Yes, *The Adventures of Pinocchio* may very well be just an entertaining fairy tale; but in the eyes of God, lying and deceiving are anything but amusing. If we don't earnestly strive to be honest people, our lies and our deceitfulness will someday become as transparent as the conspicuous nose on a lying puppet's face. Then all men will see clearly that God truly does "desire truth in the innermost being."

Asking Directions from a Dead Man

As the saying goes, "If you want free advice, you usually get what you pay for," meaning the quality of such advice will often be as low as its price. That "free" counsel can end up being very costly if it happens to give detrimental recommendations. Likewise, if the source of guidance lacks godly wisdom, making suggestions contrary to the Word of God can be very destructive. Thus, King Solomon, known for his indisputable wisdom, advocates the following:

> Trust in the Lord with all your heart and do not lean on your own understanding. In all your ways acknowledge Him, and He will make your paths straight. Do not be wise in your own eyes; fear the Lord and turn away from evil. It will be healing to your body and refreshment to your bones. (Proverbs 3:5-8)

The enlightened son of David further elucidated, "A man has joy in an apt answer, and how delightful is a timely word!" (15:23). The Word of God is the most reliable source of applicable advice anyone can possibly get. The Scriptures contain the blueprint for life and the master plan for living when it comes to making the right decision and choosing the correct paths. So why do we seldom search them for answers? Why do we rely upon ungodly advisors instead of earnestly seeking the Lord in prayer?

Alternatively, we turn to the myriads of false prophets, psychics, palm readers, mediums, witches, warlocks, and wizards who claim to possess supernatural ability to predict the future and give sound advice. From witch doctors to voodoo sorceresses, and from Ouija boards to crystal balls, people have persisted with their desperate attempts to know what lies ahead of them and to receive guidance for their uncertain lives. However, in all of man's efforts to obtain mystical advice, perhaps seeking direction from a dead man is the ultimate in stupidity.

Imagine if an individual walked up to an open casket during a funeral and audibly asked the corpse for advice and then stood there with the expectation that the lifeless body would actually converse with the inquirer? You would surely think such a person were insane. At the very least, he would appear to be extremely feebleminded in his moronic attempt to carry on a discussion with a cadaver. However, asking dead people for instruction is not as uncommon as one may think.

Saul, the very first king of Israel, asked a dead man to give him advice in regards to his war with the Philistines, as told in the Old Testament: Time and again Saul had defied God's instructions and ignored His commands to the point where the Almighty no longer answered him, "neither by dreams, nor by Urim, nor by prophets" (1 Samuel 28:6, KJV). Consequently, the rebellious king became so desperate for guidance that he violated another one of God's commands by asking a witch to summon up a dead man's spirit so that he could ask the deceased man for counsel and direction. When the soul of the dead man appeared, the Bible says:

> Then Samuel said to Saul, "Why have you disturbed me by bringing me up?" And Saul answered, "I am greatly distressed; for the Philistines are waging war against me, and God has departed from me and no longer answers me, either through prophets or by dreams; therefore I have called you, that you may make known to me what I should do." Samuel said, "Why then do you ask me, since the Lord has departed from you and has become your adversary?" (vv. 15-16)

This episode was undoubtedly the only time in human history when a medium in a séance genuinely conjured up the actual person being summoned from the grave. All other manifestations of deceased loved ones from the spirit world are demonic spirits impersonating the dead in order to draw men deeper into witchcraft and to mislead gullible individuals from the one true

God. Samuel was the only exception, because God intervened in order to pronounce his judgment and displeasure upon a foolish and arrogant king for all his rebellion and defiance against the Lord of heaven. Dead people are divinely prevented from contacting the living. However, this does not mean that the dead don't desire to speak with the living, because they do. Jesus demonstrated this when he related the story of two men. He said:

> Now there was a rich man, and he habitually dressed in purple and fine linen, joyously living in splendor every day. And a poor man named Lazarus was laid at his gate, covered with sores, and longing to be fed with the crumbs which were falling from the rich man's table; besides, even the dogs were coming and licking his sores. Now the poor man died and was carried away by the angels to Abraham's bosom; and the rich man also died and was buried. In Hades he lifted up his eyes, being in torment, and saw Abraham far away and Lazarus in his bosom. And he cried out and said, "Father Abraham, have mercy on me, and send Lazarus so that he may dip the tip of his finger in water and cool off my tongue, for I am in agony in this flame." But Abraham said, "Child, remember that during your life you received your good things, and likewise Lazarus bad things; but now he is being comforted here, and you are in agony. And besides all this, between us and you there is a great chasm fixed, so that those who wish to come over from here to you will not be able, and that none may cross over from there to us." And he said, "Then I beg you, father, that you send him to my father's house—for I have five brothers—in order that he may warn them, so that they will not also come to this place of torment." But Abraham said, "They have Moses and the Prophets; let them hear

them." But he said, "No, father Abraham, but if someone goes to them from the dead, they will repent!" But he said to him, "If they do not listen to Moses and the Prophets, they will not be persuaded even if someone rises from the dead." (Luke 16:19-31)

Yes, the dead do long to speak to their loved ones on Earth in order to give them counsel and direction, but they cannot because God has forbidden it. God has made it abundantly clear that men have Moses and the prophets from whom to seek advice, and if men will not believe what God says through them, then they won't believe even if they could communicate with a dead man returning from the grave.

Moses and the prophets, not dead people, give God's final words to men on Earth. After His resurrection, Jesus mildly rebuked two of His disciples as He walked with them on the road to Emmaus, saying, "O foolish men and slow of heart to believe in all that the prophets have spoken!" (24:25). Immediately after this incident, Christ appeared to His Apostles and said to them, "These are My words which I spoke to you while I was still with you, that all things which are written about Me in the Law of Moses and the Prophets and the Psalms must be fulfilled" (v. 44).

Regrettably, God's Word is truly despised today. It is mocked, ridiculed, denied, and vilified—sometimes even by those in the pulpit and those in the pews across this country and around the world. King Saul was neither an atheist nor an agnostic, and neither are the majority of America's political leaders or the people they govern. However, our nation and its shepherds are rebelling against God's moral commands and setting the state up as the final authority in regards to what is right and what is wrong. We stubbornly insist that the government is king and its laws (ranging from abortion to homosexuality, and from transgenders to gay marriage) are absolute—not the laws of Moses and the words of the prophets. Yet it was Samuel who said to Saul (and to all powers that be),

Behold, to obey is better than sacrifice, and to heed than the fat of rams. For rebellion is as the sin of divination, and insubordination is as iniquity and idolatry. Because you have rejected the word of the Lord, He has also rejected you from being king. (1 Samuel 15:22-23)

America's and the world's rebellion against God's words and His commands opens people up to witchcraft, and their stubborn refusal to consult the living God exposes them more and more to satanic deception and demonic control. Like King Saul of old, God no longer speaks to our leaders as they seek direction and solutions for the nation's and world's problems. Instead, He has left them to their own devices and, consequently, the more idiotic and foolish their lifeless decisions become and the more their paths lead them to disastrous destinies and tragic dead ends. Failing to sincerely ask God for guidance and direction in our lives truly becomes as foolish and idiotic as seeking advice from a corpse or asking for direction from a dead man.

Cannibalism is Merely a Matter of Taste

The great Swedish theologian, Francis Schaeffer, declared, "If there are no absolutes by which to judge society, then society is absolute."[17] Simply stated, this means that if God has not set forth a moral standard by which all men, of all time, are to live, then whatever moral commands men themselves establish are purely relative to whatever a society may decide at the moment.

According to "cultural relativism," the diversity of cultures, even those with conflicting moral beliefs, is not to be considered in terms of right and wrong or good and bad. Various practices which are condemned as morally wrong in some societies are totally acceptable in others. Similarly, "ethical relativism" views truth as variable and not absolute, so what constitutes right and wrong is determined solely by the individual or by society. Since truth is not objective, there can be no objective standard which applies to all cultures. Consequently, if there are no moral absolutes, then no individual, culture, or society is in a position to condemn other individuals, cultures, or societies for behaving in ways contrary to their own.

Actions only become morally right or wrong for someone if (and only if) a person's culture believes it to be so at any particular time. For example, there was a time in America's history when society viewed abortion, homosexuality, transsexualism, and gay marriage to be wrong, and therefore such behavior was not only objectionable, it was also unlawful. However, today all of these behaviors have now been accepted and promoted by both legislation and public approval. As a result, American society becomes the final authority, as morality simply becomes relative to the prevailing convictions or whims of its culture at the time.

One would deduce, then, that the cold-blooded murder of millions of people in the gas chambers of Nazi Germany cannot be rightfully condemned by other nations, because under Hitler, the death camps for "subhumans" became the morally acceptable thing to do by the German powers that be. Society became absolute because they made the state out to be the highest authority by which to judge morality. In the same way, the slaughtering of nearly 100 million people under these communist regimes cannot be rightfully condemned, either:

U.S.S.R: 20 million deaths (murders)
China: 65 million deaths (murders)
Vietnam: 1 million deaths (murders)
Cambodia: 2 million deaths (murders)
Eastern Europe: 1 million deaths (murders)
Africa: 1.7 million deaths (murders)
Afghanistan: 1.5 million deaths (murders)
The international communist movement and communist parties not in power: about 10,000 deaths (murders).[18]

WARNING: Faint-hearted readers may want to skip the portion of this chapter designated between the tilde (~) lines.

~ ~ ~ ~ ~ ~ ~ ~ ~ ~ ~ ~ ~ ~ ~ ~ ~ ~ ~

Consequently, then, if there are no absolutes by which to judge society, not even the depraved practice of cannibalism within some societies can be condemned by other societies. In "The Great Big Book of Horrible Things," Matthew White recorded "human sacrifice and cannibalism among the Aztecs of central Mexico was on such a vast scale that the death toll was over 1.2 million."[19] White goes on to say,

Doped prisoners by the dozens or hundreds were marched up to the top of the pyramid. At the top, in view of the gods and the city, a team of priests each grabbed a limb or a head and pulled the victim down. The sacrificial priest sawed out the prisoner's beating heart with an obsidian (dingy) knife and then burned it on the altar. The priest then pushed the body down the stairs, where it was dismantled, jointed, cooked, and carved. The owner of the sacrificed prisoner got the choicest cuts of meat to be served at a family banquet, while a stew made from the leftovers fed the masses. Pumas, wolves, and jaguars in the zoo gnawed the bones.[20]

Matthew White further reported,

Children were sacrificed to Tlaloc, the rain god. Babies born with certain physical characteristics on astrologically significant days were especially prized, but any child would do. Their throats were slit after the priest made them cry and collected their tears.[21]

In more recent years, Michael Rockefeller wrote of the Asmat people of New Guinea, having witnessed their societal customs firsthand (and who has disappeared and some believe has been killed and eaten by the Asmat people). He wrote:

In many ways, the Asmat world at times was a mirror image of every taboo of the West. In some areas, men had sex with each other. They occasionally shared wives. In bonding rituals, they sometimes drank one another's urine. They killed their neighbors, and they hunted human heads and ate human flesh.[22]

~ ~ ~ ~ ~ ~ ~ ~ ~ ~ ~ ~ ~ ~ ~ ~ ~ ~

Again, if there are no absolutes by which to judge society, then society becomes absolute; and morality merely becomes relative, not universally supreme and binding. No one can therefore denounce the atrocities of the Nazis, the Communists, the Aztecs, or the Asmats for their incredible inhumanities towards their fellow man. Even cannibalism—the ultimate depravity in human behavior—becomes just a matter of taste and not a matter of right and wrong.

Contrary to this outlook, the Bible depicts that there is a higher authority transcending the laws of men and societies, and there are moral absolutes by which to judge all men in every age and in every culture. The God of heaven has set His moral standards not only in stone with His Ten Commandments, but long before, in the hearts of every human being throughout all of history. The apostle Paul declares,

> For the wrath of God is revealed from heaven against all ungodliness and unrighteousness of men who suppress the truth in unrighteousness, *because that which is known about God is evident within them; for God made it evident to them.* For since the creation of the world His invisible attributes, His eternal power and divine nature, have been clearly seen, being understood through what has been made, *so that they are without excuse.* For even though they knew God, they did not honor Him as God or give thanks, but they became futile in their speculations, and their foolish heart was darkened. Professing to be wise, they became fools, and exchanged the glory of the incorruptible God for an image in the form of corruptible man and of birds and four-footed animals and crawling creatures. Therefore God gave them over in the lusts of their hearts to impurity, so that their bodies would be dishonored among them. For they exchanged the truth of God for a lie, and worshiped and served the creature rather than the Creator, who is blessed forever. Amen.
>
> For this reason God gave them over to degrading passions; for their women exchanged the natural function for that which is unnatural, and in

the same way also the men abandoned the natural function of the woman and burned in their desire toward one another, men with men committing indecent acts and receiving in their own persons the due penalty of their error. And *just as they did not see fit to acknowledge God any longer, God gave them over to a depraved mind, to do those things which are not proper*, being filled with all unrighteousness, wickedness, greed, evil; full of envy, murder, strife, deceit, malice; they are gossips, slanderers, haters of God, insolent, arrogant, boastful, inventors of evil, disobedient to parents, without understanding, untrustworthy, unloving, unmerciful; *and although they know the ordinance of God*, that those who practice such things are worthy of death, they not only do the same, but also give hearty approval to those who practice them. (Romans 1:18-32)

Paul goes on to say,

[B]ecause of your stubbornness and unrepentant heart you are storing up wrath for yourself in the day of wrath and revelation of the righteous judgment of God, who will render to each person according to his deeds: to those who by perseverance in doing good seek for glory and honor and immortality, eternal life; but to those who are selfishly ambitious and do not obey the truth, but obey unrighteousness, wrath and indignation. There will be tribulation and distress for every soul of man who does evil, of the Jew first and also of the Greek [Gentile or heathen], but glory and honor and peace to everyone who does good, to the Jew first and also to the Greek. *For there is no partiality with God.*

For all who have sinned without the Law [never heard of God's moral commands] will also perish without the Law, and all who have sinned under the Law will be judged by the Law; *for it is not the hearers of the Law who are just before God, but the doers of the Law will be justified.* For when Gentiles who do not have the Law do instinctively the things of the Law, these, not having the Law, are a law to themselves, in that they show the work of the Law written in their hearts, their conscience bearing witness and their thoughts alternately accusing or else defending them, on the day when, according to my gospel, God will judge the secrets of men through Christ Jesus. (2:5-16)

Therefore, according to the great apostle Paul, it is possible for people to get to heaven even if they have never heard of Jesus — but they will never get to heaven apart from Jesus. I repeat: It is possible for people to get to heaven even if they have never heard of Jesus, but they will never get to heaven apart from Jesus!

In other words, Christ is going to judge all men — the saved and the lost (2 Timothy 4:1). The believers as well as the people in cults and false religions, those who deny His existence, and those who couldn't care less about Him will be judged on the basis of how they responded to the light that He gave them. "From everyone who has been given much [a lot of light], much will be required; and to whom they entrusted much, of him they will ask all the more" (Luke 12:48).

In America, we have been given so much divine light that it is almost blinding. There are churches everywhere, an abundance of Bibles at one's disposal, and a variety of religious programming from which to choose; but as a nation and a society, we prefer darkness to light. Note what Jesus said to Nicodemus:

This is the judgment, that the Light has come into the world, and men loved the darkness rather than the Light, for their deeds were evil. For everyone who does evil hates the Light, and does not come to the Light for fear that his deeds will be exposed. But he who practices the truth comes to the Light, so that his deeds may be manifested as having been wrought in God. (John 3:19-21)

On the other hand, people who have no such spiritual advantages that Americans enjoy still know in their hearts that it is morally wrong to:

- steal, cheat, rob, loot, embezzle;
- lie, swindle, deceive, defraud, swear falsely;
- commit adultery, homosexual acts; engage in incest, prostitution, pornography, pedophilia, and fornication;
- murder, slaughter unborn children, and euthanize the aged and infirmed;
- envy, covet, and harbor malice and ill will towards others; and
- dishonor one's parents and defy lawful authorities.

Yes, men instinctively know right from wrong, even if they have never heard of the Ten Commandments. And those who attempt to live by the light, striving to obey the laws that God has written within their hearts, will be admitted into God's eternal kingdom—not because they have lived perfect moral lives, but because Christ as their judge will essentially say to them, "Because you have followed the light of the laws that I have put into your heart, I will now grant you, through My grace and through My shed blood, the glory of entering into My eternal kingdom."

But to everyone who loved darkness rather than light because their deeds were evil, He will say,

Not everyone who says to Me, "Lord, Lord," will enter the kingdom of heaven, but he who does the will of My Father who is in heaven will enter. Many will say to Me on that day, "Lord, Lord, did we not prophesy in Your name, and in Your name cast out demons, and in Your name perform many miracles?" And then I will declare to them, "I never knew you; depart from Me, you who practice lawlessness." (Matthew 7:21-23)

In conclusion, the more our society approves, legalizes, and promotes practices that violate God's commands, the more it sins against the light and the harsher its judgment. If one argues in favor of abortions, euthanasia, or other violations against God's moral commands because he believes there are no absolutes by which to judge society, then even the moral depravity of cannibalism is simply a matter of taste in a society without moral boundaries or a higher moral authority than that of its people.

Drive-by Impregnators

Perhaps of every manuscript I have ever written (published or otherwise), this chapter, above all others, is bound to generate a firestorm of criticism and an avalanche of contempt because it addresses a subject that epitomizes the slogan which states, "Fools rush in where angels dare not tread." Though there may be a fine line between courage and foolishness and between tough love and mean-spiritedness, in the face of enormous condemnation, this warning to men who produce children out of wedlock (or men who abdicate their responsibilities as fathers) needs to be said.

So let's begin with a rallying cry: "A woman needs a man like a fish needs a bicycle." It is a phrase coined by Irina Dunn and popularized by Gloria Steinem and the feminists during the 1960s. Simply put, it means that men are unnecessary in the lives of women and insignificant in the process of raising children. Men are only needed as sperm donors if women want to experience motherhood or desire fulfillment in nurturing and raising children.

However, in God's economy, men are absolutely essential when it comes to promoting the overall well-being and happiness of children. Fathers have an incredible responsibility before Almighty God and a staggering accountability to Him when it comes to the mental, emotional, moral, physical, financial, and spiritual welfare of their children. Make no mistake about it, the absence of fathers is what lies at the root of poverty and virtually every social ill that plagues our country today.

Our jails and prisons are bulging at the seams and overflowing their walls with juveniles and adults who have grown up without the powerful influence of a caring dad. To compound this tragedy, virtually no one has the courage to admit that single-parent homes are crippling our country in so many ways which are catastrophic to our nation, to our society, and especially to the ever-increasing number of fatherless boys and girls who are condemned to grow up with countless disadvantages—lifetime disadvantages—due to the self-centered irresponsibility of men. Instead, the state has replaced the father and the government has taken over the role of providing for children with absentee dads and deadbeat fathers. "Uncle Sam" has now become the sugar daddy who encourages the skyrocketing trend of illegitimacy with all of its economic and moral devastation resulting from children without fathers.

There is an old adage that says, "Understanding the problem is half solving it." Yet when it comes to the escalating crime rate, illiteracy rate, and incarceration rate today, we, as a nation, refuse to identify the real problem. Instead, these problems are blamed on poverty, lack of education, social injustice, and "racism." Above all else, racism is the battle cry of the liberal champions of societal inequality. Race baiters in the pulpits and within the halls of Congress have become the modern-day false prophets who are always claiming to speak for God but who absolutely refuse to listen to God.

The "R" word is exploited in order to silence all those who disagree and to vilify any "Uncle Tom" who doesn't toe the politically correct line. Never do we acknowledge (let alone confront) the elephant in our living room. When our schools are inundated with undisciplined, unruly, obnoxious, and rebellious children, we dare not ask, "Where is the father? Where is the father?" Rest assured, God is going to demand an answer to this all-important question out of His all-consuming fire of holiness; and no one—absolutely no one—will dare try to talk over Him or dare play the race card with this righteous and color-blind deity. Political correctness will not be a factor in His court of justice where He will display absolutely no partiality—especially when it comes to the pigmentation of a person's skin.

Men who have been little more than drive-by impregnators in the lives of their children will be terrified in His presence as He demands answers from them as to why they chose to be fatherless fathers. White, black, brown, red, and yellow will not play the slightest role in His justice and impartiality. He will lay the blame for the rebellion and moral rot within the societies and nations of the world at the feet of missing dads. Yet no one in politics or academia, and very few in the pulpits throughout our land, has the moral courage to speak the truth about this all-important fact.

However, God will not be intimidated by our politically correct talking heads in empty suits. Instead, He will tear off this hypocritical and multicultural-sensitive mask and expose the root cause of society's moral decay and spiritual rot. It is the fathers' attendance — not race — that determines a child's destiny in this life and, oftentimes, in the afterlife as well. It is the deficient paternal presence — not lack of education, or economic disparity, or prejudice — that lies at the heart of a family's and nation's moral bankruptcy and eventual collapse.

The only significance that race plays is simply this: Whatever group of people has the greatest percentage of absentee fathers, that is the group that will produce the unruliest children and manifest the greatest number of rebels against all of God's ordained authority. Without fatherly input, children are placed at enormous disadvantages so devastating that even their chances of getting into heaven become greatly reduced once they grow into adulthood.

Believe it or not, God foresaw our modern-day upsurge of unwed mothers. And in His great mercy, He will make one last attempt to confront the drive-by impregnators by sending Elijah the prophet to powerfully address this issue just before the terrible and dreadful day of Christ's return. In the last book of the Old Testament, God says through His prophet Malachi,

> For behold, the day is coming, burning like a furnace; and all the arrogant and every evildoer will be chaff; and the day that is coming will set them ablaze ... so that it will leave them neither root nor branch. ... Remember the law of Moses My servant, even the statutes and ordinances which I commanded him in Horeb for all Israel. Behold, I am going to send you Elijah the prophet before the coming of the great and terrible day of the Lord. He will *restore the hearts of the fathers to their children and*

the hearts of the children to their fathers, so that I will not come and smite the land with a curse. (Malachi 4:1, 4-6)

God, in His enormous compassion, will make one last-ditch effort (through his no-nonsense prophet Elijah) to turn fathers' hearts back to their children, demanding that they raise them up in the love, knowledge, and fear of their Creator. I can just imagine the dynamic preaching and divine warnings sounding something like this:

"You fathers need to take responsibility for your children or you are going to hell!"

"You fathers need to instruct your children in the laws and ways of God or you will be eternally damned!"

"You fathers are the cause of countless rebellious, defiant, and insolent children today, and you are going to have to answer to God for your neglectful crimes!"

"God is going to hold you drive-by impregnators responsible if your offspring end up in hell as adults!"

Additionally, in light of Revelation 11 where we are told that Elijah's message will be so offensive that for 3½ years people will repeatedly attempt to assassinate him and his fellow messenger (who I personally believe will be none other than Moses, the lawgiver himself), I am confident the message will include the condemnation of every form of immoral behavior—regardless of whether these practices are legalized or not! No doubt, they will also expose and condemn every false religion, false prophet, and heretical belief and act throughout the world. God had told Moses, "I ... am a jealous God, visiting the iniquity of the fathers on the children, on the third and the fourth generations of those who hate Me" (Exodus 20:5). If men are liars, thieves, murderers, drug

143

addicts, sluggards, or criminals, the chances are great that their iniquity will be passed on to their offspring, because "God is not mocked; for whatever a man sows, this he will also reap" (Galatians 6:7).

No wonder the populace will want these men and their message exterminated! After countless failed assassination attempts, the inhabitants of the earth will only succeed in their murderous endeavor when these two messengers from heaven "have finished their testimony" (Revelation 11:7). On that long-awaited occasion to kill these two men of God, a global celebration will take place, albeit brief.

Although some feminists may believe that women no more need a man than a fish needs a bicycle, God adamantly disagrees, as He demands that a man marry a woman before impregnating her and that he love and cherish both her and their offspring. Even when divorce is unavoidable, men are still required to wholeheartedly invest their lives into their children and raise them up in the love and knowledge of God. However, for all widowed, divorced, and single mothers, God has these encouraging words:

> Fear not, for you will not be put to shame; and do not feel humiliated, for you will not be disgraced; but you will forget the shame of your youth, and the reproach of your widowhood you will remember no more. For your husband is your Maker, whose name is the Lord of hosts; and your Redeemer is the Holy One of Israel, who is called the God of all the earth. For the Lord has called you, like a wife forsaken and grieved in spirit, even like a wife of one's youth when she is rejected. (Isaiah 54:4-6)

Thus, when single moms make God (not the government) their God and make Christ (not the state) their husband, it can go a long way in helping their disadvantaged children in this life as well as the next. The expression, "a fish rots from the head down," can be interpreted to mean if the head of the household is rotten, so will the rest of the family be. Likewise, a society follows the lead of its nation, and a nation with absent or derelict fathers will eventually die and decay; and its ensuing putridity will become the stench smelled around the world, all because fathers neglected their God-determined role as heads of their families and spiritual leaders of their children.

Dung on the Face of the Ground

WARNING: This chapter is not for the culturally refined.

Few things generate more of a disgusting and negative response from people as when they see or accidentally come into contact with human or animal excrement. We recoil in revulsion because we instinctively sense that bodily waste is both defiled and defiling; and to come into contact with such contamination is abasing.

Interestingly, the Bible speaks of a type of divine judgment involving rebellious men who literally become "dung on the face of the ground." One of the greatest insults that anyone can undergo is to have their dead body left in an open field to be devoured by the beasts of the field and the birds of the air and the insects of the earth. The corpses of such men are then transformed into abhorrent waste that is eliminated by the creatures that feed upon them. Truly, this is one of the most supreme indignities that could possibly be done to a person—the indignity of not even being given a proper burial, and then to have one's carcass transfigured into bird feces or animal manure.

Yet God's Word describes this very thing which has happened to his enemies throughout the past and foretells of this very thing transpiring on a massive scale in the very near future—the future event of Christ's second coming—and the end of the world. God told His prophet Jeremiah that because of the sins and the treachery of His chosen people Israel:

> At that time ... they will bring out the bones of the kings of Judah and the bones of its princes, and the bones of the priests and the bones of the prophets, and the bones of the inhabitants of Jerusalem from their graves. They will spread them out to the sun, the moon and to all the host of heaven, which they have loved and which they have served, and which they have gone after and which they have sought,

and which they have worshiped. They will not be gathered or buried; they will be as dung on the face of the ground. (Jeremiah 8:1-2)

Jeremiah goes on to say,

> For death has come up through our windows; it has entered our palaces to cut off the children from the streets, the young men from the town squares. Speak, "Thus says the Lord, 'The corpses of men will fall like dung on the open field, and like the sheaf after the reaper, but no one will gather them.'" (9:21-22)

The same prophet of God further states,

> For thus says the Lord concerning the sons and daughters born in this place, and concerning their mothers who bear them, and their fathers who beget them in this land: "They will die of deadly diseases, they will not be lamented or buried; they will be as dung on the surface of the ground and come to an end by sword and famine, and their carcasses will become food for the birds of the sky and for the beasts of the earth." (16:3-4)

And at the very end of the world, at the second coming of Jesus Christ, Jeremiah foretells,

> "'A clamor has come to the end of the earth, because the Lord has a controversy with the nations. He is entering into judgment with all flesh; as for the wicked, He has given them to the sword,' declares the Lord." Thus says the Lord of hosts, "Behold, evil is going forth from nation to nation, and a great storm is being stirred up from the

remotest parts of the earth. Those slain by the Lord on that day will be from one end of the earth to the other. They will not be lamented, gathered or buried; they will be like dung on the face of the ground." (25:31-33)

The prophet Ezekiel also predicts that the horrible tribulation of the last seven years before the return of Christ will begin with Magog (Russia) and her allies making an all-out invasion of Israel; but God says of their plundering armies:

> I will turn you around, drive you on, take you up from the remotest parts of the north and bring you against the mountains of Israel. I will strike your bow from your left hand and dash down your arrows from your right hand. You will fall on the mountains of Israel, you and all your troops and the peoples who are with you; I will give you as food to every kind of predatory bird and beast of the field. You will fall on the open field; for it is I who have spoken. (Ezekiel 39:2-5)

Furthermore, the apostle John predicts that when Christ physically returns to Earth:

> From His mouth comes a sharp sword, so that with it He may strike down the nations, and He will rule them with a rod of iron; and He treads the wine press of the fierce wrath of God, the Almighty. And on His robe and on His thigh He has a name written, "KING OF KINGS, AND LORD OF LORDS."
>
> Then I saw an angel standing in the sun, and he cried out with a loud voice, saying to all the birds which fly in midheaven, "Come, assemble for the great supper of God, so that you may eat the flesh

of kings and the flesh of commanders and the flesh of mighty men and the flesh of horses and of those who sit on them and the flesh of all men, both free men and slaves, and small and great." (Revelation 19:15-18)

The loving Son of God Himself also predicted this very occurrence when He said, "For just as the lightning comes from the east and flashes even to the west, so will the coming of the Son of Man be. Wherever the corpse is, there the vultures will gather" (Matthew 24:27-28).

And finally, the prophet Zephaniah proclaimed,

> Near is the great day of the Lord, near and coming very quickly; listen, the day of the Lord! In it the warrior cries out bitterly. A day of wrath is that day, a day of trouble and distress, a day of destruction and desolation, a day of darkness and gloom, a day of clouds and thick darkness, a day of trumpet and battle cry against the fortified cities and the high corner towers. I will bring distress on men so that they will walk like the blind, because they have sinned against the Lord; and their blood will be poured out like dust and their flesh like dung. Neither their silver nor their gold will be able to deliver them on the day of the Lord's wrath; and all the earth will be devoured in the fire of His jealousy, for He will make a complete end, indeed a terrifying one, of all the inhabitants of the earth. (Zephaniah 1:14-18)

There can be no greater insult to men who are at war with God and who defy His moral commands than to have their fleshly bodies turned to dung. Some of the most pompous and most arrogant men in the past have been reduced to piles of bird droppings; and many of the world's most distinguished and

149

illustrious men in the future are destined to be brought so low that they will literally become heaps of animal waste, like the wicked Queen Jezebel of old, whose body was devoured by dogs and her remains were eliminated as animal feces on the surface of the land (see 1 Kings 21:23; 2 Kings 9:10, 33-37).

What an insult! What humiliation when God fulfills His Word through His prophet Isaiah, saying, "I will punish the world for its evil and the wicked for their iniquity; I will also put an end to the arrogance of the proud and abase the haughtiness of the ruthless" (Isaiah 13:11). Unfortunately, very few people (religious or otherwise) ever contemplate this very unpleasant reality of God's holy wrath.

So the next time you are forced to clean bird droppings off the windshield of your car or to clean up the compost of your pet, let it be a reminder of the very real phenomenon of divine judgment; and realize that, although God is truly a God of love, nevertheless His indignation upon unrepentant sinners and those who are at war with Him can truly be an astonishing sight to behold and (dare I say?) smell.

Witch Doctors and Snake Oil

Most folks would agree that bad medicine has been around for centuries and has often been the prevailing "science" of the day — in spite of its many ridiculous methods. For example, in ancient Egypt, the cure for a toothache was to place a still-warm, freshly halved, dead mouse onto one's teeth. In the early 19th century, some British doctors believed that eating a fried mouse could cure whooping cough. There was a time when physicians insisted that boiled cockroaches could cure earaches and that crushed cockroaches could treat ulcers and cancer. There also was a time when the medical profession proclaimed that cow dung could aid in healing fractures.[23]

Bloodletting was also once the rage as doctors thought that draining a person's blood would actually siphon out toxins or poisons from the body and thereby heal a diseased person. (As a matter of fact, that is exactly the medical procedure that killed George Washington when all he was being treated for was a common cold. Speaking of George Washington's cold, doctors even swabbed the Founding Father's throat with beetle paste to cure his unpleasant symptoms.)

Another healing practice held by "medical experts" from various cultures was to drill a hole into a person's skull in order to relieve them of migraines, epilepsy, and other such disorders of the brain. Surgically inserting goat glands into a man's testicles or into a woman's abdomen was the procedure for curing everything from impotence to senility and from flatulence to weak eyesight. Additionally, the toxic metal, mercury, once was a popular treatment for syphilis and was also prescribed for toothaches, tuberculosis, and constipation. In the early 1900s, radioactive water was used as a treatment for lethargy, low energy, or drowsiness. Even radioactive toothpaste was promoted as a teeth whitener. Doctors once prided themselves in walking around in blood-stained aprons as they went from patient to patient without so much as washing their hands, even after doing autopsies on diseased corpses.[24]

The list can go on and on in regards to the insane medical strategies that once passed themselves off as sound science. However, one medical procedure that is sure to rank within the top 10 healing gimmicks of all time was the utterly ridiculous smoke enema. Here doctors would actually blow tobacco smoke into a hose and up a patient's rear end in order to cure everything from sour stomachs to cholera and from dysentery to drowning. This is actually the origin of the phrase "I'm not just blowing smoke up your arse [behind]."[25]

Today, we can readily laugh at so many idiotic techniques believed to be reputable science and good medicine back in its day, but unfortunately, "the more things change, the more things remain the same." Considering what plagues our infirmed society and looking at the absolutely asinine cures and worthless placebos that politicians come up with to solve the nation's dilemmas or heal our world's troubles, they are about as ludicrous as some of the absurd healing antidotes of years gone by. Because leaders the world over have rejected the God of the Bible and scoffed at His moral commands, politicians have deprived themselves of having true wisdom and understanding. They have lifted themselves and their governments up as being the final authority; as a result, their laws and their policies are altogether devoid of divine enlightenment. Instead, their indifference and their hostility towards the Creator of the universe makes them completely incapable of making common-sense decisions and producing intelligent results.

Essentially, the witch doctors of snake oil and bad medicine of the past have been resurrected in today's political high priests and legislative shamans. Their magic potions, quack remedies, and bogus cures for what ails America and the world would truly be laughable if they were not so tragic. Our nation has rejected the Divine Physician and mocked Him out of our schools, our courts, our institutions, and our political decision making; therefore, God has left the leaders of the world floundering in a sea of turmoil and confusion. God warned His people Israel that if they forsook Him:

The Lord will smite you with madness and with blindness and with bewilderment of heart; and you will grope at noon, as the blind man gropes in darkness, and you will not prosper in your ways; but you shall only be oppressed and robbed continually, with none to save you. (Deuteronomy 28:28-29)

On the other hand, God promised that "if my people, who are called by my name, will humble themselves and pray and seek my face and turn from their wicked ways, then will I hear from heaven and will forgive their sin and will heal their land" (2 Chronicles 7:14, NIV).

Furthermore, He said,

My son, do not forget my teaching, but let your heart keep my commandments; for length of days and years of life and peace they will add to you. ... Trust in the Lord with all your heart and do not lean on your own understanding. In all your ways acknowledge Him, and He will make your paths straight. Do not be wise in your own eyes; fear the Lord and turn away from evil. It will be healing to your body [or country] and refreshment to your bones [or society]. ... How blessed is the man [or nation] who finds wisdom and the man [or state] who gains understanding. For her profit is better than the profit of silver and her gain better than fine gold. She is more precious than jewels; and nothing you desire compares with her. Long life is in her right hand; in her left hand are riches and honor. Her ways are pleasant ways and all her paths are peace. She is a tree of life to those who take hold of her, and happy are all who hold her fast. ... The curse of the Lord is on the house [or nation] of the wicked, but He blesses the dwelling [or country] of the righteous. Though He scoffs at the scoffers, yet He gives grace to the afflicted [or humble]. The wise will inherit honor, but fools display dishonor. (Proverbs 3:1-2, 5-8, 13-18, 33-35)

America as a whole today does not look to God for wisdom and guidance; rather, our nation has merely reduced God to little more than a cuddly mascot whom we like to trot out at weddings, funerals, and prayer breakfasts, or in the midst of disaster, but our governments and institutions insist that He stay in His place and not make any demands upon us. With the leaders' foolish scoffing at His Word and ridiculing His commandments, God in turn mocks them through the absurd solutions they procure without Him. In Psalm 2, God says,

Why are the nations in an uproar and the peoples devising a vain thing? The kings of the earth take their stand and the rulers take counsel together against the Lord and against His Anointed, saying, "Let us tear their fetters apart and cast away their cords from us!" He who sits in the heavens laughs, the Lord scoffs at them. Then He will speak to them in His anger and terrify them in His fury, saying, "But as for Me, I have installed My King upon Zion, My holy mountain."

"I will surely tell of the decree of the Lord: He said to Me, 'You are My Son, today I have begotten You. 'Ask of Me, and I will surely give the nations as Your inheritance, and the very ends of the earth as Your possession. 'You shall break them with a rod of iron, you shall shatter them like earthenware.'"

Now therefore, O kings, show discernment; take warning, O judges of the earth. Worship the Lord with reverence and rejoice with trembling. Do homage to the Son, that He not become angry, and you perish in the way, for His wrath may soon be kindled. How blessed are all who take refuge in Him! (vv. 1-12)

Lastly, Jesus said, "apart from Me you can do nothing" (John 15:5). Consequently, our defying His moral laws and His person guarantees that our desperate attempts to solve our problems without Him will only end up in failure and humiliation. Laughably (if not pathetically), our political witch doctors today continue to offer us snake oil which could no more cure arthritis than cow dung could heal broken bones, all while making promises akin to blowing smoke in a way that is truly preposterous and foolhardy. Their solutions merely become more bloodletting that simply accelerate the demise of a country rather than actually healing what ails it.

So the next time you listen to the solutions of politicians proclaiming to have the answers to solve our nation's problems, ask yourself: "Are their prescribed methods of curing the country's troubles based on the wisdom of God's Word, or are they just blowing smoke up the nation's derriere?"

The Father of Despair

In 1942, a prominent Jewish psychiatrist was arrested, along with his newlywed wife, his parents, and his brother, by the Nazis and sent to a concentration camp. His name was Viktor Frankl, and his horrible experiences in Germany's death camps led him to write a best-selling book in just nine days. His publication was titled *Man's Search for Meaning* in which he concluded that the difference between those who lived and those who died came down to one thing: meaning. He insisted that "he [who] knows the 'why' for his existence ... will be able to bear almost any 'how.'"[26] Simply put, man must have meaning and not merely meat if he is to truly live.

Men are created for purpose and they are designed for genuine significance. Animals, on the other hand, are not. Every beast, bird, reptile, and insect on Earth may be content (and perhaps even "happy" to a degree) as long as they have their basic needs of survival met. However, man is not truly joyful or completely content simply to have good health, a full stomach, and a multitude of material possessions.

The truth of this can be seen in several ways, but nothing proclaims man's need for true meaning louder than the vastly rising number of suicides in our age of affluence and materialism. The suicide rate throughout America is rising in virtually every age category as people despair in the midst of difficult and painful circumstances. Even in the armed services, military personnel are taking their lives at alarming rates, regardless of whether they had been deployed in combat zones or not.[27][28]

Whereas, during the Great Depression of the 1930s, when people truly struggled economically and had few material possessions, the rate of self-destruction was lower in America than in our present age of abundance, easy credit, and endless entertainment.[29] It is no coincidence that the suicide rate during those hard economic times was lower, primarily because God was a priority to most people decades ago, and He was honored and His moral commands were upheld. In short, people believed that their lives had a purpose because their existence was rooted in a Creator who placed enormous value upon them. Therefore, as Victor Frankl noted, he who knows the "why" for his existence will be able to bear almost any "how."

Man was created for purpose. He needs purpose. Regrettably, this compelling need for meaning has led men everywhere to tragic and pathetic deaths. Religious fanatics who blow themselves up in their insane attempts to murder as many people as possible is in actuality a desperate attempt to give their lives purpose. Their yearning to make their lives matter and to become part of something bigger than themselves screams of desperation.

It can also be said that when most men and women join the military it is often from a desire to become part of something bigger than oneself and thereby validate their lives with a purpose. In my opinion, this is one of the major reasons for the increasing number of suicides in the armed forces. When a soldier feels like his contribution to this elite group of men and women is unappreciated and worthless, their disillusionment can be truly devastating and they can feel painfully trapped in a situation where there is no quick, easy, or honorable way out.

This is not meant to be an oversimplification of a very complex and complicated issue (when it comes to military suicides), but when military personnel begin to feel that their sacrifices for a greater cause are nothing more than a thankless task, it can truly be disheartening. On the flip side, when a soldier believes and feels that his life is solidly grounded in a noble purpose, he can endure virtually any suffering and hardship.

This brings us to the ultimate purpose for one's existence. It was the great theologian Augustine who said, "Man's heart is restless, oh Lord, until it rests in thee." In essence, he is acknowledging that searching for something other than God to satisfy them or give their lives purpose and meaning is futile. I imagine many different answers could be given (even among church members) to the profound question: "What is the meaning of your life?" or "What is the purpose to your existence?"

However, the ultimate answer to one's existence can be found in Deuteronomy 6:5 where God says, "You shall love the Lord your God with all your heart and with all your soul and with all your might." Christ reiterated this as the greatest of all the commandments, with the second being, "You shall love your neighbor as yourself" (Matthew 22:37-39). This is why man exists. This is what gives him purpose. This is the reason he was created. Every other reason is secondary and temporal—no matter how moral or excellent it may be. To commit to God's Son and to live for Him is one's ultimate purpose in life. Joining His army of heavenly soldiers is to truly be part of something much bigger and much nobler than one's self.

Yes, suicide is the father of despair, and despair has many children; but a life that is grounded in God and in obedience to Christ is truly a life worth living (regardless of how difficult it may be). In God, there is genuine meaning and true purpose; and in God, there is lasting hope. People may believe that any number of things may give their lives purpose, but apart from God, these things are merely shadows without substance and foundations of sinking sand. Life begins and ends with Christ who is "the Alpha and the Omega, the first and the last, the beginning and the end," the A to the Z (Revelation 22:13). Without Him, life is pointless and despair is inevitable, if not in this life, then most certainly in the next.

The Mother of All Screwups

An old hillbilly was sitting on a park bench one morning just munching on an apple and gazing mindlessly out in the distance. Curled up at his feet was a senile dog observing its surroundings with thoughtless indifference. An old friend of the redneck spotted him and gave out an enthusiastic greeting as he sat down beside the hillbilly and blurted out, "Hey Henry, does your dog bite?" The old man just continued to stare off into space and said with a long drawl, "Naaaaaw, my dog don't bite." Without hesitation, the old man's friend reached down to pat the mongrel on the head and immediately the hound sunk its teeth into the man's hand. The injured guy recoiled in utter shock and screamed, "Henry! I thought you said your dog doesn't bite!" The aged fellow continued to peer off into the countryside and droned, "Yeeeeah, it's true, my dog don't bite." Then, glancing down at the mutt, responded, "But that hound ain't my dog."

It's been said that "assumption is the mother of all screwups"; and like the unfortunate fellow with the punctured hand, he assumed something that was not true. He then suffered the consequences of his false conclusion that the dog belonged to his old friend. As miserable as that may have been for the man with the injured hand, far worse presumptions are made by people every day and throughout every age, and the most detrimental of all assumptions is the mistaken notion of man's "basic goodness," which postulates that if there is a heaven, one will arrive there because one is "basically good." This supposition, perhaps more than all others, has damned more souls than anything else.

If you were to ask strangers you encounter in a crowded mall, or at a sporting event, or even coming out of church this question: "If you died tonight, where do you think you would go?" I would venture that most would reply they would go to heaven if there were such a place. If asked *why* they think they would go to heaven, the overwhelming response would undoubtedly be, "because I am basically a good person." This assumption is truly the most devastating of all false assumptions because of its eternal consequences. The atheist assumes there is no God, the agnostic assumes it doesn't matter, the cultists assume their beliefs are the true beliefs, the Darwinists assume they came from apes, and the reincarnationists assume they will have an endless cycle of rebirths until the law of karma says they finally got it right. Assumptions are prevalent everywhere one turns; however, no assumption damns more souls than "I am basically good, and therefore if there is a heaven, I will surely go there."

Such an assumption flies in the face of what God says about mankind when He asserted, "There is no one who does good. The Lord has looked down from heaven upon the sons of men to see if there are any who understand, who seek after God. They have all turned aside, together they have become corrupt; there is no one who does good, not even one" (Psalm 14:1-3; see Romans 3:10-12).

Furthermore, God said through His prophet Isaiah, "[A]ll of us have become like one who is unclean, and all our righteous deeds are like a filthy garment; and all of us wither like a leaf, and our iniquities, like the wind, take us away" (Isaiah 64:6). The God of the universe avowed that even men's righteousness is nothing but "filthy rags" in His sight—let alone men's wickedness.

Most people assume they are righteous because they have set up their own standard of righteousness, and their standard is based upon their own moral criteria, not upon God's holy absolutes. What further complicates this reality is the fact that men's morality is always a moving target which can change with his feelings or fluctuate with the prevailing beliefs of the day. The assumption of personal goodness can truly be blinding, even in the midst of flagrant immorality and downright depravity. As the apostle Paul predicted:

> But realize this, that in the last days difficult times will come. For men will be lovers of self, lovers of money, boastful, arrogant, revilers, disobedient to parents, ungrateful, unholy, unloving, irreconcilable, malicious gossips, without self-control, brutal, haters of good, treacherous, reckless,

conceited, lovers of pleasure rather than lovers of God, *holding to a form of godliness, although they have denied its power.* (2 Timothy 3:1-5)

Paul also wrote:

And just as they did not see fit to acknowledge God any longer, God gave them over to a depraved mind, to do those things which are not proper, being filled with all unrighteousness, wickedness, greed, evil; full of envy, murder, strife, deceit, malice; they are gossips, slanderers, haters of God, insolent, arrogant, boastful, inventors of evil, disobedient to parents, without understanding, untrustworthy, unloving, unmerciful; and although they know the ordinance of God, that those who practice such things are worthy of death, they not only do the same, but also give hearty approval to those who practice them. (Romans 1:28-32)

In short, men can "hold to a form of godliness" and yet "not see fit to acknowledge God any longer." They like to say that they are "spiritual" or that they "worship God in their own way" and assume their "form of godliness" will get them to heaven. They have replaced God's standard of righteousness with their own, and they have presumed that their "own way" of believing is all that really matters. However, their assumptions are going to have devastating and eternal consequences because God has clearly said,

But because of your stubbornness and unrepentant heart you are storing up wrath for yourself in the day of wrath and revelation of the righteous judgment of God, who will render to each person according to his deeds: to those who by perseverance in doing good seek for glory and honor and immortality, eternal life; but to those who are selfishly ambitious and do not obey the truth, but obey unrighteousness, wrath and indignation. There will be tribulation and distress for every soul of man who does evil, of the Jew first and also of the Greek (Gentile), but glory and honor and peace to everyone who does good, to the Jew first and also to the Greek. For there is no partiality with God. (2:5-11)

Yes, assumption is truly the mother of all screwups, but no assumption is more damaging than to suppose we are "basically good" in our own eyes, while in the eyes of God, our utmost righteousness is considered to be filthy rags, let alone our sinfulness. In short, assumption may be the mother of all screwups, but nowhere are her children more abundant than in the offspring of those who assume they are righteous in and of themselves, rather than putting on Christ's righteousness in order to be truly good in the sight of God.

The Kiss of Death

The Bible speaks extensively about two kinds of death—the physical death and the spiritual death. As the saying goes: "Born once, die twice. Born twice, die once," which in essence simply means that unless a man becomes born again (by repenting of his sins and accepting Christ), he will not only experience bodily death, but his soul will undergo eternal death in the lake of fire.

When God warned through his prophet Ezekiel that "[t]he soul who sins will die" (Ezekiel 18:4), He was talking about unrepentant sinners and about the second death. He was warning of eternal death because all men die, but only unrepentant sinners die twice. The Lord proclaimed:

> The person who sins will die. ... But if the wicked man turns from all his sins which he has committed and observes all My statutes and practices justice and righteousness, he shall surely live [eternally]; he shall not die [eternally]. All his transgressions which he has committed will not be remembered against him; because of his righteousness which he has practiced, he will live [eternally]. Do I have any pleasure in the death [eternal loss] of the wicked ... rather than that he should turn from his ways and live [forever]? (Ezekiel 18:20-23)

God warned the very first man and woman on Earth that if they sinned by disobeying Him, they would "surely die" (Genesis 2:17), and James cautioned, "[E]ach one is tempted when he is carried away and enticed by his own lust. Then when lust has conceived, it gives birth to sin; and when sin is accomplished, it brings forth death" (James 1:14-15). The kiss of both physical and spiritual death is sin, and only the blood of Christ can wash away the scourge of sin and annihilate its dreaded offspring, infamously dubbed the "Grim Reaper."

At the final judgment of the damned, the apostle John said:

Then I saw a great white throne and Him who sat upon it, from whose presence earth and heaven fled away, and no place was found for them. And I saw the dead [the damned], the great and the small, standing before the throne, and books were opened; and another book was opened, which is the book of life; and the dead were judged from the things which were written in the books, according to their deeds. And the sea gave up the dead which were in it, and death [the graves] and Hades [hell] gave up the dead [lost souls] which were in them; and they were judged, every one of them according to their deeds. Then death [the Grim Reaper] and Hades were thrown into the lake of fire. *This is the second death, the lake of fire.* And if anyone's name was not found written in the book of life, he was thrown into the lake of fire. (Revelation 20:11-15)

Unfortunately, this lake of fire which is the second death is anything but soul sleep or eternal unconsciousness. Jesus warned it is a place where the "worm does not die, and the fire is not quenched" (Mark 9:42-48). John, "the apostle of love," said of this second death that the damned

will drink of the wine of the wrath of God, which is mixed in full strength in the cup of His anger; and [they] will be *tormented* with fire and brimstone in the presence of the holy angels and in the presence of the Lamb. And the smoke of their torment *goes up forever and ever;* they have no rest day and night. (Revelation 14:10-11)

A kiss can be a very pleasant experience, but we must never forget that sin can also be very pleasurable, though its pleasure is very short lived (Hebrews 11:25) and its fruit of death, eternal.

Recall how James put it: Once the seductive and enticing lust of sin is conceived, it is only a matter of time before sin is accomplished and it brings forth death. We need to also understand that to a holy God, there is no such thing as an insignificant sin, just as there is no such thing as being a little pregnant. All sin will be dealt with, either forgiven through the saving work of Christ on the cross or judged for the denial of Him.

The affectionate kiss between lovers can be very enjoyable; however, there is another kind of kiss—the kiss of death, whose fruit is damnation if its spell is not broken by the blood of Christ. The curse of the kiss of death can only be broken by the kiss of Christ.

Finally, let's heed the psalmist's advice:

> Now therefore, O kings, show discernment; take warning, O judges of the earth. Worship the Lord with reverence and rejoice with trembling. Do homage to the Son [Kiss the Son, KJV], that He not become angry, and you perish [second death] in the way, for His wrath may soon be kindled. How blessed are all who take refuge in Him! (Psalm 2:10-12)

Everybody's Got One

Our modern world has become a global Tower of Babel where confusion and division reign supreme. The earth is fragmented with warring factions where the slightest of differences can lead to hostility expressed through arguments, fist fights, riots, homicides, and ultimately to all-out wars. The litany of the world's diversities invariably generates multitudes of prejudices, animosities, and serious conflicts. However, there is one thing that all people of all ages have in common, which is rarely, if ever, thought about (let alone argued over). This common denominator is the belly button — yes, a belly button. Everybody's got one! Yet, have you ever paid attention to it or reflected upon its profound physical and spiritual significance?

In a cynical sense, belly buttons are like excuses because "everybody's got one." This analogy is especially true when it comes to one's relationship with God. In short, there is not one person on Earth who doesn't have a navel, and when it comes to man's countless failures in living up to God's commands, it is a very rare individual indeed who doesn't make up an excuse. As a matter of fact, excuses were made even before the first umbilicus came into existence.

Adam and Eve were the only human beings that were divinely fashioned outside of a woman's womb, and therefore never had the necessary umbilical cord which leaves its indelible mark on every newborn when it is detached from the baby's body. Furthermore, it was a woman who gave birth to the very first infant, but it was a man who gave birth to the very first excuse.

The conception, formation, and delivery of the very first excuse in the universe, delivered by the only man on Earth, only took seconds; and it was quickly followed by the instant creation of another excuse composed by the woman. These original excuses have since cascaded into an ocean of endless excuses. The world is now swimming in a deluge of rationalizations when it comes to commitment to Christ and obedience to God.

When God asked Adam if he had eaten of the forbidden fruit in the Garden of Eden, the man immediately said, "The woman whom You gave to be with me, she gave me from the tree, and I ate." Then the Lord God said to the woman, "What is this you have done?" And the woman said, "The serpent deceived me, and I ate" (Genesis 3:12-13). These first two excuses have now given rise to the never-ending blame game throughout all of human history. However, the Lord God did not accept either one of their excuses. Instead, He judged them severely for their transgression. They not only lost paradise, but the curse of their fallen nature has now been passed on to their innumerable descendants.

Everyone now possesses a navel that is a constant reminder of their inherited fallen and sinful condition. Their sinfulness has been transmitted through the man's sperm and the woman's ovary, and the DNA of both parents is nourished to maturity through the umbilical cord attached to the navel. As David proclaimed in the Psalms, "Behold, I was brought forth in iniquity, and in sin my mother conceived me" (Psalm 51:5).

To reiterate, all men and women are born sinners. We are not sinners because we sin; we sin because we are sinners, and we have the navel to prove it. Our sinfulness is in our very DNA, in our genes, and the only thing that can possibly change this corrupt predicament is a new nature—a new heart, a new birth—a birth without the telltale sign of a belly button. Jesus spoke of this concept to Nicodemus: "Truly, truly, I say to you, unless one is born of water and the Spirit he cannot enter into the kingdom of God. That which is born of the flesh is flesh, and that which is born of the Spirit is spirit. Do not be amazed that I said to you, 'You must be born again'" (John 3:5-7).

A change in heart can only come from God and only His Spirit can give man a new nature, a new birth without a navel. A good start in achieving this would be praying David's prayer: "Hide Your face from my sins and blot out all my iniquities. Create in me a clean heart, O God, and renew a steadfast spirit within me" (Psalm 51:9-10). However, this transformation is not possible in the midst of excuses, and playing the blame game will never make a man right before God, nor excuse man's accountability to Him. Pointing the finger at one another did not exonerate our first parents and neither will it acquit any of us.

Not only is God calling all men to repentance without any excuses, He is also inviting everyone to His heavenly and eternal banquet, and He will not accept any excuses. This is apparent in a story told by Jesus:

> A man was giving a big dinner, and he invited many; and at the dinner hour he sent his slave to say to those who had been invited, "Come; for everything is ready now." But they all alike began to make excuses. The first one said to him, "I have bought a piece of land and I need to go out and look at it; please consider me excused." Another said, "I have bought five yoke of oxen, and I am going to try them out; please consider me excused." Another one said, "I have married a wife, and for that reason I cannot come." And the slave came back and reported this to his master. Then the head of the household became angry and said to his slave, "Go out at once into the streets and lanes of the city and bring in here the poor and crippled and blind and lame." And the slave said, "Master, what you commanded has been done, and still there is room." And the master said to the slave, "Go out into the highways and along the hedges, and compel them to come in, so that my house may be filled. For I tell you, none of those men who were invited shall taste of my dinner." (Luke 14:16-24)

Excuses are as ubiquitous as belly buttons; everyone has one — no exceptions! They are so commonplace that rarely does anyone notice them, on others or even themselves. Similarly, man's excuses for ignoring or disobeying God's moral demands become so habitual that he thinks little or nothing of them, either. However, he will not be excused from his accountability to God.

Navels are God's reminder to all people that just as we were once totally dependent on the life of our mother while in her womb, so navels are outward signs of everyone's dependence upon God for everything—including our next breath. As the apostle Paul put it: "He Himself gives to all people life and breath and all things ... He is not far from each one of us; for in Him we live and move and exist" (Acts 17:25, 27-28).

In light of this, two very important questions to reflect upon are: First, "Do I merely make up excuses when it comes to obeying God?" and second, "Do I truly realize just how dependent I am upon God, so dependent that I cannot even take my next breath without Him?" When it comes to excuses, simply because everybody's got one, doesn't mean we need to use them, especially in our relationship with our heavenly Father.

The Power of Weakness

Did you ever stop to consider just how strong a newborn infant really is, or exactly how powerful a little child can be? Ironically, their strength is nothing short of miraculous because it lies at the very heart of their weaknesses. Their helplessness becomes absolutely nothing short of brute force as it moves a mother with such tenderness and compassion that she will expend all of her energy to care for her powerless child. In times of danger, a mother will put her own life in jeopardy in order to defend or protect her vulnerable infant. Virtually any lost and frightened child becomes a powerful magnet drawing total strangers to come to its aid, sometimes even at the risk of their own welfare.

Also, women can possess a mysterious power over men due to the fact that by nature, females are—more often than not—physically weaker than males; and oddly enough, it is a woman's charm, beauty, and gracefulness, not her muscles, strength, and dominance that the majority of men find most attractive. I realize this is not a politically correct statement and may ruffle the feathers of some of my readers; nonetheless, it was God who said, "You husbands ... live with your wives in an understanding way, *as with someone weaker*, since she is a woman" (1 Peter 3:7).

It is a woman's physical weakness that often elicits her power over a man. In times of crises, women and children are almost always given priority and first consideration. Whether being rescued from a burning building, a sinking ship, or a natural disaster, the weaker ones are invariably always given preeminence; and any man who pushes aside women and children in order to save himself will never live down his cowardly acts of self-preservation.

In our day and age, chivalry may be said to be dead, and the demands and claims of feminists may abound, but the human instinct to protect the weak and care for the helpless is an unspoken and universal code. It is a divine law that is chiseled not on some slab of political correctness, but written within the very heart of humanity; and nowhere is this divine law seen more clearly than in God Himself. The apostle Paul proclaimed:

> For the word of the cross is foolishness to those who are perishing, but to us who are being saved it is the power of God. For it is written, "I will destroy the wisdom of the wise, and the cleverness of the clever I will set aside." Where is the wise man? Where is the scribe? Where is the debater of this age? Has not God made foolish the wisdom of the world? For since in the wisdom of God the world through its wisdom did not come to know God, God was well-pleased through the foolishness of the message preached to save those who believe. For indeed Jews ask for signs and Greeks search for wisdom; but we preach Christ crucified, to Jews a stumbling block and to Gentiles foolishness, but to those who are the called, both Jews and Greeks, Christ the power of God and the wisdom of God. *Because the foolishness of God is wiser than men, and the weakness of God is stronger than men.* (1 Corinthians 1:18-25)

The true power of God is actually manifested in the "weakness of God," as when He drank the last dregs of pain and humiliation in order to save a lost and helpless humanity. Similarly, the true power of a soul will always be found within the soul's humility. Jesus instructed us, "[L]earn from Me, for I am gentle [meek] and humble in heart" and "Blessed are the gentle, for they shall inherit the earth" (Matthew 11:29; 5:5). In the same manner:

> [C]lothe yourselves with humility toward one another, for "God is opposed to the proud, but gives grace to the humble." Therefore humble yourselves under the mighty hand of God, that He may exalt you at the proper time. (1 Peter 5:5-6; see James 4:6)

When the disciples asked the Son of God who was the "greatest in the kingdom of heaven," Jesus called a child to Himself and emphatically said, "Truly I say to you, unless you are converted and become like children, you will not enter the kingdom of heaven. Whoever then humbles himself as this child, he is the greatest in the kingdom of heaven" (see Matthew 18:1-4). We can appreciate how a child instinctively realizes he is dependent upon his parents for everything, and it is this weakness that makes a child humble while paradoxically empowering him with great strength.

When the apostle Paul implored the Lord three different times to be relieved of his "thorn in the flesh," Jesus said to him, "My grace is sufficient for you, for [My] power is perfected in weakness." Paul then responded by humbly declaring, "Most gladly, therefore, I will rather boast about my weaknesses, so that the power of Christ may dwell in me. Therefore I am well content with weaknesses, with insults, with distresses, with persecutions, with difficulties, for Christ's sake; for when I am weak, then I am strong" (see 2 Corinthians 12:7-10).

Yes, there is great power in weakness, and a humble spirit unleashes God's perfect power in us. With it, we have a strength beyond reckoning, while appearing as innocent and helpless as a baby. We are the bride of Christ and as such, the weaker vessel, cherished coheirs to new life together with Him. To God be the glory for the great things He has done through the weakness of humble men in furthering His kingdom, both now and forevermore.

Beware of Beds, Baskets, and Basements

Light is a phenomenon seldom examined while carrying out our daily routines, even when we are bathed in the sun's radiance for hours at a time. It is only when people find themselves surrounded by unwelcome darkness that they even begin to think about light, because darkness can quickly and easily produce anxiety and desperation, especially in a time of danger or emergency. Without light of one kind or another, even 20/20 vision becomes useless in the midst of blackness. The lack of illumination will inevitably find one groping around like the blind do in their attempts to find something or to arrive at a desired destination.

Consequently, it is no accident that the remarkable aspect of light is used when describing Jesus, as well as His followers and spiritual matters. The apostle John referred to Christ as being the light of the world when he wrote, "In [Jesus] was life, and the life was the Light of men. The Light shines in the darkness, and the darkness did not comprehend it" (John 1:4-5). The apostle went on to say that although John the Baptist was not himself the light, he came to testify about the light and to lead them to this light.

Then Jesus said of Himself, "I am the Light of the world; he who follows Me will not walk in the darkness, but will have the Light of life'" (8:12). The Lord went on to say, "We must work the works of Him who sent Me as long as it is day; night is coming when no one can work. While I am in the world, I am the Light of the world" (9:4-5). He continued, saying, "For a little while longer the Light is among you. Walk while you have the Light, so that darkness will not overtake you; he who walks in the darkness does not know where he goes. While you have the Light, believe in the Light, so that you may become sons of Light" (12:35-36).

Not only did the Son of God proclaim to be the light of mankind shining in the darkness, He has passed this very same heavenly torch off to His followers who have a moral obligation to let the light of Christ shine through them. However, He also warned of three things that would greatly diminish or even extinguish this divine light: beds, baskets, and basements!

Jesus pointed out that no one takes a lighted lamp and puts it "under a bed" (Mark 4:21, Luke 8:16). A bed symbolizes slothfulness, ease, comfort, sensuality, sleep, and dreaming. All of these can greatly diminish or extinguish altogether a Christian's light. As a matter of fact, slothfulness was listed as being one of the seven deadly sins by the early church leaders, and the sacred writings strongly condemn the sin of indolence. Twice in the book of Proverbs, Solomon (the wisest of wise men) addresses this:

> How long will you lie down, O sluggard? When will you arise from your sleep? "A little sleep, a little slumber, a little folding of the hands to rest" — your poverty will come in like a vagabond and your need like an armed man. (6:9-11)

Later he re-addresses the matter:

> I passed by the field of the sluggard and by the vineyard of the man lacking sense, and behold, it was completely overgrown with thistles; its surface was covered with nettles, and its stone wall was broken down. When I saw, I reflected upon it; I looked, and received instruction. "A little sleep, a little slumber, a little folding of the hands to rest," then your poverty will come as a robber and your want like an armed man. (24:30-34)

God does not put a premium on laziness, but rather exhorts His followers over and over again to be diligent in their relationship with Him, or their light will surely dwindle and their commitment to Him will disappear like the sun at sunset.

Furthermore, it goes without saying, sensuality and immoral passions that a bed can generate will certainly curtail even the brightest of lights. King David was a man who loved God with all of his heart, yet the desire to sleep with another man's wife was his undoing and brought tremendous judgment upon him and his entire household. Although God forgave him, his spiritual light was greatly diminished because of a bed, and much of his moral authority faded in the eyes of his nation.

The next object that Christ warned could reduce the illumination of a Christian's light was a basket (Matthew 5:15, Mark 4:21). Baskets represent commerce, money, and materialism. They symbolize prosperity and abundance as they are used to sell and exchange wheat, barley, grain, and other food staples or valuable commodities. Christ cautioned that wealth and the pursuit of riches have enormous potential to overshadow a Christian's light for God.

In Jesus' famous parable of the sower and the seed, He explained that the seed which falls among the thistles and thorns symbolizes "the man who hears the word, and the worry of the world and the *deceitfulness of wealth* choke the word, and it becomes unfruitful" (Matthew 13:22). In Luke 8:14, Jesus said that the thorns also exemplify the "pleasures of this life." In other words, prospering Christians can have their light choked out through their preoccupation with making money and in the pursuit of pleasures that are both legitimate and illegitimate in the eyes of God. Notice that Jesus said there is a deceitfulness of wealth, suggesting that once a man sets his heart on money, there is never enough—because no matter how much he accumulates, he is always going to desire more.

Consequently, placing a basket of commerce over a lighted lamp is sure to obscure that light, and it does not take a great deal of money to do so. Bring one thin dime close enough to a person's eye, and that ten-cent piece can blot out the sun which is almost 900,000 miles wide!

Lastly, Jesus warned of basements, or cellars, as being something that can also hide the spiritual light of His followers. He said, "No one, after lighting a lamp, puts it away in a cellar" (11:33). To put a lighted lamp down in a basement rather than in plain view of everyone is to imply that such an individual is ashamed of it, and therefore he senses a need to hide it—to relocate it in a place where only they themselves see it. In other words, their relationship with Christ is a "personal thing," and no one else needs to know of it or see it.

Another reason why a person may want to camouflage their light around others is to avoid having to live up to that light. They can break any of God's moral laws and never be accused of being a hypocrite or a charlatan. Their hidden light will never expose their ungodly behavior as being a sham and a mockery. Nevertheless, to those who hide their light, Jesus warned, "For whoever is ashamed of Me and My words in this adulterous and sinful generation, the Son of Man will also be ashamed of him when He comes in the glory of His Father with the holy angels" (Mark 8:38). In contrast, He said, "You are the light of the world. A city set on a hill cannot be hidden. ... Let your light shine before men in such a way that they may see your good works, and glorify your Father who is in heaven" (Matthew 5:14, 16).

In conclusion, if we are to shine brightly for the Lord Jesus Christ, we must get out of the basements to light the way for others, avoiding beds of ease and baskets of affluence along the path. The more mindful we are of the dangers of the three B's, the less ability they will have in overcoming us and diminishing the very light that a world shrouded in darkness desperately needs.

The Awesome Power of a Two-letter Word

The God of the Bible is the only true God. He is the God of gods, the Lord of lords, and the King of kings. His power has no limits and His intelligence, no bounds. The only things that are His equal are the very words He speaks. The apostle John says of this one and only God:

> In the beginning was the Word, and the Word was with God, and the Word was God. He was in the beginning with God. All things came into being through Him, and apart from Him nothing came into being that has come into being. In Him was life, and the life was the Light of men. ... He was in the world, and the world was made through Him, and the world did not know Him. ... And the Word became flesh, and dwelt among us, and we saw His glory, glory as of the only begotten from the Father, full of grace and truth. (John 1:1-4, 10, 14)

When Christ came into this world, which He Himself created, He came as an infant and grew into a man who embodied the very words of God as He spoke His message to men. Furthermore, when He returns to this world in great power and great glory, John says of Him:

> And I saw heaven opened, and behold, a white horse, and He who sat on it is called Faithful and True, and in righteousness He judges and wages war. His eyes are a flame of fire, and on His head are many diadems; and He has a name written on Him which no one knows except Himself. He is clothed with a robe dipped in blood, and His name is called The Word of God. ... And on His robe and on His thigh He has a name written, "KING OF

KINGS, AND LORD OF LORDS." (Revelation 19:11-13, 16)

This God of the Bible is infinite, omnipotent, and omniscient. His vocabulary is without measure. He can speak every language known to angels, devils, and men. He can articulate any words in any accent, dialect, or vernacular that has ever existed or that ever will exist. This same "Word of God" can also communicate in thoughts, dreams, and visions. He can speak His words through nature, through circumstances, through joys and sorrows, and through life and death. This Great Communicator has even been known to speak through the mouth of a jackass, as when He rebuked His wayward prophet Balaam (see Numbers 22:22-35).

In view of these amazing facts, the power of a divinely spoken word can never be overestimated or taken for granted. In addition, God uses a lot of words over and over again in the Bible, but few words are used more numerously than the word "if." This one-syllable, subordinating conjunction can be used as a noun ("the future is full of ifs") or even as an idiom ("no ifs, ands, or buts"). However, when God uses this little two-letter word, it is almost always as part of a condition, saying, "If you do this, I'll do that" or "If you do that, I'll do this."

He frequently told His people in the Old Testament that "if" they obeyed Him, and honored Him, and walked in His commandments and statutes, then He would bless, prosper, and multiply them and allow them to live long in the land that He gave to them. However, He also warned them time and again that "if" they worshipped other gods, or trampled underfoot His laws, or began to act with hostility towards Him, then He would bring curse after curse upon them until they were destroyed, with very few survivors remaining.

The shallow thinker will argue that such curses only applied to God's people in the Old Testament; however, conditional promises with corresponding curses can be found in the New Testament as well:

"If we do not repent ...
"If we do not accept Christ ...
"If we do not obey Him ...
"If we do not follow Him ...
"If we ignore God's commands ...
"If we disregard His warnings ...
"If we refuse to listen ... then we will be eternally
   lost and separated from God in the lake of fire."

On the other hand:

"If we repent of our sins ...
"If we believe in the Son of God ...
"If we accept Jesus Christ ...
"If we follow Him ...
"If we obey Him ... then we will live forever with
   Him in heaven."

The power of that one little word used again and again is truly awesome. It possesses the power of blessings and curses, life and death, and heaven and hell. The word "if" may be a very, very small word but when applied by God, its length, breadth, width, and weight stretches into eternity where every lost soul will be forever saying, "If only ... if only ... if only. ..."

Legion of the Expendables

Did you ever wonder how many cells in the human body are shed and replaced in just a single day? The numbers are incomprehensible — in the tens of billions. Some have even claimed that approximately 70-90% of all household dust is comprised of human skin cells. It has been estimated that between 30-40,000 skin cells fall off our bodies every minute, which averages out to roughly 8.8 pounds per year. It's not too surprising then, that God referred to mankind as dust when He cursed the ground because of Adam's disobedience and said to him, "By the sweat of your face you will eat bread, till you return to the ground, because from it you were taken; for you are dust, and to dust you shall return" (Genesis 3:19). Men are but dust.

Although nearly every type of cell within the human body is replaced many times over during one's lifetime, the fact that skin cells shed every day and completely regenerate themselves between 10 to 30 days, each year of one's life.[30] Consequently, it would be easy to conclude that the sheer volume of human skin cells makes them very expendable. However, the skin is actually an essential organ that happens to be the largest of the 78 organs of the human body.

Based upon the volume and density of each type of cell in the human anatomy, scientists have concluded the average human being is made up of around 37.2 trillion cells in total, of which the skin makes up about 6.0 trillion.[31] Of course these numbers fluctuate, depending upon the size of the individual; but as a rule, 16% of one's body weight consists of a single organ, the skin. Therefore, the significance of this organ should never be underestimated or taken for granted.

Joseph Stalin was one of the biggest mass murderers in history, and he was known to say, "The death of one man is a tragedy. The death of millions is a statistic." Unfortunately, if people fail to see the value of one individual (or the value of one simple cell), their worthwhileness can easily be obscured when hearing or reading reports of voluminous numbers and statistics.

The brain, heart, kidneys, liver, and lungs are essential for survival, but the skin is the first and most important line of defense in protecting all body parts. Therefore, it is no coincidence that the people of God are referred to as a "body" where Christ is the head and the believers are defined as members of the Lord's spiritual anatomy:

> For the body is not one member, but many. If the foot says, "Because I am not a hand, I am not a part of the body," it is not for this reason any the less a part of the body. And if the ear says, "Because I am not an eye, I am not a part of the body," it is not for this reason any the less a part of the body. If the whole body were an eye, where would the hearing be? If the whole were hearing, where would the sense of smell be?
>
> But now God has placed the members, each one of them, in the body, just as He desired. If they were all one member, where would the body be? But now there are many members, but one body. And the eye cannot say to the hand, "I have no need of you"; or again the head to the feet, "I have no need of you." On the contrary, it is much truer that the members of the body which seem to be weaker are necessary; and those members of the body which we deem less honorable, on these we bestow more abundant honor, and our less presentable members become much more presentable, whereas our more presentable members have no need of it
>
> But God has so composed the body, giving more abundant honor to that member which lacked, so that there may be no division in the body, but that the members may have the same care for one another. And if one member suffers, all the members suffer with it; if one member is honored, all the members rejoice with it. Now you are

Christ's body, and individually members of it.
(1 Corinthians 12:14-27)

In view of this incredible analogy, it becomes apparent that it is the Holy Spirit acting as the very DNA molecule which determines how each and every cell of the body will function. The fact that God assigns so many cells to be just one part of the body, powerfully proclaims their importance. Their vast numbers may give the appearance that they are expendable and simply serve in the legion of the expendables; but in God's design, their value cannot be overemphasized.

So the next time you see household dust in the corner of a room or layered upon a piece of furniture, instead of mindlessly sweeping it away, we would do well to recall the incredible sacrifice which those unsightly piles of cells have made in order to assure our very survival. Dead skin cells may appear to be very expendable as we discard them, but that dust was once more valuable than gold nuggets and more precious than bars of silver because they gave their very lives that we might live.

Likewise, in the body of Christ, we may feel very unimportant and expendable; but in God's economy, our sacrificial contributions are absolutely necessary for the life of His Church and for the well-being of His body. Consequently, if household dust can be more valuable than granules of gold, it is God's way of saying that no one is expendable to Him, and that the importance of each individual church member should never be underestimated or underappreciated. Only men and demons can make us feel worthless in the vast sea of humanity that makes up Christ's body, but the Almighty and His angels know the true significance of just a single cell. Therefore, in God's evaluation, no one who happens to serve in the "legion of the expendables" is truly expendable.

The Curse of the "God Gene"

Decades ago, the Federal Food and Drug Administration required every tobacco company in the nation to warn their customers of the dangers and ill effects of their noxious products. Every carton of cigarettes, every can of chewing tobacco, and every package of cigars must carry a bold warning label declaring something to the effect of: "Caution: Smoking can be hazardous to your health." Smoking and tobacco products have become so demonized by the healthcare industry and so vilified by political correctness that no one can plead ignorance to the negative consequences of sucking on "cancer sticks," chewing wads of tobacco, or puffing on large stogies.

Let's face it, there is no real redeeming factor to tobacco use; nevertheless, it is still the habit of many. A far better habit to develop would be that of prayer, although it, too, should come with a warning label, because praying can do more harm than good spiritually if it is not grounded in the truth of the one legitimate God. Nonetheless, it is notable that men and women the world over and throughout all of human history have been known to pray and seek spiritual guidance from a divine source.

Research by a geneticist named Dean Hamer has led him to believe there is a specific gene which predisposes people towards spiritual or mystical experiences. He authored the book titled, *The God Gene: How Faith Is Hard-Wired into Our Genes*, in which he claims that man is hardwired to believe in the supernatural. He bases his God gene hypothesis on a combination of behavioral, genetic, neurological, and psychological studies and remarks, "Religious believers can point to the existence of God genes as one more sign of the Creator's ingenuity—a clever way to help humans acknowledge and embrace a divine presence."[32]

Interestingly, the greatest theologian in all of history, the apostle Paul, wrote of this God gene long before all of the research and findings of Dean Hamer. He relayed, "that which is known about God is evident within them; for God made it evident to them. For since the creation of the world His invisible attributes,

His eternal power and divine nature, have been clearly seen, being understood through what has been made, so that they are without excuse" (Romans 1:19-20). Only "[t]he fool says in his heart, 'there is no God'" (Psalm 14:1, NIV) and yet Paul says that people can be fools even if they profess to believe in God (or a god) or in gods. The epistle of James tells us that even demons believe in God—so much so that they fear and shudder at the very thought of Him (James 2:19). Therefore, whether or not men actually possess a God gene is not the issue; rather, what men do in regards to the concept of God is what really matters.

The Bible teaches that God created man in His own image and likeness (Genesis 1:26-27), but people have tried desperately to remake Him into their own image and likeness. Naturally, men prefer a god of their own liking—one who will bless them and prosper them in all their fleshly desires and worldly ambitions. While their God gene may convince them there is a god, their fallen nature compels them to make him into a Divine Being with whom they are most comfortable. Paul put it this way:

> For even though they knew God, they did not honor Him as God or give thanks, but they became futile in their speculations, and their foolish heart was darkened. Professing to be wise, they became fools, and *exchanged the glory of the incorruptible God for an image in the form of corruptible man and of birds and four-footed animals and crawling creatures.* ... For they exchanged the truth of God for a lie, and worshiped and served the creature rather than the Creator, who is blessed forever. (Romans 1:21-23, 25)

This divinely infused God gene can become as deadly as any cancer cell if it mutates into a distortion of who God truly is and what He has clearly said in His Word. Consequently, men have been known to worship virtually everything in the heavens and on Earth. From insects to galaxies and from the moon to money, men will give homage to almost anything that accommodates their wishes and fulfills their earthly desires. However, did you know that when the heathen worship idols, we are told in Deuteronomy 32:16-17 and 1 Corinthians 10:20, they are actually invoking the power of demons? Regardless, people are without excuse when it comes to their idolatrous practices because the truth about God is known to men intuitively. Isaiah the prophet announced:

> Thus says the Lord, your Redeemer, and the one who formed you from the womb, "I, the Lord, am the maker of all things, stretching out the heavens by Myself and spreading out the earth all alone. ... I am the Lord, and there is no other; besides Me there is no God .... that men may know from the rising to the setting of the sun that there is no one besides Me. I am the Lord, and there is no other, the One forming light and creating darkness, causing well-being and creating calamity; I am the Lord who does all these." (Isaiah 44:24; 45:5-7)

The Bible tells us that King Belshazzar of Babylon went out of his way one night to insult this one and only true God of heaven by desecrating the sacred bowls and cups from Solomon's temple. While he and a thousand of his nobles were having a drunken bash and praising a variety of gods, suddenly a mysterious hand began writing on one of the walls of the king's palace, and the arrogant king was terrified! Although he did not understand the inscription, under the weight of his guilty conscience, he knew that such a supernatural revelation could not be a good thing. In desperation, Belshazzar sought for anyone who could interpret the mysterious message, and it wasn't until the prophet Daniel was summoned that it could be deciphered for the king and his revelers. When Daniel read the divine caption, he rebuked the king, saying:

[Y]ou have exalted yourself against the Lord of heaven; and they have brought the vessels of His house before you, and you and your nobles, your wives and your concubines have been drinking wine from them; and you have praised the gods of silver and gold, of bronze, iron, wood and stone, which do not see, hear or understand. But the God in whose hand are your life-breath and your ways, you have not glorified. (Daniel 5:23)

Daniel then relayed the message to the foolish monarch that God was putting an end to his kingdom and was giving it over to the Medes and the Persians because the king had "been weighed on the scales and found deficient" (vv. 24-28). Likewise, all men who use their divinely infused God gene to manufacture gods to their own liking will also be weighed in the balances of God's eternal justice and be found eternally condemned.

Suffice it to say, the God gene can definitely be a curse when men deliberately pervert what they instinctively know to be true. This begs the question then, "Why would anyone want to distort the truth about God?" Most likely because they do not want to be accountable to Him. One such person was Karl Marx, the godless and atheistic father of communism, who declared that "religion is the opiate of the masses"; meaning that belief in God is merely a drug to which people become addicted for solace and comfort. Well, Karl Marx may have been an all-time fool, but he wasn't completely deranged when he considered religion to be an opiate, because even when people pray to the one true God, it can inoculate them with just enough spiritual dope to make them feel comfortable in their sins and secure in their unrepentant lifestyles and to mistakenly think that all is well between them and the Almighty. Jesus validated this truth when He said,

Not everyone who says to Me, "Lord, Lord," will enter the kingdom of heaven, but he who does the will of My Father who is in heaven will enter. Many will say to Me on that day, "Lord, Lord, did we not prophesy in Your name, and in Your name cast out demons, and in Your name perform many miracles?" And then I will declare to them, "I never knew you; depart from Me, you who practice lawlessness." (Matthew 7:21-23)

In conclusion, then, if administered as an opiate, prayer can truly be hazardous to one's soul, as we exchange the truth about God for a lie and insist upon fashioning deities that are more palatable to our taste buds. So, feel free to make prayer a daily habit but in so doing, remember this warning: "Beware of the curse of the God gene" — because it can easily turn into a fatal drug that may produce a spiritual high, but it has no genuine connection with the one and only God of heaven and Earth.

Just Imagine

John Lennon, the famous rock star of the Beatles band wrote his acclaimed song titled "Imagine" with the following lyrics:

Imagine there's no heaven; it's easy if you try.
No hell below us and above us, only sky.
Imagine all the people living for today.

Imagine there's no countries; it isn't hard to do.
Nothing to kill or die for and no religion, too.
Imagine all the people living life in peace.

You may say I'm a dreamer, but I'm not the only one.
I hope someday you'll join us, and the world will be as one.

Imagine no possessions; I wonder if you can.
No need for greed or hunger, a Brotherhood of Man.
Imagine all the people sharing all the world.

You may say I'm a dreamer, but I'm not the only one.
I hope someday you'll join us, and the world will be as one.

These humanistic lyrics accompanied by their catchy tune have been heard and sung, and believed in, for decades. They invite mankind to envision what a wonderful and peaceful world the earth would be, if only men would deny the existence of God and the afterlife and instead focus on a Brotherhood of Man—a brotherhood of mankind living under the Utopia of a one-world government or global community where men genuinely care for one another and promote the welfare of every person.

While a world such as this may sound ideal, it is impossible apart from the Prince of Peace. We will not experience Utopia on Earth until the Holy Spirit enters each of us and does away with our sinful nature. Now I've come up with some lyrics here to my own song, in contrast to John Lennon's:

Just Imagine

Imagine only one commandment; imagine if you
    can.
Only one commandment to live by, and all the
    world obeys.
Imagine only one commandment; it isn't hard to do;
Because this single commandment applies to me
    and you.

Now imagine all of men's possessions, free from
    thieves and envy;
Never being burglarized or embezzled, no matter
    how tempting it might be.
Just imagine what the world would be like, for you
    as well as me;
If only that one commandment were followed,
    making men glad and free.
Then peace on Earth would be just a breath away;
If only all the people would honor God this way.

You may say I'm a dreamer, but in heaven it
    already is that way.
Just that one commandment could change our
    world in a single day.

And when Christ is ruling and reigning,
All men will follow that one commandment,
Forbidding men to steal, then peace will be forever.

Simply by obeying just one teaching, the world
would become as one.

You may say I'm a dreamer, but I'm not the only
one.
I hope someday you'll join us, the ones who follow
and obey.
And in keeping that commandment, the world will
be as one.

The Ten Commandments of God are as follows (albeit with
differing sequences):

	Catholic	Protestant
1	Have no other gods but me	Have no other gods but me
2	Don't take God's name in vain	Make no graven images
3	Keep holy the Sabbath day	Don't take God's name in vain
4	Honor your father and mother	Keep holy the Sabbath day
5	Do not kill	Honor your father and mother
6	Do not commit adultery	Do not kill
7	Do not steal	Do not commit adultery
8	Do not bear false witness against your neighbor	Do not steal
9	Do not covet your neighbor's wife	Do not bear false witness against your neighbor
10	Do not covet your neighbor's goods	Do not covet anything

(Exodus 20:3-17; Deuteronomy 5:7-21)

Now, regardless of which list you choose, "Thou shalt not steal" means "Do not steal" — whether it is read as the 7th or as the 8th Commandment. (I only say this, so that the arrangement does not become the focus but rather the commandment itself.) Imagine every man on Earth keeping this commandment of God in both the letter and the spirit. Our world would truly become a virtual paradise overnight without wars, poverty, hunger, prisons, and murders because, if you think about it, these perils basically stem from the selfish desire of wanting what someone else has and committing crimes in order to obtain what rightfully belongs to others. The epistle of James illuminates this with his penetrating question and answer:

> What is the source of quarrels and conflicts among you? Is not the source your pleasures that wage war in your members? You lust and do not have; so you commit murder. You are envious and cannot obtain; so you fight and quarrel. You do not have because you do not ask. You ask and do not receive, because you ask with wrong motives, so that you may spend it on your pleasures. (James 4:1-3)

In addition, just imagine the trillions of dollars that could be saved annually if just the one commandment that prohibits every form of larceny was obeyed. Insurance premiums would tumble due to no longer needing to compensate for thefts. The costs of armies, police departments, healthcare (currently riddled with theft via fraud), correctional institutions, surveillance cameras, armored vehicles, security guards, and a host of other high costs relating to anti-theft devices and safeguards would be radically reduced as they become far less necessary; and even grocery stores and retailers would no longer need to inflate prices to cover shoplifting losses. This vast and incomprehensible saving could go a long way, if not all the way, in eradicating hunger and poverty on a global scale.

John Lennon may have wanted men to imagine how dreaming of no possessions, no hunger, and no God or afterlife would usher in peace and brotherhood, but I challenge men to imagine how keeping just one of God's Commandments would effectively guarantee a world that would indeed be as one.

The Powerful Charm and Influence of a Woman

Anyone who believes there are no major differences between men and women other than anatomically has obviously not spent much time with the opposite sex! The very popular book, authored by John Gray, called *Men are from Mars, Women are from Venus* has sold over 50 million copies and spent 121 weeks on the bestseller list. As the title suggests, men and women's variances are so vast that it is as if they came from two different planets. To name one, Gray asserts there are fundamental psychological differences between the genders, and evidently these are the cause of most problems between men and women.

So many marital conflicts and eventual divorces are the result of misunderstanding the needs, perceptions, and expectations of one's spouse. Much ink has been spilt in the writing of numerous books, gender studies, and scientific research cataloging and expounding upon all of these contrasting characteristics; however, rarely (if ever) has gender research explored the mystifying effect that women have over men in general.

A biblical sage by the name of Agur lists four things that perplex him:

> There are three things which are too wonderful for me, four which I do not understand: the way of an eagle in the sky, the way of a serpent on a rock, the way of a ship in the middle of the sea, and the way of a man with a maid. (Proverbs 30:18-19)

Who can thoroughly describe the way of a man with a woman? Men can become so intoxicated with the beauty, charm, and intrigue of a woman that they can be reduced to utter fools. Exactly what is this bewitching power that women have over men? It is a power that has no equal; a mesmerizing influence that can lead a man to heaven or can damn a man to hell.

In Greek mythology, the beauty of Helen of Troy was so over-powering that Paris, the prince of Troy, felt compelled to abduct her from King Menelaus of Sparta, Greece. Her face launched a thousand ships and ignited the ten-year Trojan War—the beauty and charm of one woman dispatched tens of hundreds of war vessels and propelled tens of thousands of men into a death struggle that lasted for over a decade. Only after the Spartans deceitfully entered Troy while hiding in the bowels of the infamous Trojan Horse did the war finally come to an end.

Granted, the tale of Helen of Troy is merely a myth, but it is based upon the known truth that a woman's beauty can motivate men into action in ways that perhaps nothing else can compare. Regardless of a man's intellect, strength, or bravery, the effect—one way or another—of a woman is remarkable. Men know this, not only from personal experience but from several examples given in the Bible.

For starters, consider Adam, created directly from the hand of God, who was perfect in every way. In my opinion, he had to be the most intelligent man to ever walk the earth, as his profound understanding of living organisms enabled him to identify and label the myriads of different species of plants, trees, animals, birds, reptiles, spiders, and insects accordingly (Genesis 2:19-20). Correspondingly, Eve's intellect and beauty had to be beyond comparison as well.

However, in spite of their perfection, they were profoundly unique in their differences as male and female, and although the devil is the greatest champion of political correctness, he is nevertheless nobody's fool when it comes to identifying and exploiting the gender differences of men and women. He could see clearly that the man and the woman were anything but identical, and he immediately recognized that the divinely created female nature possessed a greater inclination to filter things through her emotions, more so than the male nature, for "it was not Adam who was deceived, but the woman being deceived, fell into transgression" (see 1 Timothy 2:12-14). Satan knew by suggesting to Eve that God was lying to her and was deliberately withholding a greater degree of happiness from her, that he (Satan) would be playing more upon the woman's emotions rather than her intellect.

The devil also knew that the woman possessed a power and influence over the man that defies all comprehension. Instinctively, the father of lies knew that this man would not fall for his deceptions, but that Adam would most likely act against his better judgment once the enticement and the seductive powers of the woman entered the situation. Consequently, the intellectual powers of one of the most intelligent men who ever lived was no match when it came to the hypnotic spell of the female gender.

Likewise, the strongest man who ever lived was the powerful and mighty Samson. He was unquestionably the most able-bodied man throughout all of human history. He single-handedly ran down and caught 300 foxes, and he killed 1,000 charging Philistines at one time; and he ran for over 25 miles to the top of a mountain with a one-ton city gate on his shoulders (see Judges 14-16). However, Samson's incredible masculine powers were weakened by the tears and the pleading of his fiancée, which compelled him to reveal the answer to his mysterious riddle and lose a sizable wager to the Philistines.

Additionally, his blind love and attraction for a cunning and deceitful woman named Delilah proved to be his final undoing. She, too, managed to wear down and overthrow the strongest man on Earth with her feminine power and spellbinding seductiveness. As the Bible reveals, "[S]he pressed him daily with her words and urged him, that his soul was annoyed to death. So he told her all that was in his heart" (16:16-17). No man, or army of men, could stand before Samson, but he ended up under a pile of rocks due to the power of one enchanting woman.

Now let's consider the wisest man to ever live, apart from Christ: the legendary Solomon. God said to him, "Behold, I have given you a wise and discerning heart, so that there has been no one like you before you, nor shall one like you arise after you" (1 Kings 3:12; see 2 Chronicles 1:11-12). Yet, in spite of this, his marriage to many heathen women seduced him into becoming an utter fool as they led him into many idolatrous practices (see 1 Kings 11:1-13). His father, King David, was one of the bravest warriors and greatest kings. He also loved and followed God with all of his heart. Nevertheless, his heroic, political, and spiritual leadership was overthrown in just one night by the moonlit beauty of a gorgeous female (see 2 Samuel 11).

So too, the amazing prophet Elijah was the greatest of all the prophets as he stood alone against 450 prophets of Baal and 400 prophets of Asherah, and called down fire from heaven to consume the water-drenched sacrifice on Mount Carmel, defying physics. After having the 850 men killed for their idolatry, he ran 26 miles at night in the pouring rain. In his soaking-wet clothes, he outran the horses of King Ahab, which suggests that he ran the fastest marathon on record as the spirit of the Lord was upon him (see 1 Kings 18:19-46). Furthermore, Elijah twice called down fire from heaven to destroy a hundred pursuing soldiers (see 2 Kings 1:1-16).

However, just one woman threatened his life, and he immediately ran away in such confusion and discouragement that he actually prayed to die. The great prophet demonstrated again and again that he was afraid of no man and that not even pursuing armies could intimidate him, but a crabby queen by the name of Jezebel drove him to despair and helplessness (see 1 Kings 19).

One may claim there is no difference between male and female other than the physical, but the devil laughs at such foolishness. He exploits to the fullest the profound gender differences, while convincing gullible men and women that there are none. Satan is well aware that the power women possess in their relationships with men can likewise be used of God to influence a man in many ways for good—as in the case of Queen Esther. Her beauty and charm melted the heart of a king notorious for his callousness and cruelty, and she was used by God to save the entire population of the Jewish race from the sentence of death.

Certainly, the elusive and mysterious power the Creator has infused into the nature of the female is a divinely incredible force she possesses for good or for evil. The devil knows it and exploits these distinctions between men and women to our detriment, often under the guise of the politically correct notion that there are no differences!

Preach to the Choir!

Since I am just a layman, the chances of me ever being given the opportunity to address a convention of pastors or to speak to a room full of preachers is slim to none. Nevertheless, if such a privilege ever presented itself, I would not hesitate in selecting a topic for my presentation. I would wholeheartedly exhort all pastors, preachers, ministers, and priests to "preach to the choir!" This phrase may have a bad connotation to it because preaching to the choir implies that a preacher has little or nothing new to say since the most loyal congregants (i.e., the choir) have heard the pastor's message many times before. The ramification is they begin to grow stagnant in their relationship with God due to the mere fact that the bread of life becomes stale and the living water begins to evaporate in a lifeless pool of familiar words.

Regardless, preaching to the choir is exactly what every pastor, no matter the denomination, needs to do. The reason is simple: If the choir goes home edified, challenged, and motivated, then virtually every person in the pew (whether of newfound faith or well established in their walk with the Lord) will also leave the church service inspired and spiritually invigorated.

Consequently, preaching to the choir demands an enormous amount of prayer and a tremendous supply of blood, sweat, and tears. When it comes to delivering sermons, no more shooting from the hip when a preacher ascends the pulpit and no more dusting off and rehashing old sermons. No more speaking to the lowest common denominator (considering the biblical literacy of the saved and the scriptural ignorance of the unsaved) which loses its impact.

The apostle Paul knew the importance of a preacher's words and also that prophesying (proclaiming God's Word through preaching) is the most important of the spiritual gifts. He said, "Pursue love, yet desire earnestly spiritual gifts, but especially that you may prophesy" (1 Corinthians 14:1). The great apostle valued preaching above signs, wonders, healings, and other miracles. He said, "[I]n the church I would rather speak five intelligible words *to instruct others* than ten thousand words in a tongue" (v. 19, NIV).

The manifestation of different gifts may very well be spiritually beneficial; worship is very important, music can be thoroughly uplifting, and singing is often edifying. Nevertheless, it is preaching that is most important--especially when preaching to the choir. It is noteworthy today that some seminaries are employing professional actors to coach seminarians on how to become more dynamic and electrifying in their sermons and teachings. Although hiring professional entertainers can be helpful in coaxing pastors to be more expressive, no amount of theological training or attendance of drama classes can substitute for God's anointing.

Neither John the Baptist nor the Lord Jesus Himself ever went to acting school or received instructions from debating coaches. Yet, time and time again, people would marvel at Christ's exhortations and say that He speaks as one having authority, not as the scribes or religious leaders of His day (Matthew 7:28-29). Furthermore, the preaching of John the Baptist was so energetic that both the saved and the lost came from miles around in order to go into the wilderness to hear him preach. It wasn't formal education or professional mentoring that made Jesus and John such powerful and moving preachers; it was the Spirit of God speaking through them as they expounded upon the Scriptures and divided the Word of God correctly. Without question, they understood that

> the Word of God is living and active and sharper than any two-edged sword, and piercing as far as the division of soul and spirit, of both joints and marrow, and able to judge the thoughts and intentions of the heart. (Hebrews 4:12)

Unfortunately, a growing number of preachers today no longer view the Bible as the infallible Word of God, but as just another "literary work" or nice collection of stories and legends that somehow possess deeper meanings in the face of Darwinism, political correctness, and progressive morality. However, such preaching will rarely, if ever, be endowed with the powerful anointing of God's Spirit, regardless of how high a preacher's IQ might be or how many educational degrees he may acquire. It was Jesus who said of the intelligentsia of His day:

> I praise You, O Father, Lord of heaven and earth that You have hidden these things from the wise and intelligent and have revealed them to infants. Yes, Father, for this way was well-pleasing in Your sight. (Luke 10:21; see Matthew 11:25-26)

The religious leaders of Christ's day may have been highly educated, but their air of superiority, as well as their refusal to fully believe in God's words, disqualified them when it came to being His spokesmen. In short, "God is opposed to the proud, but gives grace to the humble" (James 4:6), so when preachers put more confidence in their own understanding than in what God has said, they become like the high priest Zacharias. He was told by the angel, Gabriel, that God was going to give him and his wife, Elizabeth, a son and that they were to name him "John." Nevertheless, the rabbinical preacher doubted God's messenger, and he was struck dumb until the day he demonstrated to others that he was truly convinced of the truth of God's words (see Luke 1:5-80).

It is true that "familiarity breeds contempt," and it can also breed contempt even at the very altar of God. Therefore, it is not uncommon for those who preach to become stale with age whenever they unconsciously begin to view their high calling as merely a job with certain expectations. The everyday duties and responsibilities of a job can become so routine that passion and intensity begin to fade when sermons are delivered simply in exchange for a paycheck. In contrast, from the beginning of Christ's public ministry right up to the very end of His life, the zeal for His Father's house consumed Him (see John 2:13-17; Matthew 21:12-13).

Zeal for God and the things of God can never be purchased with money but it can always be bought off with wages when preaching becomes a profession rather than a calling.

Lastly, Solomon refers to himself as "the Preacher" with the duty of delivering God's truth accurately; and in the concluding words of his book, he says:

> In addition to being a wise man, the Preacher also taught the people knowledge; and he pondered, searched out and arranged many proverbs. *The Preacher sought to find delightful words and to write words of truth correctly.* The words of wise men are like goads, and masters of these collections are like well-driven nails; they are given by one Shepherd. (Ecclesiastes 12:9-11)

The "one Shepherd" is, of course, Jesus Christ. It is He who anoints a preacher's words, but it is the preacher's responsibility to "ponder," to "search out," to "arrange," to "find delightful words," and to "[teach] truth correctly," to the point where his words become like "well-driven nails" and powerful goads to motivate people to pursue God with greater intensity. This requires zeal, thoroughness, and conviction about what God has said. The Lord of hosts Himself emphasized the importance of this when He acknowledged:

> My people are destroyed for lack of knowledge. Because you have rejected knowledge, I also will reject you from being My priest. Since you have forgotten the law of your God, I also will forget your children [spiritual offspring]. (Hosea 4:6)

Preachers who replace God's words with a social gospel, or a prosperity gospel, or a politically correct gospel are certain to end up with congregations that begin to perish because of lack of knowledge. Therefore, the message to preachers is simple — but the challenge is great: Preach to the choir! Preach to the choir!! Preach to the choir!!! Zero in on the most spiritually mature and biblically informed member of your congregation and make sure that he or she returns home challenged and edified, and then the entire assembly will leave inspired as well.

The Godless Church

An oxymoron is essentially a contradiction of terms that suggests an absurdity on at least some level of understanding, such as "dry water," or "cold heat," or a "live corpse." The words of an oxymoron are totally mismatched and just don't make sense in reality. Nevertheless, there is now a growing movement that started in England and is sweeping across America, referred to as the "Sunday Assembly," where people gather together for church services without God, and because the presence of God is not allowed during these church assemblies, it is referred to as the "godless church," which of course epitomizes an oxymoron.

In short, people want the benefits of going to church without actually worshiping God or without the obligations of obeying Him in regards to His commandments. Recent studies have discovered that some of the benefits associated with regular churchgoing are reduced risks of depression, of loneliness, and even of getting cancer. Routine church attendance has also been a determining factor in promoting better heart health and more satisfactory sex.[33] And though people today are leaving the church and formal religion in droves, many of these same individuals still desire the positive byproducts of religious gatherings. Therefore, they assemble together on Sundays to enjoy a service typically consisting of pop music, poetry reading, speeches of some kind, and a moment of reflection. In essence, it is a completely secular church where God and His moral demands have no place, and where worship of Him is not welcome.

It is interesting, therefore, that the apostle Paul foretold of this coming godless church when he wrote:

> But realize this, that in the last days difficult times will come. For men will be lovers of self ... lovers of pleasure rather than lovers of God, *holding to a form of godliness, although they have denied its power*; avoid such men as these. (2 Timothy 3:1-2, 4-5)

Paul foretold that just prior to the return of Christ and the end of the age, men would hold to a form of spirituality but deny the truth about God and the saving power of His Son, Jesus Christ. "Holding to a form of godliness" epitomizes the godless church, and the godless church exemplifies the absurdity of those who attempt to reinvent the wheel. Regardless of how many different designs they come up with to replace the circular wheel, they end up going nowhere and accomplishing nothing.

Instead, by kicking God out of their assemblies, they have merely created a vacuum, and as the saying goes, "nature abhors a vacuum," meaning every empty space needs to be filled with something. Consequently, the spiritual vacuum that the godless church creates opens it up for Satan and the powers of darkness to rush in and fill it. As Paul said:

> For even though they knew God, they did not honor Him as God or give thanks, but they became futile in their speculations, and their foolish heart was darkened. Professing to be wise, they became fools. ... And just as they did not see fit to acknowledge God any longer, God gave them over to a depraved mind, to do those things which are not proper, being filled with all unrighteousness ... [and giving] hearty approval to those who practice them. (Romans 1:21-22, 28-29, 32)

In Paul's second letter to the Thessalonians, he tells us that Satan is going to deceive the whole world "with all power and signs and false wonders," manifested through a coming world leader—a leader the Bible refers to as the antichrist or the beast. However, this "man of lawlessness" cannot appear until apostasy comes first (2 Thessalonians 2:1-12). (Apostasy is a falling away from the truth; it is forsaking sound biblical doctrine.)

Consequently, the growing popularity of the godless church is just one more example of the predicted apostasy that will help generate the very vacuum that the forces of darkness are destined to fill. However, the godless church does not only exist in the fellowships that run God out of their gatherings, but also in assemblies where God Himself chooses to leave due to the moral decline and unrepentance of its members. This happened in the days of Israel when God's presence left the temple just before the city was destroyed because of the wickedness of God's people (see Ezekiel 10). Another time, the "religious" people of Ezekiel's day had no idea that the glory of God's presence had departed from the famous temple of Solomon, and in 70 AD, the Orthodox Jews had no idea that the presence of God had departed from Herod's magnificent temple just prior to its destruction by the Roman commander, Titus.

Whether God's presence is intentionally prohibited in the church assembly or whether God Himself chooses to leave a particular church, either way it becomes a vacuum that is quickly filled by the god of this age. Consequently, the "godless church" may seem like an oxymoron, but in truth, it really does have a god in its midst—"the god of this world" (2 Corinthians 4:4).

Global Bickerfest

> [T]he wicked are like the tossing sea, for it cannot be quiet, and its waters toss up refuse and mud. "There is no peace," says my God, "for the wicked." (Isaiah 57:20-21)

As history unfolds, there appear to be more and more people pleading for peace, marching for peace, fighting for peace, preaching for peace, and promising peace than ever before. Yet, ironically, the world has never been in as much unrest as it is in the present day. Planet Earth is unquestionably becoming a global symphony of feuding and bickering, where the very notion of world peace seems to be just a cruel illusion. Is peace just an absurd delusion that simply exists in a fool's paradise, or is it actually something that can be achieved and experienced the world over? The answer is both yes and no.

It may come as a surprise to you, but apart from God, peace does not exist and it is therefore just a ludicrous concept and a bizarre dream. On the other hand, one of the titles of Jesus Christ is the Prince of Peace (Isaiah 9:6) and it was the Prince of Peace who said:

> Peace I leave with you; My peace I give to you; not as the world gives do I give to you. Do not let your heart be troubled, nor let it be fearful. ... These things I have spoken to you, so that in Me you may have peace. In the world you have tribulation, but take courage; I have overcome the world. (John 14:27, 16:33)

Jesus Christ "Himself is our peace" and "the peace of God, which surpasses all comprehension, will guard [our] hearts and [our] minds in Christ Jesus" (Ephesians 2:14; Philippians 4:7); and as the apostle Paul relates, Jesus Christ "will come to have first place in everything. For it was the Father's good pleasure for all the fullness to dwell in Him, and through Him to reconcile all things to Himself, *having made peace through the blood of His cross; through Him ... whether things on earth or things in heaven"* (Colossians 1:18-20).

Apart from Christ, there will never be peace on Earth as long as people remain at war with God by refusing to submit to His will. Separated from God, all the peace marches, all the peace talks, and all attempts to promote peace become meaningless exercises in futility. In the days of Asa, a rebellious king of Judah, God said to him through the prophet Azariah:

> [T]he Lord is with you when you are with Him. And if you seek Him, He will let you find Him; but if you forsake Him, He will forsake you. ... *In those times there was no peace to him who went out or to him who came in, for many disturbances afflicted all the inhabitants of the lands.* Nation was crushed by nation, and city by city, for God troubled them with every kind of distress. (2 Chronicles 15:2, 5-6)

Remember that Satan is "the god of this world" (2 Corinthians 4:4), and when people forsake God through their rebellion and disobedience, God permits the devil to rob men and nations of their peace. Keep in mind, too, that witchcraft always opens the door to demonic influence and that idolatry is actually the worship of demons (Deuteronomy 32:16-17; 1 Corinthians 10:20). As such, the prophet Samuel rebuked King Saul, saying:

> Has the Lord as much delight in burnt offerings and sacrifices as in obeying the voice of the Lord? Behold, to obey is better than sacrifice, and to heed than the fat of rams. For rebellion is as the sin of divination [witchcraft], and insubordination [stubbornness] is as iniquity and idolatry. Because you have rejected the word of the Lord, He has also rejected you from being king. (1 Samuel 15:22-23)

Saul's defiance not only robbed him of his peace but resulted in the Spirit of the Lord departing from him and an evil spirit from the Lord terrorizing him; and the only thing which could rid King Saul of his torment was when a god-fearing man (David) played a particular instrument in Saul's presence, most likely while singing praises to God (16:14-23). Consequently, unless the wickedness of mankind is replaced with godly righteousness, the global bickerfest and the endless feuding of nations will continue until the unrest literally vaporizes in what appears to be a nuclear holocaust, as predicted through God's prophet Isaiah:

> Wail, for the day of the Lord is near! It will come as destruction from the Almighty. Therefore all hands will fall limp, and every man's heart will melt. They will be terrified, pains and anguish will take hold of them; they will writhe like a woman in labor, they will look at one another in astonishment, *their faces aflame.* Behold, the day of the Lord is coming, cruel, with fury and burning anger, to make the land a desolation; *and He will exterminate its sinners from it.* For the stars of heaven and their constellations will not flash forth their light; the sun will be dark when it rises and the moon will not shed its light. Thus I will punish the world for its evil and the wicked for their iniquity; I will also put an end to the arrogance of the proud and abase the haughtiness of the ruthless. *I will make mortal man scarcer than pure gold* ... I will make the heavens tremble, and the earth will be shaken from its place at the fury of the Lord of hosts in the day of His burning anger. (Isaiah 13:6-13)

There is no peace today, no peace in the hearts of men, and no peace in the home or the society or the nation. Again, there is no peace because we have forsaken the Prince of Peace, and unless we come to Him, and submit to His lordship, peace will continue to elude us like a phantom until the end of time.

The Bigot Bomb

"At first we were silent, and then we were silenced," said one of the few surviving Jews under Hitler's reign of terror. With communism, Nazism, fascism, and beneath the heels of any ruthless dictator, the freedom to speak one's mind or to express an opposing view is one of the first liberties to be eliminated when it comes to human rights. Hitler had his death camps, Stalin had his gulags, Pol Pot had his killing fields, Ho Chi Minh had his reeducation asylums, and North Korea has their torture chambers. All of them brutally suppressed or continue to crush the individual's right to disagree.

Mao Zedong has the unique distinction of being the biggest mass murderer in history, and he was fond of saying, "Political power grows out of the barrel of a gun."[34] However, in America (the "land of the free" with its Statue of Liberty, Bill of Rights, freedom of the press, and freedom of religion), the power to control and to silence others comes with words and not bullets.

It's been said that "the pen is mightier than the sword," meaning that in many cases, words can be more effective in silencing enemies than bloodshed. The childhood rhyme declaring, "Sticks and stones can break my bones but words can never hurt me" fails to take into account just how deadly words can become in the face of political correctness. Instead, the "bigot bomb" has become a very destructive weapon of name-calling today. It denigrates anyone holding different convictions than those of the P.C. crowd, and it has become the arsenal of choice on university and college campuses.

Consequently, the bigot bomb can be as powerful as the barrel of a gun when it comes to killing all intelligent debate and silencing all reasonable arguments. Anyone refusing to goosestep with the politically correct mob is attacked and stigmatized by the words "racist," "hateful," "intolerant," "homophobic," "sexist," or "bigoted." From being "mean-spirited" to "dim-witted," the list of vilifying epithets can be endless, but nowhere is the name-calling more evident than when it comes to the verbal assaults on the true followers of Christ.

Jesus warned his disciples of this unfortunate truth when he said, "Blessed are you when people insult you and persecute you, and falsely say all kinds of evil against you because of Me ... for in the same way they persecuted the prophets who were before you." Christ said of the name-callers of his day: "John [the Baptist] came neither eating nor drinking, and they say, 'He has a demon!' The Son of Man came eating and drinking, and they say, 'Behold, a gluttonous man and a drunkard, a friend of tax collectors and sinners!'" He also declared, "A disciple is not above his teacher, nor a slave above his master. ... If they have called the head of the house [Jesus] Beelzebub [Satan], how much more will they malign the members of his household!" (Matthew 5:11-12; 11:18-19; 10:24-25).

Two thousand years have come and gone since the name-callers of Christ's day concluded that verbal attacks were not effective enough to destroy Him. Their insulting words and all their mudslinging could not keep Him quiet. Consequently, they resorted to torturing Him to death in order to silence Him. Name-calling and slandering are always the first salvo of attacks by the politically correct camp before they resort to persecution, imprisonment, and finally to the execution of all those who fail to regurgitate the beliefs of the group.

In short, failure to go along with the P.C. band is sure to make one a walking target for all the bigot-bomb enthusiasts, especially the bomb throwers in the media. Genuine Christians, in particular, who hold fast to God's moral laws and insist that we all need to repent of our sins and commit to Jesus, become prime targets of journalists and newscasters as well. Although "group think" may be fashionable at the moment and political correctness the key to popularity and acceptance, Jesus said, "Woe to you when all men speak well of you, for their fathers used to treat the false prophets in the same way" (Luke 6:26).

Therefore, when today's army of group thinkers bombard you with slanderous words because of your stance for Jesus, consider the barrage of their bigot bombs as a badge of honor. There is no greater nobility than joining the legion of faithful warriors in God's kingdom. "Rejoice and be glad, for your reward in heaven is great" (Matthew 5:12).

Flying by the Seat of Your Pants

Before the 12 tribes of Israel had a king who could galvanize them into one nation, the Jews had various judges appointed by God to be their liberators and their leaders. Nevertheless, it was the crucial duty of the priestly tribe of Levi to instruct God's people in understanding and obeying the laws that He had ordained through Moses. Unfortunately, the Levitical priests, as a whole, failed miserably in their religious responsibilities of directing Israel's people in the ways of God. Consequently, without strong political or religious leadership, "every man did what was right in his own eyes" (Judges 17:6). It's not that the priests and the Jewish people were without God's moral laws; they basically just disregarded them, and each person began to rely upon one's own feelings and opinions about ethics and morality.

When it comes to everyone doing what is right in their own eyes, very little has changed since the days of Israel's judges, and the results can be summed up by the phrase, "flying by the seat of your pants." This was an expression that became well known to pilots during the early days of aviation. It was a saying that came to signify three different things: First, it meant flying an aircraft by one's feelings rather than depending upon the plane's instrument panel for guidance and direction. Second, flying by the seat of your pants referred to the practice of cutting out pieces of one's pants and using the cloth to patch up a tear in the woven fabric of the plane's wings or fuselage. Third, it came to mean flying without a plan, simply flying as you go and changing course based on a whim.

Whichever explanation one chooses, flying by the seat of one's pants is what many people are doing today, disregarding the words of God and choosing instead to be morally guided by sentimentality and human reasoning. For example, the moral justifications of the homosexual lifestyle, gay marriages, assisted suicide, gender reversals, and doing away with unborn children are but a few of the hot-button issues that are sanctioned and promoted based on emotions, rather than upon what God has

213

declared in the Bible. Instead, God's Word and His moral absolutes are tossed aside as being old-fashioned and outmoded—even hateful—in the face of modern humanism and contemporary preferences. However, passing laws based upon feelings rather than divine absolutes will inevitably result in disaster.

When pilots of primitive aviation flew at night, or through clouds, or in bad weather, the lack of visibility made them totally dependent upon their instruments for navigation and piloting. However, without the aid of sight, their equilibrium would often become distorted and they would begin to depend on their feelings and their contorted mental impressions, rather than relying solely upon their mechanical measuring devices. As a result, crash after crash would occur for no other reason than disregarding the plane's guidance system.

The Bible clearly warns, "There is a way which seems right to a man, but its end is the way of death," and, "The way of a fool is right in his own eyes, but a wise man is he who listens to counsel," as well as, "Grievous punishment is for him who forsakes the way; he who hates reproof will die," and, "Every man's way is right in his own eyes, but the Lord weighs the hearts" (Proverbs 14:12; 12:15; 15:10; and 21:2). On the other hand, it is the wise man who lives by the advice given in Proverbs 3:5-6, which says, "Trust in the Lord with all your heart and do not lean on your own understanding. In all your ways acknowledge Him, and He will make your paths straight."

There was once a time when God's Word was honored in much of Europe and America, and a time when both Britain and the United States sent missionaries throughout the world to proclaim the gospel. Today, however, both the United Kingdom and the United States have thrown God's words overboard. Humanism has replaced Christianity as the preferred religion of the masses, and God's moral laws have been supplanted with the teachings of tolerance, acceptance, inclusiveness, social justice, and broad-mindedness. Permissiveness has become the order of the day, and moral absolutes have been condemned to the dustbin of ancient history. Consequently, when it comes to religious beliefs and ethical standards, we are just flying by the seat of our pants.

Jesus once spoke of a rich man who completely ignored God's words, and after the foolish man died, he found himself condemned forever to the place of torments. Christ tells us that this rich man in hell then saw Abraham far off in the distance and pleaded with him to send Lazarus back from the dead in order to warn the rich man's five brothers of his infernal realm of anguish, lest they too become condemned to this fiery abode. Abraham said that the rich man's brothers had Moses and the prophets to warn them. However, the damned soul insisted that his brothers would not listen to Moses and the prophets, but that his relatives would believe if someone came back from the grave and admonished them. However, Abraham maintained that if his brothers did not believe Moses and the prophets, then they would not be persuaded even if someone returned from the dead to exhort them (Luke 16:19-31).

In short, the words of the prophets, the apostles, and Christ are God's guidance system to direct people to heaven. Thus, all those who disregard the truth and the warnings of Scripture are inevitably destined to the same eternal fate as that of the unbelieving rich man. Consequently, flying by the seat of our pants may feel right, but when it comes to heeding God's words, choosing His moral compass is what will keep us en route to heaven and steered clear from hell.

The Magic Bubble

"Hell no—There ain't no hell!" Or so declare today's illiterate bumpkins, right along with the world's progressive theologians. The scriptural notion of hell has become a mythical concept, in spite of the fact that the incarnate Son of God spoke of such a literal place more than anyone else in Scripture. Jesus Christ warned of hell, He described hell, and He identified the type of people who are going to end up in hell. He had no illusions when it came to the reality of hell and He fervently cautioned how to avoid it.

Some would insist that Jesus was only speaking figuratively and that since God is love, hell cannot, does not, and will not ever exist because an eternal hell and a merciful God are incompatible. In essence, they believe that love, compassion, and forgiveness negate the very notion of eternal punishment for unrepentant sinners. So, like magic, hell has ceased to exist—never mind what the Eternal God says about such a place, because in the end, "love wins."

Therefore, everyone—regardless of what they believe or how they act or what they fail to do—is destined for heaven; because the God of forgiveness and compassion would never condemn anyone to such a horrible place of eternal punishment or everlasting torment. The fact is, though, we are condemned already (see John 3:18). As such, God is not sending anyone to hell; we are choosing to stay on the path that leads to it. In His mercy, however, when we accept His Son as our Savior, He plucks us off this path of eternal destruction and welcomes us into His kingdom.

While we can debate the existence of hell until hell itself freezes over, a deeper and closer look at the concept of hell powerfully suggests that if hell does not exist, then God Himself cannot be a just God, nor can He be a holy God, let alone One who cannot tell an untruth. If God does not punish evildoers for their lawless deeds, He would be amoral, having no moral standards. Instead, a price must be paid before He can overlook or forgive transgressions. That price "is death, but the free gift of God is eternal life in Christ Jesus our Lord" (Romans 6:23). However, insulating ourselves in some kind of magic bubble—no matter how big and beautiful it may appear to be—blinds us to the fact that God is absolutely holy and altogether just.

Only death can ultimately prove or disprove the existence of hell, but no magic bubble can invalidate the profound warnings of an utterly holy and truthful God:

> [D]o you think lightly of the riches of His kindness and tolerance and patience, not knowing that the kindness of God leads you to repentance? But because of your stubbornness and unrepentant heart you are storing up wrath for yourself in the day of wrath and revelation of the righteous judgment of God, who will render to each person according to his deeds ... There will be tribulation and distress for every soul of man who does evil ... but glory and honor and peace to everyone who does good ... For there is no partiality with God. (2:4-6, 9-11)

We must never mistake God's patience and kindness for tolerance or indifference.

> "But by His word the present heavens and earth are being reserved for fire, kept for the day of judgment and destruction of ungodly men. But do not let this one fact escape your notice, beloved, that with the Lord one day is like a thousand years, and a thousand years like one day. The Lord is not slow about His promise, as some count slowness, but is patient toward you, not wishing for any to perish but for all to come to repentance" (2 Peter 3:7-9).

Therefore, in order to get off this road to hell, we must first come to repentance. Only then can God exercise complete forgiveness due to the shed blood of His Son which paid the ultimate price to redeem man from this place of fiery torment. Consequently, we either heed the divine warnings of damnation which are clearly proclaimed throughout the Bible, or we disregard them. However, if we choose rather to believe the soothing and comforting and reassuring words of the preachers and teachers that deny what God has declared on the subject of hell, then we are simply living in a magical bubble — a colorful and mesmerizing bubble that is not filled with sound doctrine but one that is filled with hot air heated by the very hell fire that we so adamantly deny exists.

The Deeper Need

"God sees not as man sees, for man looks at the
outward appearance, but the Lord looks at the
heart." (1 Samuel 16:7)

The Gospel of Mark records an incident in the healing ministry
of Jesus involving a paralyzed man who was lowered from a hole
in a roof. The friends of the paralytic wanted desperately for Christ
to see the unfortunate condition of their companion and thereby
heal him of his infirmary. Unfortunately, dropping the sick man
through an opening in the roof was the only way they could reach
Jesus who was surrounded by pressing crowds. As the impaired
man descended into the overflowing room, everyone no doubt
expected the Lord to heal him, or maybe wondered if He would,
or even could, make him whole again. However, when the Son of
God gazed into the man's eyes, He saw a deeper need and
immediately addressed it before He dealt with the obvious
problem. The Lord said to the stricken individual, "Son, your sins
are forgiven" (Mark 2:1-5).

When questioned about His authority to forgive sins, Jesus
said to his critics: "'Which is easier, to say to the paralytic, "Your
sins are forgiven" or to say, "Get up, and pick up your pallet and
walk"? But so that you may know that the Son of Man has
authority on earth to forgive sins' — He said to the paralytic, 'I say
to you, get up, pick up your pallet and go home.'" And he got up
and went home. But when the crowds saw this, they were
awestruck and "glorifying God" who had given such authority to
men (2:9-12).

This episode epitomizes how Almighty God is far more
concerned about a person's spiritual condition than about one's
physical well-being. Christ patently demonstrated His ability to
heal any infirmity but knew that if He only healed this man
physically, the healing would be all for naught if the man's soul
ended up being lost for eternity.

Our Father considers the deeper, or the unseen, need when people come to Him with their prayer requests. He restores some people physically, knowing their healing will have a positive effect upon them spiritually. Others remain in their sickness, as it can either lead them to salvation or, for those already trusting their Creator, deepen their relationship with Him. Nevertheless, regardless if one's prayers for healing are answered or remain unaddressed, what's important is, "the Lord looks at the heart."

Another recorded incident of Christ's healing ministry involved a bedridden man who lay helplessly impaired for 38 long years. No doubt he spent many hours in prayer asking God to heal him, but it never happened. All the while, others around him were being divinely healed in his presence. When Jesus came upon him, He asked the stricken man if he wanted to be healed and subsequently told him, "Get up, pick up your pallet and walk" (see John 5:5-8). After the cured and ecstatic man left the presence of Christ, Jesus saw him again in the temple area and said to him, "Behold, you have become well; do not sin anymore, so that nothing worse happens to you" (5:14).

Jesus' admonition suggests that *this* man's illness may have been a divine judgment upon his life for living in rebellion against God's moral laws. The same kind of judgment can be seen when the apostle Paul handed over to Satan an incestuous and adulterous man in the Corinthian church. Paul demanded that the man be excommunicated from the assembly and delivered him "to Satan for the destruction of his flesh, so that his spirit may be saved in the day of the Lord Jesus" (see 1 Corinthians 5:1-5). From Paul's second letter to the Corinthians, it appears the man's ailments motivated him to repent and that the man's repentance broke the physical infirmity the devil was allowed to inflict upon him (see 2 Corinthians 2:4-8).

Having said all of this, it is absolutely crucial that people understand I am in no way suggesting that every sickness, disease, handicap, or infirmity is the result of sin or the work of Satan. On the contrary, the Gospel of John tells us:

As [Jesus] passed by, He saw a man blind from birth. And His disciples asked Him, "Rabbi, who sinned, this man or his parents, that he would be born blind?" Jesus answered, "It was neither that this man sinned, nor his parents; *but it was so that the works of God might be displayed in him.*" (John 9:1-3)

In summary, it is always the deeper need, the heavenly need, about which God is most concerned when it comes to people's prayer requests. Jesus' admonition, "so that nothing worse happens to you," further implies there is something worse than physical sicknesses; i.e., spiritual damnation to hell. Therefore, as we place our petitions before our Father, know that He is too good to be unkind and too wise to make mistakes while He considers the invisible — the condition of our hearts — before taking visible action.

Murder Has Changed Its Name

In 1932, Aldous Huxley published his best-selling novel titled, *Brave New World*. Within the pages of his book, Huxley anticipates a future setting in London in the year 2540 where reproductive technology, sleep learning, psychological manipulation, and societal conditioning all work together to create a world where government is all important and all controlling.

Similarly, in 1949, George Orwell published his novel, *1984*, in which he foretells of a coming totalitarian government, the leader of which is "Big Brother," and describes the routine use of deception by officials, abusive secret surveillance, and the manipulation of recorded history, in addition to the presence of thought police everywhere. The language was filled with doublespeak using words composed of two mutually contradictory meanings, and boldly claiming that something is true, in contradiction to the plain facts. Some examples are these three slogans from the book:

"War is Peace"
"Freedom is Slavery"
"Ignorance is Strength" [35]

Alas, the future predictions of Huxley and Orwell have fused into a 21st century brave-new-world reality. Not only is big government becoming more and more overshadowing and omnipresent, but doublespeak has become the official language of the state where:

men can become women (Bruce Jenner),
women can become men (Chaz Bono);
blacks can become white (Michael Jackson),
whites can become black (Rachel Dolezal);
homosexual marriages are all the rage,
traditional marriages are antiquated;

the Bible has become a hate book,
    political correctness has become the Bible;
infanticide has become pro-choice,
    baby killing has become a personal right;
God has become the government,
    the government has become God;
lies have become truth, and
    truth has become lies.

And in the midst of our brave new world, even homicide has fallen prey to doublespeak; murder has now changed its name to "mercy," and killing has adopted the alias of "compassion." Furthermore, anyone who happens to disagree with this new terminology of Big Brother is vilified as a hateful, bigoted, racist, and homophobic blasphemer who is a threat to the governmental powers that be.

However, all the doublespeak of our brave new world cannot change the fact that God — and God alone — has the power over life and death. Man may proclaim all he wants that he is being compassionate and merciful when it comes to his numerous arguments and legislation that promote assisted suicide, but neither men nor their governments have the authority to end the life of anyone, simply because they are suffering. Psalm 139 tells us that from each person's conception, God determines the number of years, months, weeks, minutes, and seconds that each individual is divinely allotted on Earth (v. 16). Of course, man can always cut his allotted time short through suicide or living in defiance of God's moral laws. For instance, if someone overdoses on drugs, or gets killed in a gunfight while robbing a bank, or dies from a sexually transmitted disease, his rebellion against God's commands result in diminishing his predetermined days in this life.

In addition, God has placed such an enormous value upon human beings that in the Old Testament, he required the ultimate punishment for the crime of murder: "life for life" (Exodus 21:23;

see Leviticus 24:17); and when it comes to assisted suicide, the only recorded incident of mercy killing in the Bible is very enlightening. It was when King Saul lay dying from a battle injury and then from a self-inflicted wound in his attempt to end his own life before the Philistines captured him. Coincidentally, an Amalekite happened to come upon the suffering king, and he related his encounter to David, telling him:

> "By chance I happened to be on Mount Gilboa, and behold, Saul was leaning on his spear. And behold, the chariots and the horsemen pursued him closely. When he looked behind him, he saw me and called to me. And I said, 'Here I am.' He said to me, 'Who are you?' And I answered him, 'I am an Amalekite.' Then he said to me, *'Please stand beside me and kill me, for agony has seized me because my life still lingers in me.'* So *I stood beside him and killed him, because I knew that he could not live after he had fallen."* (2 Samuel 1:6-10)

When David learned of the assisted suicide performed by the Amalekite, David had him executed for murder. It did not matter that Saul had only moments of life left and would have died anyway, and it did not matter that Saul was suffering and wanted to die; and even though thousands of years have come and gone since the "compassionate" killing of King Saul, God's attitude toward mercy killing has not altered. Today, murder may have changed its name to mercy, but in the eyes of man's Creator, it is still premeditated murder and cold-blooded killing. However, God in His benevolence does permit those who are suffering a painful death (as well as their loved ones) to do all in their power to lessen the misery of the terminally ill. The Bible says:

> Give strong drink to him who is perishing, and wine to him whose life is bitter. Let him drink and forget his poverty [or his distress] and remember

his trouble no more. Open your mouth for the mute, for the rights of all the unfortunate. Open your mouth, judge righteously, and defend the rights of the afflicted and needy. (Proverbs 31:6-9)

We need to realize that God is the Author of all life, and that only He has the authority to decide when and how a person must die. We must also understand that, among other justifiable reasons, God often uses suffering to draw us closer to Him, knowing that without pain, some may never turn to Him. Therefore, in our brave new world, no amount of doublespeak can change murder into mercy, and no amount of rhetoric can transform killing into compassion.

Nevertheless, because men refuse to recognize God's sovereignty when it comes to life and death, He is going to bring a judgment upon unrepentant mankind that is totally and utterly unique. Jesus Christ said that He (and He alone) has "the keys of death and [hell]" (Revelation 1:18). Consequently, because Big Brother refuses to acknowledge this fact, Christ is going to give His keys of death and hell to Satan, who will in turn unlock a special door in hell. This door will unleash a multitude of demonic creatures from the bottomless pit, and these satanic beings will then be permitted to inflict upon men (who are living in rebellion against God) a very painful sickness or disease. The apostle John says:

And they were not permitted to kill anyone, but to torment for five months; and their torment was like the torment of a scorpion when it stings a man. And in those days men will seek death and will not find it; they will long to die, and death flees from them. (Revelation 9:5-6)

Nothing in the history of mankind compares with this divine judgment where men try to kill themselves because of their sufferings, but death escapes them. All attempts of suicide or mercy killing will fail, as the One who holds the keys of death powerfully demonstrates His authority over the living and the dead.

Well, we may be living in a brave new world where doublespeak has become the language of the land, but in the end, both men and governments will discover that God alone has the authority to decide who lives and who dies. Murder can masquerade as mercy, and killing may wear the mask of compassion, but the real Author of life and death will soon uncover the true identity beneath the disguise of assisted suicide and behind the veneer of mercy killing—and all men will see clearly that extinguishing life in the name of compassion is simply cold-blooded murder parading around in the fancy clothing of doublespeak.

The Ghosts of Winchester

Satan has many titles, and one which Christ gave him is "the father of lies." Jesus said that "there is no truth in him" (John 8:44); and unfortunately, speaking in his native tongue of deception, the devil has managed to con untold multitudes into believing his lies and into behaving foolishly and self-destructively for ages. This is especially true when it comes to spiritism, or man's attempts to contact the spirits of the dead. So many well-intentioned people have spent their lives and their treasures trying to communicate with the dead and placate the deceased. However, few people have been more victimized and hoodwinked by the lies of the powers of darkness than Sarah Winchester.

Most historians believe that Sarah Winchester was born in 1840 as Sarah Pardee in New Haven, Connecticut. At the height of the Civil War, Sarah met and fell in love with William Winchester, whose gun company developed the first repeating rifle; and his Henry rifles were purchased in vast numbers by the Northern troops during the Civil War. Sarah and William married in September of 1862 and four years later, Sarah gave birth to a daughter, Annie. Sadly, their daughter died as an infant and William died some 15 years later from tuberculosis. As a result, Sarah inherited over $20 million from the Winchester empire and received about $1,000 a day from the revenues of the repeating rifle.[36]

Needless to say, Sarah became incredibly wealthy from the proceeds of her husband's gun manufacturing business, but her newfound fortune could not ease the devastating loss of her daughter and her husband. Unfortunately, Sarah did not seek the God of heaven, nor did she consult the Bible, for comfort or guidance throughout her grievous heartbreak. Instead, it has been reported that a friend suggested she speak to a spiritist, or a medium, about her calamity. In so doing, either knowingly or unwittingly, she closed her eyes to the Bible's clear warnings against the use of sorcery:

227

There shall not be found among you anyone who makes his son or his daughter pass through the fire [child sacrifice], one who uses divination, one who practices witchcraft, or one who interprets omens, or a sorcerer, or one who casts a spell, or a medium, or a spiritist, or one who calls up the dead. For whoever does these things is detestable to the Lord; and because of these detestable things the Lord your God will drive them out before you. You shall be blameless before the Lord your God. (Deuteronomy 18:10-13)

Sarah's violation of God's direct warnings to stay away from mediums opened her soul up to a lifetime of diabolical deceit and spiritual fraud, the likes of which the world has seldom seen.

In consultation with the spiritist, Sarah was told that the Winchester family had been struck with a terrible curse, and that the departed spirits of all those who were killed by the Winchester rifle were seeking vengeance upon the Winchester family for their deaths. The demon speaking through the medium told Sarah that the only way to appease the dead souls was to build a house for them. She was told she must sell her property in New Haven and head towards the setting sun, relying upon the ghost of her dead husband to give her guidance as to where to settle. The medium advised that once there, she must build, and continue to build, a house for all of the victims slain by the Winchester rifles. She was warned that she must never stop building her dwelling place for the dead, for if she did, she herself would die.

So Sarah headed west and ultimately bought a 6-room house on 162 acres of prime real estate. She lived in the house until her death some 38 years later, having never stopped expanding the size of her home, in keeping with the advice given to her. Rooms were added to rooms, making up entire wings; and the structure reached 7 stories high with 3 elevators and 47 fireplaces. There were staircases leading to nowhere, closets opening to blank walls, a blind chimney stopping short of the ceiling, and a number of trap doors and double-back hallways. The house had been designed into a maze in order to disorient any spirits with evil intent. By the time of its completion, it had become a convoluted labyrinth with an estimated 160 rooms, but the real number is unknown due to the very confusing layout of the entire complex.

For over 36 years, around the clock, workers built and rebuilt, altered and re-altered, and demolished one section of the house after another, per Sarah's instructions after consulting the spirit world. Sarah spent millions and millions of dollars in her insane attempts to placate the dead. In the end, she exhausted her fortune on a fool's errand from hell, and died in her sleep on September 4, 1922, at the approximate age of 83.

Sarah spent decades dancing to the tune of the devil's lies because she refused to walk in the truth of God's light. Little did she know that the conjured-up ghosts communicating with her were not those of human beings, but were deceitful demons of the supernatural powers of darkness. Satan's lying spirits ruined her life and have undoubtedly destroyed her soul through her well-intentioned, but nevertheless defiant, actions against the God of heaven.

However, Satan's tactics and lies to bankrupt Sarah's soul were child's play in comparison to the deceptions that he is about to employ in order to damn multitudes in the very near future. The apostle Paul forewarns that there is coming a man of lawlessness and deception:

> [T]he one whose coming is in accord with the activity of Satan, with all power and signs and false wonders, and with all the deception of wickedness for those who perish, because they did not receive the love of the truth so as to be saved. For this reason God will send upon them a deluding influence so that they will believe what is false, in order that they all may be judged who did not believe the truth, but took pleasure in wickedness. (2 Thessalonians 2:9-12)

229

Consequently, the eccentric life of Sarah Winchester can easily be dismissed as the outlandish behavior of an insane, demented woman, but for those who believe what God has said in His Word, she has become a dark warning of just how effective the father of lies can be in his relentless endeavor to deceive and ruin all mankind. In truth, the "ghosts" of Winchester were not the departed spirits of men killed in battle, but rather demonic spirits who continue today in their infernal malice to damn as many souls as possible, in order to spite the God of heaven; and their lies, deceptions, and false wonders are most effective in doing just that — damning gullible men and women to eternal hell.

The Wheel Has Come Full Circle

In William Shakespeare's play entitled "King Lear" (Act 5, scene 3), the villainous acts of Edmund eventually return to haunt him, and thus Edmund coins the phrase, "The wheel has come full circle." These words epitomize how negative consequences are not always the result of bad luck or awful fate, but can be the fruit of poetic justice. Basically, the laws of karma taught in Hinduism and Buddhism reflect the same concept, claiming that when we exhibit a negative force in thought, word, or action, that negative energy will come back to us; and even though these false religions are demonically inspired, they nevertheless reflect the divine principle of reaping what one sows—which is an immutable law of God, as depicted in the words of the apostle Paul:

> Do not be deceived, God is not mocked; for whatever a man sows, this he will also reap. For the one who sows to his own flesh will from the flesh reap corruption, but the one who sows to the Spirit will from the Spirit reap eternal life. Let us not lose heart in doing good, for in due time we will reap if we do not grow weary. So then, while we have opportunity, let us do good to all people, and especially to those who are of the household of the faith. (Galatians 6:7-10)

This applies to nations as well as churches, and individuals as well as generations. Take, for example, the baby boomer generation: Almost exactly nine months after World War II ended, more babies were born in 1946 than ever before (3.4 million or 20% more than in 1945). This was the beginning of the so-called baby boom. In 1947, almost 3.8 million children were born. In 1952, another 4 million, and an additional 4 million were born every year from 1954 until 1964 when the population explosion in the United States finally tapered off. By then, there were 76.4 million baby boomers in America, which made up almost 40% of the nation's citizenry.[37]

However, in January of 1973, the Supreme Court of the land declared that the killing of unborn children was now a constitutional right of any woman who desired to terminate the life of the child in her womb. Coincidentally, it was the baby boomer generation that began the wholesale genocide and mass execution of unborn children. Presently, the carnage has exceeded over 70 million exterminated children[38] in the land whose Declaration of Independence proclaimed that all men are created equal and are endowed by their Creator with certain unalienable rights—rights that include life, liberty, and the pursuit of happiness.

The baby boomers have now grown to become the largest group of senior citizens in our country's history. Simultaneously retiring by the millions, they are beginning to overwhelm our nation's healthcare provisions and governmental services, including Social Security benefits. Consequently, today's vast numbers of baby boomers are quickly becoming an excessive strain on the younger taxpayers of America who, before long, will view the graying, balding, fatiguing, and unproductive members of this aging populace as being a financial burden and an utter inconvenience—just as so many boomers had considered their unborn children before aborting them.

Furthermore, in the face of this unfortunate reality, more and more states are legalizing or promoting legislation that sponsors assisted suicide laws, granting suffering people the "right to die" rather than prolonging their suffering until natural death. Nevertheless, few people realize how the wheel is truly coming full circle as this so-called "right to die" will eventually become "the responsibility to die." Most assuredly, in the face of a nation that is about to be financially bankrupted by its senior citizens, the responsibility to die is inevitable, yet rarely do people have the good grace to see the truth of this. It is money, not values, that always has the final say in any nation that has devalued human life to the degree that America has.

Therefore, it is becoming inevitable that in time, the younger generations (which are compelled to finance the medical and social welfare of the elderly boomers) will judge them the same as Adolf Hitler did, as "useless eaters" who are a burden to the state and dead weight to the productive members of society. Ironically, had the millions of aborted babies been allowed to live and contribute to the workforce, the funds would now be available to provide for this aging generation, and the baby boomers would have raised their future caregivers instead of their future undertakers.

Truly, what goes around comes around, and the wheel is about to complete its full revolution because "God is not mocked. For whatever a man sows, this he will also reap."

The Lunar Lunacy Effect

On December 5, 2012, the US House of Representatives passed a joint resolution approved earlier by the US Senate, removing the word "lunatic" from all federal laws in the United States, and it was signed into law by President Obama on December 28, 2012. However, putting all "political correctness" aside, when describing one of the worst cases of demon possession recorded in the Scriptures, the Bible uses the word "lunatic":

> When [Jesus and his disciples] came to the crowd, a man came up to Jesus, falling on his knees before Him and saying, "Lord, have mercy on my son, for he is a *lunatic* and is very ill; for he often falls into the fire and often into the water. I brought him to Your disciples, and they could not cure him." And Jesus answered and said, "You unbelieving and perverted generation, how long shall I be with you? How long shall I put up with you? Bring him here to Me." And Jesus rebuked him, and the demon came out of him, and the boy was cured at once. Then the disciples came to Jesus privately and said, "Why could we not drive it out?" And He said to them, "Because of the littleness of your faith ... But this kind [of demon] does not go out except by prayer and fasting." (Matthew 17:14-21)

The Bible uses the term "lunatic" when referring to people who are considered mentally ill, dangerous, or foolish and unpredictable. The expression "lunatic" may be considered insulting or demeaning in our modern times, but the term is actually derived from the Latin word "lunaticus" which originally and primarily referred to epilepsy or a disease of madness *caused by the moon*. In short, the word "lunacy" comes from "Luna" who was the moon goddess in the Roman pantheon of deities.

Still today we use the word lunar when speaking of the moon's surface or of its various phases, revolutions, and gravitational pull upon the earth. The force of the moon's gravity upon the world is so powerful that it moves the massive weight of our entire oceans in the formation of tides. And, therefore, people have often believed the moon's pull could also affect the mental state of people due to the watery composition of an individual's brain and body. Even the Greek philosopher Aristotle suggested that the brain was the "moistest" organ in the body and, therefore, was very susceptible to the negative influences of the moon's gravity. Such beliefs were called the "lunar lunacy effect" or the "Transylvania effect," where humans were widely reputed to transform into werewolves or vampires during a full moon.[39]

Even in our scientific age, many people think that the mystical powers of the full moon induce erratic behavior, suicides, traffic accidents, an increase in psychiatric admissions, and an influx of emergency room patients, as well as a spike in crime and violent behavior during a full moon. However, over the last half-century, thousands of studies have looked at the moon's effect on human behavior and have systematically determined that the gravitational effects of the moon upon individuals are far too minuscule to generate any meaningful consequences on brain activity, let alone human behavior. In short, scientists have investigated all of these claims of lunacy caused by the moon and have repeatedly discredited them.[40]

Nonetheless, there is one explanation our modern science and research will never consider, and that is demonic possession and influence which can increase during a full moon. In the Old Testament, God commanded His people to schedule the religious feast days according to a lunar calendar instead of a solar timetable. Their religious calendar was based upon the 30-day cycle of the moon's revolution around the earth, rather than the world's 365-day orbit around the sun. In the book of Numbers, God said:

Also in the day of your gladness and in your appointed feasts, *and on the first days of your months* [the new moon], you shall blow the trumpets over your burnt offerings, and over the sacrifices of your peace offerings; and they shall be as a reminder of you before your God. I am the Lord your God. (Numbers 10:10)

In addition, His people were instructed to

[s]ing for joy to God our strength; shout joyfully to the God of Jacob. Raise a song, strike the timbrel, the sweet sounding lyre with the harp. Blow the trumpet *at the new moon, at the full moon, on our feast day*. For it is a statute for Israel, an ordinance of the God of Jacob. He established it for a testimony in Joseph when he went throughout the land of Egypt ... "I relieved his shoulder of the burden, his hands were freed from the basket." (Psalm 81:1-6)

Consequently, the day of the new moon became a special day of worship and fellowship, with animal sacrifices pointing to a new beginning in one's relationship with God. It was as if the past 29 days of moral failures and spiritual shortcomings of God's people were to be forgiven and forgotten through all the animal sacrifices, which pointed to Jesus Christ; and people were to rejoice and celebrate their new moons with a fresh start and a renewed commitment to the Lord.

The very beginning of the Jewish religious calendar started with a new moon (see Exodus 12) and the full moon does not appear until the 14th day after the new moon. The phases of the moon (new, half, full, and back again) culminate with the moon at its fullest. The greatest conflict between the spiritual forces of darkness and light occurs when the moon is completely full. In fact, the Bible relates one of the most severe judgments from God occurring during a full moon, against the idolatrous nation of Egypt:

> Your lamb shall be an unblemished male a year old; you may take it from the sheep or from the goats. *You shall keep it until the fourteenth day of the same month* [the full moon], then the whole assembly of the congregation of Israel is to kill it at twilight. Moreover, they shall take some of the blood and put it on the two doorposts and on the lintel of the houses in which they eat it. They shall eat the flesh *that same night,* roasted with fire, and they shall eat it with unleavened bread and bitter herbs. ... For I will go through the land of Egypt on that night, and will strike down all the firstborn in the land of Egypt, both man and beast; and *against all the gods of Egypt* I will execute judgments—I am the Lord. The blood shall be a sign for you on the houses where you live; and when I see the blood I will pass over you, and no plague will befall you to destroy you when I strike the land of Egypt. (Exodus 12:5-13)

It is the apostle Paul who tells us there is a very intense and real spiritual conflict going on throughout our world today. He said that "our struggle is not against flesh and blood, but against the rulers, against the powers, against the world forces of this darkness, against the spiritual forces of wickedness in the heavenly places" (Ephesians 6:12). Therefore, the so-called "lunar effect" of the full moon is not actually physical, but spiritual. The new moon was meant by God to signal a clean start, a fresh beginning, and a renewed commitment in one's relationship with their Maker. So, of course, Satan and his fallen angels are doing everything in their power to counteract Him. Many satanic rituals and worship of the devil increase during full moons; and if there is any truth to the spike of wicked deeds or bizarre behavior during this time, it is due to the influence of the dark forces and not to the gravitational sway of the moon.

Now it is also very important for people to realize that not all mental illness is due to demonic influence, and symptoms of mind disorders can often be treated with medication and professional assistance. Nevertheless, it is incredible to me that reports of human behavior which can only be described as "criminally insane" are never attributed to the possibility of demonic exploitation, but instead are deemed psychological disturbances.

However, the lunacy of the lunatic that Christ encountered was the direct result of demon possession, and Jesus said that this particular demon was so powerful that only prayer and fasting could drive him out (which suggests to me that the evil spirit was a fallen archangel). Clearly, what is wreaking havoc in our world is not the gravitational pull of the moon; rather, it is the true "lunar lunacy effect" of the spirit realm; but so few people have the good grace to see it, let alone believe it.

Bada Bing, Bada Boom!

Our fast-paced world has become a pressure cooker of activities, schedules, and deadlines. It is also a world where we (especially as Americans) have come to expect and demand prompt results and instantaneous fulfillment in virtually every area of our lives. From wanting our food prepared and served in a moment's notice to counting on rapid weight loss, and from fast computers and quick fixes to speedy travel, modern man has come to anticipate rapid results and immediate gratification.

Unfortunately, this mindset has crept into the Church, where spiritual growth and religious maturity are expected to happen from listening to "dine-and-dash" sermons on Sundays or motivational speakers who promote a gospel of "health, wealth, and prosperity." Alas, when it comes to personal growth in Christ, many church members today have become like professional lawn mowers who pull up to their designated landscapes and expend as little time and effort as possible cutting the grass before moving on to their next scheduled "mow-blow-and-go" assignment.

However, being transformed into images of Christ is a lifelong process that requires faithful diligence and effort in order to become spiritually mature and fruitful. Consider this parable told by Jesus:

A man had a fig tree which had been planted in his vineyard; and he came looking for fruit on it and did not find any. And he said to the vineyard-keeper, "Behold, for three years I have come looking for fruit on this fig tree without finding any. Cut it down! Why does it even use up the ground?" And he answered and said to him, "Let it alone, sir, for this year too, until I dig around it and put in fertilizer; and if it bears fruit next year, fine; but if not, cut it down." (Luke 13:6-9)

There is no quick remedy to being Christ-like. It takes the consistent nourishment of prayer, Bible studies, fellowship, and spiritual exercises, in addition to the work of the Holy Spirit, to produce and develop flourishing Christians (not merely the routine of attending church services once a week or twice a year). As such, Jesus used the analogy of a grapevine to describe the need to cling to Him in order to produce fruit:

> I am the true vine, and My Father is the vinedresser. Every branch in Me that does not bear fruit, He takes away; and every branch that bears fruit, He prunes it so that it may bear more fruit. You are already clean because of the word which I have spoken to you. Abide in Me, and I in you. As the branch cannot bear fruit of itself unless it abides in the vine, so neither can you unless you abide in Me. I am the vine, you are the branches; he who abides in Me and I in him, he bears much fruit, for apart from Me you can do nothing. If anyone does not abide in Me, he is thrown away as a branch and dries up; and they gather them, and cast them into the fire and they are burned. ... If you keep My commandments, you will abide in My love; just as I have kept My Father's commandments and abide in His love. These things I have spoken to you so that My joy may be in you, and that your joy may be made full. (John 15:1-6, 10-11)

Christian maturity takes laborious care and maintenance. Becoming "born again" may happen in an instant, but spiritual growth can never be accomplished in a bada-bing-bada-boom moment, or by the wave of a magic wand. No, it will always require great effort on the part of God and man. "Abracadabra" and "Hocus Pocus" are not in God's vocabulary when it comes to being transformed spiritually. Instead, He says:

Now for this very reason also, applying all diligence, in your faith supply moral excellence, and in your moral excellence, knowledge, and in your knowledge, self-control, and in your self-control, perseverance, and in your perseverance, godliness, and in your godliness, brotherly kindness, and in your brotherly kindness, love. For if these qualities are yours *and are increasing*, they render you neither useless nor unfruitful in the true knowledge of our Lord Jesus Christ. For he who lacks these qualities is blind or short-sighted, having forgotten his purification from his former sins. Therefore, brethren, *be all the more diligent* to make certain about His calling and choosing you; for as long as you *practice* these things, you will never stumble; for in this way the entrance into the eternal kingdom of our Lord and Savior Jesus Christ will be abundantly supplied to you. (2 Peter 1:5-11)

In short, when it comes to spiritual growth and fruitfulness, God is not in the "mow-blow-and-go" business; neither is He in the "dine-and-dash" industry. With Him, there is no "bada-bing-bada-boom" moment when it comes to transforming men into images of His Son Jesus Christ.

If it's Free, it's for Me!

Aesop is best known for his collection of fables (numbering some 725 stories according to the Perry Index).[41] His fairy tales were essentially allegorical myths written for the purpose of teaching life lessons and moral principles, by often using animals and insects to convey his ethical messages. The following fable, however, was not written by Aesop, yet it contains an absolute truth and timeless precept that is worth pondering just the same:

> There was once a very wise and knowledgeable king who had an insatiable thirst for enlightenment, wisdom, and understanding. His appetite for insight and discernment was so great that he called together all of the scribes and officials in his administration and commanded them to go throughout the entire known world and collect all of the wisest things that had ever been written, and to assemble them into one book.
>
> After years of research and investigation, the king's servants compiled all of the wisdom of the ages into one extensive volume and presented it to the emperor. The ruler was truly astonished by the depth of prudence and the breadth of perceptiveness that the publication contained; however, the king then told his administrators that he wanted them to condense the volume down to its barest essence and to summarize the manuscript into as brief and as concise a writing as possible. After months of intense labor, the king's assistants revised the volume down to a single chapter.
>
> Now the king was very impressed and appreciative of their work, but he demanded that they reduce the chapter down still further. Weeks later, they presented the king with just one paragraph containing the wisest sayings ever

written. Nevertheless, the monarch still insisted that his scribes boil down all the wisdom of mankind into just one sentence. After many revisions and much thought, the officials finally provided the king with all of the wisdom of history condensed down to this one simple statement: "THERE IS NO SUCH THING AS A FREE LUNCH!"

It's true! Nothing, whether provided by man or God, can be given away as truly free. It doesn't matter what it is; if it has any value at all, it always, always comes at a cost. A person may rejoice if given a "free steak dinner," but in actuality, it cost someone something to provide a free meal to another. Even if it were genuinely possible to bequeath a free steak dinner to another, the obvious truth is that the source of the complimentary meal — the cow — paid an incredibly high price for it.

Consequently, absolutely nothing worthwhile is free — not even a beautiful sunset or the very air we breathe, because the expenditure of God's power is required to provide mankind with these things, which may appear so ordinary but in reality are essential for life and happiness. If this principle is true in our physical universe, how much more accurate it must be in the spiritual world!

Christians often talk about the "free gift of salvation" without reflecting upon the infinite cost that was expended by God in redeeming man. In Paul's epistle to the Romans, he proclaimed that "the wages of sin is death, but the free gift of God is eternal life in Christ Jesus our Lord" (Romans 6:23). The apostle also declared, "For by grace you have been saved through faith; and that not of yourselves, it is the gift of God; not as a result of works, so that no one may boast" (Ephesians 2:8-9). God's grace is His undeserved favor that cannot be earned or purchased by anyone. In this respect, it becomes a "free gift," but in reality it is the most costly "free" gift in all of history, especially when it cost God His Son to grant man eternal life. It is not cheap grace!

As the psalmist wrote, "No man can by any means redeem his brother or give to God a ransom for him—for the redemption of his soul is costly, and he should cease trying forever—that he should live on eternally, that he should not undergo decay" (Psalm 49:7-9). Isaiah the prophet spoke of the incredible cost of man's salvation when he predicted of Christ:

> Behold, My servant will prosper, He will be high and lifted up and greatly exalted. Just as many were astonished at you, My people, so His appearance was marred more than any man and His form more than the sons of men. Thus He will sprinkle many nations, kings will shut their mouths on account of Him; for what had not been told them they will see, and what they had not heard they will understand. (Isaiah 52:13-15)

Read carefully the following text from Isaiah as it pertains to the Messiah's redemptive work on the cross at Calvary, yet it was written nearly 800 years before Christ was born on Earth:

> He was despised and forsaken of men, a man of sorrows and acquainted with grief; and like one from whom men hide their face He was despised, and we did not esteem Him. Surely our griefs He Himself bore, and our sorrows He carried; yet we ourselves esteemed Him stricken, smitten of God, and afflicted. But He was pierced through for our transgressions, He was crushed for our iniquities; the chastening for our well-being fell upon Him, and by His scourging we are healed. All of us like sheep have gone astray, each of us has turned to his own way; but the Lord has caused the iniquity of us all to fall on Him. He was oppressed and He was afflicted, yet He did not open His mouth; like a lamb that is led to slaughter, and like a sheep that is

silent before its shearers, so He did not open His mouth. By oppression and judgment He was taken away; and as for His generation, who considered that He was cut off out of the land of the living for the transgression of my people, to whom the stroke was due? ... But the Lord was pleased to crush Him, putting Him to grief; if He would render Himself as a guilt offering. ... He poured out Himself to death, and was numbered with the transgressors; yet He Himself bore the sin of many, and interceded for the transgressors. (53: 3-8, 10, 12)

Accepting this awesome "free gift of salvation" will not, however, be free for man; just as it cost Christ His life, it will cost man his own life in more ways than one. Jesus said that we cannot be His disciples unless we deny ourselves and commit to Him completely. He said that we must count the cost and pay the cost with our lives if we are going to enter the kingdom of God (see Luke 14:25-35); and it was the writer of Hebrews who asked: "[H]ow will we escape [hell] if we neglect so great a salvation?" (Hebrews 2:3).

Christ asserted that salvation was a free gift when He said, "I will give to the one who thirsts from the spring of the water of life without cost," but immediately after having said this, he said, "He who *overcomes* will inherit these things, and I will be his God and he will be My son" (Revelation 21:6-7). To overcome something, one must exert energy and effort. In sacrificing Himself on the cross, Christ granted us our free gift of salvation; however, to live for Christ will also come at a great cost—that of our own lives. Therefore, all those who say, "If it's free, it's for me!" should consider that nothing of value in life is truly free. All the wisdom of the ages continues to assert that "THERE IS NO SUCH THING AS A FREE LUNCH!"

The Collapse of a Star

A star explodes when it reaches the end of its life, violently bursting into brilliant points of light. Instantly, it blazes into a stellar explosion referred to as a supernova. Such supernovas can briefly outshine entire galaxies and radiate more energy than our sun will in its entire lifespan. Throughout our universe, supernovas occur millions and perhaps billions of times each and every year, and the combined energy that they release is truly beyond man's ability to fully comprehend.[42]

However, no exploding star has ever produced more of a damaging force or released more ruinous energy than "the star of the morning, son of the dawn." The Bible refers to this "star of the morning, son of the dawn" as Lucifer, or light-bearer, which is clearly Satan, or the devil himself. Referring to him, Isaiah the prophet wrote:

> How you have fallen from heaven, O star of the morning, son of the dawn! You have been cut down to the earth, you who have weakened the nations! But you said in your heart, "I will ascend to heaven; I will raise my throne above the stars of God, and I will sit on the mount of assembly in the recesses of the north. I will ascend above the heights of the clouds; I will make myself like the Most High." Nevertheless you will be thrust down to Sheol [hell], to the recesses of the pit. (Isaiah 14:12-15)

Regarding this same Lucifer, the word of the Lord came to Ezekiel, saying:

> Son of man, take up a lamentation over the king of Tyre [Satan] and say to him, "Thus says the Lord God, 'You had the seal of perfection, full of wisdom and perfect in beauty. You were in Eden, the garden of God [not Eden, the garden of Adam and Eve, but

the Eden in heaven]; every precious stone was your covering: the ruby, the topaz and the diamond; the beryl, the onyx and the jasper; the lapis lazuli, the turquoise and the emerald; and the gold, the workmanship of your settings and sockets, was in you. On the day that you were created they were prepared. You were the anointed cherub who *covers* [was over all the angels], and I placed you there. You were on the holy mountain of God; you walked in the midst of the stones of fire. You were blameless in your ways from the day you were created until unrighteousness was found in you. By the abundance of your *trade* [his angelic authority], you were internally filled with violence, and you sinned; therefore I have cast you as profane from the mountain of God. And I have destroyed you, O covering cherub, from the midst of the stones of fire. Your heart was lifted up because of your beauty; you corrupted your wisdom by reason of your splendor.'" (Ezekiel 28:11-17)

Furthermore, when Jesus' disciples rejoiced over the fact that demons were subject to them, Christ said to them:

I was watching Satan fall from heaven like lightning. Behold, I have given you authority to tread on serpents and scorpions, and over all the power of the enemy, and nothing will injure you. Nevertheless do not rejoice in this, that the spirits are subject to you, but rejoice that your names are recorded in heaven. (Luke 10:18-20)

During the revolt of "the star of the morning, son of the dawn" against God, Satan persuaded a third of the *stars of heaven* (angels) to throw in their lot with him. These angels were instantly transformed into demons and cast into eternal hell as a divine punishment for their blasphemy. They now possess natures that are filled with an infernal hatred towards God and a depraved malice towards all men and women who are created in God's image.

The collapse of this once-magnificent star has truly generated the most destructive force in all of history that will also last for all eternity. This fallen star has been the driving force behind every war, every murder, every lie, every theft, and each and every violation of the moral laws of Almighty God. Few people realize the magnitude of this formidable, evil being who will stop at nothing to strike back at the heart of God by damning as many souls as possible, and flooding the world with all manner of wickedness and devastation. Instead, many church leaders and laypeople deny the very existence of Satan or have reduced him into simply being a nonentity, an abstract form of evil, or a sinister clown with horns and a pitchfork. The apostle Paul, however, had no such illusions when he wrote to

> be strong in the Lord and in the strength of His might. Put on the full armor of God, so that you will be able to stand firm against the schemes of the devil. ... For our struggle is not against flesh and blood, but ... *against the spiritual forces of wickedness in the heavenly places.* (Ephesians 6:10-12)

No one on Earth knows for sure just when this celestial revolt took place, but it appears to have occurred shortly after the creation of the cosmos and the forming of man. We are given this remarkable insight when the Lord addressed Job out of a whirlwind: God challenged Job to answer the questions that He was about to ask him, in order to show Job that he was in no position to question the ways and the righteousness of God:

> Who is this that darkens counsel by words without knowledge? Now gird up your loins like a man, and I will ask you, and you instruct Me! Where

were you when I laid the foundation of the earth? Tell Me, if you have understanding, who set its measurements? Since you know. Or who stretched the line on it? On what were its bases sunk? Or who laid its cornerstone, *when the morning stars sang together and all the sons of God shouted for joy?* (Job 38:2-7)

Did you catch that? When God created the universe, the angels sang and shouted for joy. Angels are "ministering spirits, sent out to render service for the sake of those who will inherit salvation [mankind]" (Hebrews 1:14). Knowing this, my supposition is that Lucifer began to resent the notion that he was to serve men and not rule over them. Consequently, his place of importance began to fill him with envy and resentment, as noted in the Ezekiel passage quoted near the beginning of this chapter. His rallying cry to all the angelic hosts was to convince them that they would not need to serve or minister to men, but they could instead rule and reign with him as he raised his throne above the stars of God and made himself like the Most High. Much to their surprise and dismay, however, God created hell and threw Lucifer—and all the angels who followed him—into it as everlasting punishment for their foul uprising.

On the other hand, Christ is "the Bright Morning Star" that has eclipsed the star of the morning (Revelation 22:16). He has come to destroy the works of the devil and to redeem man from his infernal grip (Hebrews 2:14-18). At the close of the Bible, we are given a glimpse of the new heavenly Jerusalem, a magnificent city that will have

no need of the sun or of the moon to shine on it, for the glory of God has illumined it, and its lamp is the Lamb. The nations will walk by its light, and the kings of the earth will bring their glory into it. In the daytime (for there will be no night there) its gates will never be closed; and they will bring the glory and the honor of the nations into it; and nothing unclean, and no one who practices abomination and lying, shall ever come into it, but only those whose names are written in the Lamb's book of life. (Revelation 21:23-27)

Hell was originally designed for Satan and his angels, but anyone whose name is not written in the book of life will join them there (Matthew 25:41; Revelation 20:14-15). Nevertheless, Jesus Christ was victorious over all fallen angels and made a way for mankind to join Him in His kingdom. He said, "I am the way, and the truth, and the life; no one comes to the Father but through Me" and "He who believes in the Son has eternal life; but he who does not obey the Son will not see life, but the wrath of God abides on him" (John 14:6, 3:36).

In conclusion, eternity awaits every one of us, and each of us makes the choice as to where we will spend it—and in whose company, meaning the company of either Christ, "the Bright Morning Star" or Lucifer—the collapsed "star of the morning, son of the dawn."

Hide and Seek

Generation after generation, boys and girls the world over have enjoyed playing Hide and Seek. Children delight in the excitement and suspense of hiding from each other in places where they feel secure and are confident they will not be discovered, regardless of how fervently their playmates search for them.

However, the very first hide-and-seek adventure was not played by children and it was anything but an amusing pastime. Instead, it was enacted by two very mature adults who tried desperately to hide from the all-seeing God of the universe. Both Eve (having been deceived by Satan) and Adam defied God's command to not eat of the tree of knowledge of good and evil. This resulted in their foolhardy attempt to cover over their nakedness with fig leaves and then fearfully run and hide from the presence of their Creator. As the Scriptures reveal:

> Then the eyes of both of them were opened, and they knew that they were naked; and they sewed fig leaves together and made themselves loin coverings. They heard the sound of the Lord God walking in the garden in the cool of the day, and the man and his wife hid themselves from the presence of the Lord God among the trees of the garden. Then the Lord God called to the man, and said to him, "Where are you?" [Adam] said, "I heard the sound of You in the garden, and I was afraid because I was naked; so I hid myself." (Genesis 3:7-10)

This was the beginning of Hide and Seek, and the spectacle has been repeated ad infinitum, ad nauseam, between God and man the world over and throughout all ages. History is filled with examples of men and women constantly trying to hide from God because of their wickedness, and God in turn hiding His face from men and women for the exact same reason. Over and over and over again, God says in His Word that He will hide His face from those who seek Him in their times of need and desperation while at the same time refusing to obey Him and repent of their sins:

> The Lord said to Moses, "Behold, you are about to lie down with your fathers; and this people will arise and play the harlot with the strange gods of the land, into the midst of which they are going, and will forsake Me and break My covenant which I have made with them. Then My anger will be kindled against them in that day, *and I will forsake them and hide My face from them. ... But I will surely hide My face in that day because of all the evil which they will do,* for they will turn to other gods. (Deuteronomy 31:16-18)

And again:

> Alas, sinful nation, people weighed down with iniquity, offspring of evildoers, sons who act corruptly! They have abandoned the Lord, they have despised the Holy One of Israel, they have turned away from Him. ... So when you spread out your hands in prayer, *I will hide My eyes from you;* yes, even though you multiply prayers, I will not listen. Your hands are covered with blood. (Isaiah 1:4,15)

And again: "Because of the iniquity of his unjust gain I was angry and struck him; I hid My face and was angry, and he went on turning away, in the way of his heart" (57:17). And again: "I have hidden My face from this city because of all their wickedness" (Jeremiah 33:5).

And yet again:

The nations will know that the house of Israel went into exile for their iniquity because they acted treacherously against Me, and *I hid My face from them*; so I gave them into the hand of their adversaries, and all of them fell by the sword. According to their uncleanness and according to their transgressions I dealt with them, *and I hid My face from them*. (Ezekiel 39:23-24)

And still another time: "Then they will cry out to the Lord, but He will not answer them. Instead, He will hide His face from them at that time because they have practiced evil deeds" (Micah 3:4). Even in the gospels, Jesus Christ hid Himself from evil men, as the apostle John writes:

So the Jews said to Him, "You are not yet fifty years old, and have You seen Abraham?" Jesus said to them, "Truly, truly, I say to you, before Abraham was born, I am." Therefore they picked up stones to throw at Him, but Jesus hid Himself and went out of the temple. (John 8:57-59)

And:

While you have the Light, believe in the Light, so that you may become sons of the Light. These things Jesus spoke, and He went away and hid Himself from them. But though He had performed so many signs before them, yet they were not believing in Him. (12:36-37)

Time and time again, God has hidden Himself from evil men. However, in the end, God will not be the one who hides from men, but evil men will be in an absolute panic and will want to hide when they see Jesus Christ returning in awesome power and glory to judge the world for all of its wickedness:

Then the kings of the earth and the great men and the commanders and the rich and the strong and every slave and free man *hid themselves in the caves and among the rocks of the mountains;* and they said to the mountains and to the rocks, *"Fall on us and hide us from the presence of Him who sits on the throne,* and from the wrath of the Lamb; for the great day of their wrath has come, and who is able to stand?" (Revelation 6:15-17)

And:

Enter the rock and hide in the dust from the terror of the Lord and from the splendor of His majesty. The proud look of man will be abased and the loftiness of man will be humbled, and the Lord alone will be exalted in that day. For the Lord of hosts will have a day of reckoning against everyone who is proud and lofty and against everyone who is lifted up, that he may be abased. ... The pride of man will be humbled and the loftiness of men will be abased; and the Lord alone will be exalted in that day, but the idols will completely vanish. *Men will go into caves of the rocks and into holes of the ground* before the terror of the Lord and the splendor of His majesty, when He arises to make the earth tremble. In that day men will cast away to the moles and the bats their idols of silver and their idols of gold, which they made for themselves to worship, in order *to go into the caverns of the rocks and the clefts of the cliffs* before the terror of the Lord and the splendor of His majesty, when He arises to make the earth tremble. (Isaiah 2:10-12, 17-21)

254

In the end, unrepentant sinners will be utterly terrified as they discover too late that there is no place to hide from God and there is no way to run from Him. Instead, in their desperation, they will be wishing and praying for the rocks and the mountains to fall upon them and to crush them into oblivion, rather than face His holy wrath. Consequently, people everywhere and throughout all ages need to know that their only hope is to hide *in* God rather than *from* God; and that playing Hide and Seek with an angry God will definitely not be a game. Instead, it will be a terrifying experience where unrepentant men will most certainly suffer never-ending torment for their arrogance, defiance, and foolishness.

So the next time you happen to see little children playing their delightful game of Hide and Seek, remember that there will some-day be a global incident of Hide and Seek which will be anything but fun or enjoyable when those who are at war with God attempt to hide from His angry countenance and from His holy justice.

The King of Terrors

Death has been given many nicknames: "lights out," "the last roundup," "the Grim Reaper," and "bought the farm." Annihilation, darkness, demise, deceased, expired, fatality, and passed away all refer to the process of dying and the final act of drawing one's last breath. The Bible also has many different words and phrases to describe death, such as "the king of terrors" and "the last enemy" (Job 18:14; 1 Corinthians 15:26). However, there is one term that the Scriptures use more than any other when referring to death and that is "sleep." As a matter of fact, there are over 100 references throughout the Bible that use some form of the word "sleep" when referring to death or being deceased.

"Sleep" is defined as a suspension of voluntary bodily functions and the natural cessation of consciousness. It is a state of being dormant, inactive, and unaware of one's surroundings and environment. Nevertheless, the very nature of sleep implies that at some point there will be an awakening. The same is true of the billions of people who have died throughout the ages. Their bodies are now asleep even though their spirit which houses their soul is very much conscious and alive, regardless of whether the person is saved or lost.

King Solomon best described what happens when a person dies, stating that "the dust [or body] will return to the earth as it was, and the spirit will return to God who gave it" (Ecclesiastes 12:7). When Adam rebelled against God's command, He said to him: "By the sweat of your face you will eat bread, till you return to the ground, because from it you were taken; for you are dust, and to dust you shall return" (Genesis 3:19).

In contrast, the apostle Paul best summed up the death experience of the committed Christian when he wrote:

> For to me, to live is Christ and to die is gain. But if I am to live on in the flesh, this will mean fruitful labor for me; and I do not know which to choose. But I am hard-pressed from both directions, *having*

the desire to depart and be with Christ, for that is very much better; yet to remain on in the flesh is more necessary for your sake. (Philippians 1:21-24)

In addition, Paul proclaimed to the Thessalonian Christians:

But we do not want you to be uninformed, brethren, about those who are asleep, so that you will not grieve as do the rest who have no hope. For if we believe that Jesus died and rose again, even so God will bring with Him those who have fallen asleep in Jesus. For this we say to you by the word of the Lord, that we who are alive and remain until the coming of the Lord, will not precede those who have fallen asleep. For the Lord Himself will descend from heaven with a shout, with the voice of the archangel and with the trumpet of God, and the dead in Christ will rise first. Then we who are alive and remain will be caught up together with them in the clouds to meet the Lord in the air, and so we shall always be with the Lord. Therefore comfort one another with these words. (1 Thessalonians 4:13-18)

Furthermore, Jesus spoke of two dead men and their very different experiences after they died. Christ said one was a very poor and sick man named Lazarus, while the other was a very wealthy and self-centered man who had no concern for either God or men:

Now the poor man died and was carried away by the angels to Abraham's bosom; and the rich man also died and was buried. In Hades he lifted up his eyes, being in torment, and saw Abraham far away and Lazarus in his bosom. And he cried out and said, "Father Abraham, have mercy on me, and send Lazarus so that he may dip the tip of his finger

257

in water and cool off my tongue, for I am in agony in this flame." But Abraham said, "Child, remember that during your life you received your good things, and likewise Lazarus bad things; but now he is being comforted here, and you are in agony. And besides all this, between us and you there is a great chasm fixed, so that those who wish to come over from here to you will not be able, and that none may cross over from there to us." And he said, "Then I beg you, father, that you send him to my father's house—for I have five brothers—in order that he may warn them, so that they will not also come to this place of torment." But Abraham said, "They have Moses and the Prophets; let them hear them." But he said, "No, father Abraham, but if someone goes to them from the dead, they will repent!" But he said to him, "If they do not listen to Moses and the Prophets, they will not be persuaded even if someone rises from the dead." (Luke 16:22-31)

The bodies of both of these men were buried and returned to dust, but they were without question very much alive in the spiritual realm. Jesus also used the term "asleep" when speaking of the death of a synagogue official's daughter (see 8:52). So, too, when Lazarus (the brother of Martha and Mary) died:

"Our friend Lazarus has fallen asleep; but I go, so that I may awaken him out of sleep." The disciples then said to Him, "Lord, if he has fallen asleep, he will recover." Now Jesus had spoken of his death, but they thought that He was speaking of literal sleep. So Jesus then said to them plainly, "Lazarus is dead." (John 11:11-14)

After saying this, Christ stood before the grave of Lazarus and said: "Lazarus, come forth." The man who had died came forth, bound hand and foot with wrappings, and his face was wrapped around with a cloth. Jesus said to them, "Unbind him, and let him go" (vv. 43-44). God also said through the prophet Isaiah, "Your dead will live; their corpses will rise. You who lie in the dust, awake and shout for joy, for your dew is as the dew of the dawn, and the earth will give birth to the departed spirits" (Isaiah 26:19).

One's decomposing body will eventually turn to dust, but at Christ's command that same dust of the earth will be transformed into a resurrected body as man's spirit reenters it. The resurrection of the righteous will truly be a glorious thing to behold and to experience; however, the resurrection of the damned will be anything but majestic, as the prophet Daniel predicts:

> Many of those who sleep in the dust of the ground will awake, these to everlasting life, but the others to disgrace and everlasting contempt. Those who have insight will shine brightly like the brightness of the expanse of heaven, and those who lead the many to righteousness, like the stars forever and ever. (Daniel 12:2-3)

The apostle John gave more details when he wrote:

> And the sea gave up the dead which were in it, and death [the grave] and Hades [hell] gave up the dead which were in them; and they were judged, every one of them according to their deeds. Then death and Hades were thrown into the lake of fire. This is the second death, the lake of fire. And if anyone's name was not found written in the book of life, he was thrown into the lake of fire. (Revelation 20:13-15)

Death truly is the king of terrors and the last enemy, but it is never man's termination. Rather, it is his transition, and his resurrection will finalize his eternal destination.

For this perishable must put on the imperishable, and this mortal must put on immortality. But when this perishable will have put on the imperishable, and this mortal will have put on immortality, then will come about the saying that is written, "Death is swallowed up in victory. O death, where is your victory? O death, where is your sting?" The sting of death is sin, and the power of sin is the law; but thanks be to God, who gives us the victory through our Lord Jesus Christ. Therefore, my beloved brethren, be steadfast, immovable, always abounding in the work of the Lord, knowing that your toil is not in vain in the Lord. (1 Corinthians 15:53-58)

In conclusion, since Jesus Christ is the "King of kings, and Lord of lords" (Revelation 19:16), neither the king of terrors nor the lord of death can overpower Him because in the end,

the tabernacle of God is among men, and He will dwell among them, and they shall be His people, and God Himself will be among them, and He will wipe away every tear from their eyes; *and there will no longer be any death*; there will no longer be any mourning, or crying, or pain; the first things have passed away." And He who sits on the throne said, "Behold, I am making all things new." And He said, "Write, for these words are faithful and true." (21:3-5)

The Dead Man Who Resurrected a Dead Man

Throughout the Bible, we can read about a number of individuals who had been resurrected from the dead. Both the prophet Elijah and the prophet Elisha raised children from their sleep of death. Likewise, Jesus Himself raised Jairus' daughter from the dead, along with the widow of Nain's son, as well as Lazarus, the brother of Martha and Mary. Even the apostle Paul brought life back into a boy who had fallen to his death, and it appears that the Spirit of God also raised Paul himself from the sleep of death after he was stoned with rocks and left for dead (see 1 Kings 17:17-24; 2 Kings 4:8-37; Mark 5:35-43; Luke 8:49-56; 7:11-17; John 11:1-46; Acts 20:7-12; 14:8-20; 2 Corinthians 12:1-6).

There is one incident in the Old Testament however, where the dried bones of a dead prophet of God raised a dead man from the grip of death as well:

> Elisha died, and they buried him. Now the bands of the Moabites would invade the land in the spring of the year. As they were burying a man, behold, they saw a marauding band; and they cast the man into the grave of Elisha. And when the man touched the bones of Elisha he revived and stood up on his feet. (2 Kings 13:20-21)

In just two verses buried deep within the historical episodes of the book of Kings, we see a flash of light illuminating a profound spiritual reality before disappearing back into the blackness of a very penetrating and mysterious biblical truth. Elisha was God's prophet to both kings and priests, and to both Jews and Gentiles. As God's spokesman, he was a type of Christ; he was a prefigurement of the coming Jesus Christ who is the ultimate "Word of God" (Revelation 19:13; see John 1:1-5;). Even though the prophet had died and his flesh had turned to dust; nevertheless, his bones continued to proclaim the truth of God's Word regarding the resurrection of all men.

This incredible miracle involving Elisha's dead bones was God's way of demonstrating the coming power of His Son Jesus Christ, how his death will in turn impart eternal life to multitudes of spiritually dead people who would be transformed by their contact with Him. As the apostle Paul said:

> For if the dead are not raised, not even Christ has been raised; and if Christ has not been raised, your faith is worthless; you are still in your sins. Then those also who have fallen asleep in Christ have perished. If we have hoped in Christ in this life only, we are of all men most to be pitied. But now Christ has been raised from the dead, the first fruits of those who are asleep. For since by a man came death, by a man also came the resurrection of the dead. For as in Adam all die, so also in Christ all will be made alive. But each in his own order: Christ the first fruits, after that those who are Christ's at His coming, then comes the end, when He hands over the kingdom to the God and Father, when He has abolished all rule and all authority and power. For He must reign until He has put all His enemies under His feet. The last enemy that will be abolished is death. (1 Corinthians 15:16-26)

When Jesus expired on the cross we are told:

> Jesus cried out again with a loud voice, and yielded up His spirit. And behold, the veil of the temple was torn in two from top to bottom; and the earth shook and the rocks were split. The tombs were opened, and many bodies of the saints who had fallen asleep were raised; and coming out of the tombs after His resurrection they entered the holy city and appeared to many. (Matthew 27:50-53)

We don't know exactly how many dead people came to life when Christ breathed His last on Calvary, but they were people whose faith was counted as righteousness, so their dead bodies were transformed by the death of Christ and became a living testimony to the coming resurrection of all men (both the saved and the lost).

In conclusion, grieving the loss of a loved one is natural and expected while attending a funeral service or standing at a gravesite. However, by believing in the death and resurrection of One Man—Jesus Christ—we can be assured of the future resurrection of all people, but His death can only give eternal life in heaven to those who touch Him and who are touched by Him.

It's Déjà Vu All Over Again

The famous New York Yankees catcher, Yogi Berra, has made so many humorous-sounding statements that they have been given the collective term of "Yogiisms." One well-known quote that has been attributed to him is: "It's déjà vu all over again!"[43] Its redundancy is what makes the sentence funny; however, the overuse of needless repetition can become annoying, at the very least, and tragic, at worst. Furthermore, when mistakes are repeated without learning from them, it becomes a living déjà-vu tragedy.

Wise, old King Solomon summed up this concept best when he wrote:

> "Vanity of vanities! All is vanity." What advantage does man have in all his work which he does under the sun? A generation goes and a generation comes, but the earth remains forever. Also, the sun rises and the sun sets; and hastening to its place it rises there again. Blowing toward the south, then turning toward the north, the wind continues swirling along; and on its circular courses the wind returns. All the rivers flow into the sea, yet the sea is not full. To the place where the rivers flow, there they flow again. All things are wearisome; man is not able to tell it. The eye is not satisfied with seeing, nor is the ear filled with hearing. That which has been is that which will be, and that which has been done is that which will be done. So there is nothing new under the sun. (Ecclesiastes 1:2-9)

Simply a surface glance at mankind's past proclaims the truth of Solomon's words, as the shores of man's history are strewn with the wreckage of wars, insurrections, revolutions, and conflicts that have done little or nothing to significantly change the world for the better. In the past 150 years alone, the amount of blood shed in man's vain attempt to alter the course of humanity for the better is truly astounding. Over 600,000 men died in the American Civil War in order to preserve the union and to abolish slavery; nevertheless, a century-and-a-half later, America is more divided than ever, experiencing incomparable racial tension and hatred. World War I was termed "the war to end all wars," yet more people have been killed in subsequent wars than in all recorded history of mankind.[44] The Armistice (Latin meaning "arma" or "arms" and "stitum" or "stopping") of the First World War was signed at the 11th hour on the 11th day of the 11th month in 1918. The phrase "at the 11th hour" means the last possible moment for doing something; thus, this was thought to be the last chance for ending war before war ended the human race.

Unfortunately, the ceaseless parade of revolts marches on as the world's nations continue their death dance of musical chairs. However, regardless of how much blood is spilt, the disputes never end. Short-lived alliances proceed to mutate and morph into the same old regimes with different labels, because people are never long satisfied. Solomon noted this as well:

> A poor yet wise lad is better than an old and foolish king who no longer knows how to receive instruction. For he has come out of prison to become king, even though he was born poor in his kingdom. I have seen all the living under the sun throng to the side of the second lad who replaces him. There is no end to all the people, to all who were before them, and even the ones who will come later will not be happy with him, for this too is vanity and striving after wind. (4:13-16)

Irrespective of whom "he" is that "has come out of prison" (whether the poor lad or the old king), of interest is Solomon's observation of the cycle where men continuously lead revolutions to overthrow the authorities, only to be overthrown themselves by succeeding generations. It becomes "a déjà vu all over again."

Well, the succession of wars will not stop until the people and their governments acknowledge Christ as the Supreme King and the God above all other so-called gods. Indeed, this will come to pass when Christ returns to change the course of mankind's repulsive treadmill. As the prophet Isaiah proclaimed:

> For a child will be born to us, a son will be given to us; and the government will rest on His shoulders; and His name will be called Wonderful Counselor, Mighty God, Eternal Father, Prince of Peace. There will be no end to the increase of His government or of peace, on the throne of David and over his kingdom, to establish it and to uphold it with justice and righteousness from then on and forevermore. The zeal of the Lord of hosts will accomplish this. (Isaiah 9:6-7)

Isaiah also predicted:

> Then a shoot will spring from the stem of Jesse, and a branch from his roots will bear fruit. The Spirit of the Lord will rest on Him, the spirit of wisdom and understanding, the spirit of counsel and strength, the spirit of knowledge and the fear of the Lord. And He will delight in the fear of the Lord, and He will not judge by what His eyes see, nor make a decision by what His ears hear; but with righteousness He will judge the poor, and decide with fairness for the afflicted of the earth ... and with the breath of His lips He will slay the wicked. ... And the wolf will dwell with the lamb, and the leopard will lie down with the young goat, and the calf and the young lion and the fatling together. ... and the lion will eat straw like the ox. The nursing child will play by the hole of the cobra. ... They will not hurt or destroy in all My holy mountain, for the

earth will be full of the knowledge of the Lord as the waters cover the sea. Then in that day the nations will resort to the root of Jesse, who will stand as a signal for the peoples; and His resting place will be glorious. (11:1-4, 6-10)

Yes, there is coming a day when history will cease to be "déjà vu all over again," at which time there will finally, finally be peace on Earth under the worldwide reign and lordship of the Prince of Peace.

Eaters of the Dead

Vultures are truly amazing creatures, no matter which of the 23 different existing species to which a particular one may belong. They are the only land-based vertebrates that can survive solely on scavenging carcasses and devouring decomposing bodies. Much of the following fascinating facts were reported in the article, "Vultures are Repulsive. Here's Why We Need to Save Them" in the January 2016 *National Geographic Magazine*:

Their anatomy is designed in such a way as to enable them to expend as little energy as possible when soaring on thermals over 12,000 feet in their search of cadavers and dying animals. Moreover, their powerful hooked beaks enable them to rip apart the rotting remains of the dead, and they also have tongues with deep grooves and backward-facing barbs for quickly gulping down hefty portions of the deceased.

Besides these attributes, they have flatter feet and shorter, less-curved claws than any other predatory bird, which enables them to spend more time walking on the ground than most raptors. They also have extremely keen eyesight, empowering them to excel at spotting a carcass from great distances. Furthermore, some vultures can store up to 20% of their body weight in consumed flesh within their enlarged esophagus, and then expunge their vile stomach contents in an instant in order to quickly escape the sudden threat of an attack by a predator.

Additionally, their bald crown enables the ultraviolet light of the sun to kill off the myriads of deadly microbes which cling to their face and head as they devour diseased bodies, but most amazing of all about these eaters of the dead is their mysterious gut. They have highly corrosive, bacteria-killing stomach acids that neutralize pathogens and deadly diseases as potent as anthrax, rabies, influenza, smallpox, Ebola, and the plague. Virtually no toxic bacterium can live in their extremely lethal stomach acids. Consequently, they have become the ideal killing machine when it comes to limiting the spread of harmful bacteria and diseases that threaten the very lives of both men and beasts.

As a result, where there is an absence of vultures, decaying carcasses can take three times longer to decompose, which then increases the chances of other animals contracting malignant diseases — diseases which would otherwise die within the digestive juices of the eaters of the dead. Vultures also prevent cattle from contracting fatal herpes viruses by reducing the dead remains to bones within hours. Their rapid devouring of decaying corpses also suppresses insect populations linked with eye diseases in both humans and livestock; and of course, the pestilence of flies multiplying exponentially, and therefore spreading even more debilitating infirmities.[45]

Therefore, vultures are crucial in the survival of humanity as well as the preservation of many different animal species, and without them, an unparalleled ecological disaster would follow (not to mention the economic catastrophe resulting from staggering healthcare costs and hindered productivity from the unchecked spread of pandemics).

In light of these amazing facts, it's very interesting to note what God has to say about vultures. Not surprisingly, the Bible classifies these birds as unclean (Leviticus 11:13; Deuteronomy 14:12). Even so, God plans to use them as a powerful cleansing agent at the end of the age when the highest count of dead bodies will be concentrated in one place — among the armies of Armageddon in Israel:

A clamor has come to the end of the earth, because the Lord has a controversy with the nations. He is entering into judgment with all flesh; as for the wicked, He has given them to the sword ... Behold, evil is going forth from nation to nation, and a great storm is being stirred up from the remotest parts of the earth. *Those slain by the Lord on that day will be from one end of the earth to the other. They will not be* lamented, gathered *or buried*; they will be like dung on the face of the ground. (Jeremiah 25:31-33)

The Lord God also said to His prophet Ezekiel:

Speak to every kind of bird and to every beast of the field, "Assemble and come, gather from every side to My sacrifice which I am going to sacrifice for you, as a great sacrifice on the mountains of Israel, that you may eat flesh and drink blood. You will eat the flesh of mighty men and drink the blood of the princes of the earth. ... So you will eat fat until you are glutted, and drink blood until you are drunk, from My sacrifice which I have sacrificed for you. You will be glutted at My table with horses and charioteers, with mighty men and all the men of war. ... And I will set My glory among the nations; and all the nations will see My judgment which I have executed and My hand which I have laid on them." (Ezekiel 39:17-21)

Finally, the apostle John reveals his vision of the future:

And I saw heaven opened, and behold, a white horse, and He who sat on it is called Faithful and True, and in righteousness He judges and wages war. ... From His mouth comes a sharp sword, so that with it He may strike down the nations, and He will rule them with a rod of iron; and He treads the wine press of the fierce wrath of God, the Almighty. And on His robe and on His thigh He has a name written, "King of kings, and Lord of lords." Then I saw an angel standing in the sun, and he cried out *with a loud voice, saying to all the birds which fly in midheaven, "Come, assemble for the great supper of God, so that you may eat the flesh of kings* and the *flesh of commanders* and the *flesh of mighty men* and the *flesh of horses and of those who sit on them* and the *flesh of all men*, both free men and slaves, and small and great." (Revelation 19:11, 15-18)

This will be the final judgment upon the spiritually dead and morally rotten men on Earth. God will call forth all the vultures and predatory birds throughout the globe to cleanse this planet of every carcass of man who was at war with Him, and who insisted on living in defiance of His moral laws. No longer will they be in a position to contaminate others spiritually with their twisted philosophies, adulterous practices, and depraved lifestyles. In addition, Satan and his army of unclean spirits will be confined to the depths of hell, where they will be unable to infect and spread their deadly spiritual pathogens through rebellious people anymore.

Granted, vultures' gruesome feasting can be really revolting to watch; however, it epitomizes the need to cleanse the world of physical defilement, and in the end, spiritual defilement when God will use these eaters of the dead to eradicate the globe of those who rebelled against Him and were in constant conflict with His people (Revelation 20:12-13; 2 Timothy 4:1; Matthew 8:21-22; Luke 9:59-60).

Rage is All the Rage

Bitterness, animosity, hatred, resentment, and indignation are manifesting themselves like never before. Killing and rioting have become all too frequent, and road rage is becoming more and more commonplace as people of compassion and forbearance become fewer and fewer. Racial rage has now reached its tipping point and economic rage is growing exponentially in the face of monetary disparity. Political rage, gender rage, rage in the media, rage on campuses, environmental rage, and rages everywhere have reached their boiling points.

Being outraged at the outrage of others is escalating at an alarming rate, as well. Both umbrage and indignation march across the globe like a massive invading army, unleashing its venomous hatred at every turn and leaving in its wake even more vengeful people who retaliate with still more escalating violence and growing spitefulness. Rage may be all the rage today, but it comes at a great price to individuals, families, societies, nations, and ultimately the world. It is the polar opposite of peace and harmony, negatively affecting people's immune systems and overall well-being. In short, rage is clearly toxic to others and it is completely destructive to oneself.

The first episode of rage and its negative effect upon one's health and happiness is recorded in the fourth chapter of Genesis. It was when Cain began to seethe with resentment towards his brother, Abel, due to the fact that God accepted Abel's animal sacrifices while rejecting Cain's offerings from his harvest. Consequently, Cain's jealousy and ill-will towards his brother festered to such an extent that God appealed to Cain, saying:

> "Why are you angry? And why has your countenance fallen? If you do well, will not your countenance be lifted up? And if you do not do well, sin is crouching at the door; and its desire is for you, but you must master it." ... And it came about when they were in the field, that Cain rose up

against Abel his brother and killed him. (Genesis 4:6-8)

God Himself inferred that being righteous and doing good in His sight will have a positive effect upon one's overall health and basic quality of life. This is because having an uplifted countenance actually boosts one's immune system and the general vigor of one's mind and anatomy. As wise King Solomon said, "Anxiety in a man's heart weighs it down, but a good word makes it glad," as well as, "A joyful heart makes a cheerful face, but when the heart is sad, the spirit is broken," and "A joyful heart is good medicine, but a broken spirit dries up the bones" (Proverbs 12:25; 15:13; 17:22).

A lifted-up countenance and a joyful heart act as a medicine and a powerful healing tonic that restores and refreshes the spirit, soul, and body. On the other hand, rage produces nothing but stress, anxiety, and apprehension—all of which wreak havoc on one's physiology, peace of mind, and longevity of life. God knows this, and that is why He told Cain that if he wanted to enjoy his life, he needed to master his sinful nature and to manifest righteous deeds. This, and only this, will genuinely lift a man's countenance; however, it takes the power of God to replace explosive anger with a lasting peace.

Christ said, "Peace I leave with you; My peace I give to you; not as the world gives do I give to you. Do not let your heart be troubled, nor let it be fearful" (John 14:27). He also asserted:

> You have heard that it was said, "An eye for an eye, and a tooth for a tooth." But I say to you, do not resist an evil person; but whoever slaps you on your right cheek, turn the other to him also. If anyone wants to sue you and take your shirt, let him have your coat also. Whoever forces you to go one mile, go with him two. ... You have heard that it was said, "You shall love your neighbor and hate your enemy." But I say to you, love your enemies and

pray for those who persecute you, so that you may be sons of your Father who is in heaven; for He causes His sun to rise on the evil and the good, and sends rain on the righteous and the unrighteous. For if you love those who love you, what reward do you have? Do not even the tax collectors do the same? If you greet only your brothers, what more are you doing than others? Do not even the Gentiles do the same? Therefore you are to be perfect, as your heavenly Father is perfect. (Matthew 5:38-41, 43-48)

Let's face it, men do not have the power within themselves to love their enemies, or to give more than is demanded, or to turn the other cheek, or to go the extra mile. Nonetheless, Paul said, "I can do all things through [Christ] who strengthens me" (Philippians 4:13). Only through His power can our countenance be lifted up by mastering our fallen natures and doing the right thing in the sight of God. He says, "Bless those who persecute you; bless and do not curse. ... Never pay back evil for evil to anyone" (Romans 12:14, 17). Of course, this goes contrary to our instinct for revenge, which is why rage is still all the rage today, and rage only begets more rage. Eventually, rage is what will destroy the world, and the only antidote for rage is peace — "the Prince of Peace"!

Fool's Gold

From Genesis to Revelation, gold is spoken of hundreds of times, as both God and man place enormous value upon this very rare and precious metal. The first mention of gold in the Bible is in Genesis 2:8-12 when the Scriptures speak of its purity and its abundance surrounding the Garden of Eden, while the last reference to gold can be found in Revelation 21:18 describing the tremendous quantity of gold within the new and eternal city of Jerusalem where God will rule and reign forever.

However, there are two different types of gold whose values are as different as day and night: pure gold and fool's gold. Symbolically, God uses gold as a very costly element pointing to both His deity and His righteous works. For example, gold is used extensively in the construction of the Tabernacle furnishings, including the Ark of the Covenant, the altar of incense, the table of showbread, and the seven-branched candlestick, all of which symbolically pointed to Jesus Christ and to His holy works. In Solomon's Temple, huge amounts of gold overlaid the interior walls, as well as the two majestic cherubim that stood guard before the veil separating the holy place from the holy of holies (1 Kings 6:19-35; 2 Chronicles 3-4). The God of heaven essentially surrounds Himself with gold to emphasize His eternal worth and the value of His holiness.

God also places great value on His very words because He has elevated His every word to be equal with Himself, referring to Christ as "The Word of God" and "the Word made flesh," or God's Word in human form (Revelation 19:13; John 1:1-14). His Word imparts wisdom and understanding, two incredibly valuable traits: "How blessed is the man who finds wisdom and the man who gains understanding. For her profit is better than the profit of silver and her gain better than fine gold. She is more precious than jewels; and nothing you desire compares with her" (Proverbs 3:13-15). Solomon goes on to say:

Does not wisdom call, and understanding lift up her voice? ... she cries out: "To you, O men, I call, and my voice is to the sons of men. O naïve ones, understand prudence; and, O fools, understand wisdom. Listen, for I will speak noble things; and the opening of my lips will reveal right things. ... *Take my instruction and not silver, and knowledge rather than choicest gold. For wisdom is better than jewels; and all desirable things cannot compare with her* ... I love those who love me; and those who diligently seek me will find me. Riches and honor are with me, enduring wealth and righteousness. *My fruit is better than gold, even pure gold, and my yield better than choicest silver.* ... Now therefore, O sons, listen to me, for blessed are they who keep my ways. Heed instruction and be wise, and do not neglect it. ... For he who finds me finds life and obtains favor from the Lord. But he who sins against me injures himself; all those who hate me love death." (8:1, 3-6, 10-11, 17-19, 32-33, 35-36)

Also more precious than gold is a man's faith in God and in His words, as well as having a good reputation in His sight (see 1 Peter 1:7; Proverbs 22:1). As for the deeds of believers, the apostle Paul describes how they can be either as precious as gold or as worthless as stubble:

For we are God's fellow workers; you are God's field, God's building. According to the grace of God which was given to me, like a wise master builder I laid a foundation, and another is building on it. But each man must be careful how he builds on it. For no man can lay a foundation other than the one which is laid, which is Jesus Christ. Now *if any man builds on the foundation with gold, silver, precious stones, wood, hay, straw, each man's work will become evident; for* the day will show it because *it is to be revealed with fire, and the fire itself will test the quality of each man's work. If any man's work* which he has built on it *remains, he will receive a reward. If any man's work is burned up, he will suffer loss; but he himself will be saved,* yet so as through fire. (1 Corinthians 3:9-15)

In summary, God's personhood, His Word, and His holiness are like gold; and a man's faith in Him, and a man's sterling reputation, and a man's righteous deeds are all more valuable in the sight of God than the purest of fine gold. These are true riches—riches with an eternal value that is beyond all measure.

The second type of gold is "fool's gold," or pyrite, which is a mineral with a superficial resemblance to real gold. It is an iron sulfide with a metallic luster and a bright yellow hue that glitters like genuine gold but is absolutely worthless in both its monetary value and its bargaining power. Jesus warned of spiritual pyrite when he said:

Do not store up for yourselves treasures on earth, where moth and rust destroy, and where thieves break in and steal. But store up for yourselves treasures in heaven, where neither moth nor rust destroys, and where thieves do not break in or steal; for where your treasure is, there your heart will be also. ... You cannot serve God and wealth [gold]. (Matthew 6:19-21, 24)

Jesus also alluded to this fool's gold when He gave the parable of the rich man whose wealth had increased to the point where he said to himself:

"Soul, you have many goods laid up for many years to come; take your ease, eat, drink and be merry." But God said to him, "You fool! This very night your soul is required of you; and now who will own what you have prepared?" So is the man who stores up treasure for himself, and is not rich toward God. (Luke 12:19-21)

Christ prefaced this parable with the warning to: "beware, and be on your guard against every form of greed; for not even when one has an abundance does his life consist of his possessions." Therefore, storing up treasures here, rather than in heaven, is as foolish and ignorant as storing up pyrite in a bank's safety deposit box. Nonetheless, the Bible predicts that there will be a sharp increase in the last days of the number of greedy and ignorant people who will hoard their fool's gold in their disregard for heavenly riches:

> Come now, you rich, weep and howl for your miseries which are coming upon you. Your riches have rotted and your garments have become moth-eaten. Your gold and your silver have rusted; and their rust will be a witness against you and will consume your flesh like fire. It is in the last days that you have stored up your treasure! ... You have lived luxuriously on the earth and led a life of wanton pleasure; you have fattened your hearts in a day of slaughter. (James 5:1-3, 5)

There will be a multitude of wealthy individuals in the last days who will amass their worthless fortunes of spiritual pyrite, even in the face of global poverty. However, people do not have to be rich to make riches their idol or wealthy to make gold their god, because counterfeit gold has been an idol for all ages, and a deity of even the poorest of the poor for thousands of years. For example, over 600 years before Christ, the cultural elite of Daniel's day "praised the gods of gold and silver, of bronze, iron, wood and stone" (Daniel 5:4); and in the closing days of history, both rich and poor alike will "not repent of the works of their hands, so as not to worship demons, *and the idols of gold and of silver and of brass and of stone and of wood,* which can neither see nor hear nor walk; and they did not repent of their murders nor of their sorceries nor of their immorality nor of their thefts" (Revelation 9:20-21).

Men of all ages and of all backgrounds have been seduced by the glitter of fool's gold and will lie, cheat, steal, or kill to get it. They will strive to accumulate it in vast quantities and will sacrifice their soul, their family and friends, and their futures to acquire it. Nevertheless, when Christ returns in great power and great glory, the Bible predicts:

> Enter the rock and hide in the dust from the terror of the Lord and from the splendor of His majesty. The proud look of man will be abased and the loftiness of man will be humbled, and the Lord alone will be exalted in that day. For the Lord of hosts will have a day of reckoning against everyone who is lifted up, that he may be abased. ... but the idols will completely vanish. ... In that day men will cast away ... their idols of silver and their idols of gold, which they made for themselves to worship, in order to go into the caverns of the rocks and the clefts of the cliffs before the terror of the Lord and the splendor of His majesty, when He arises to make the earth tremble. Stop regarding man, whose breath of life is in his nostrils; for why should he be esteemed? (Isaiah 2:10-12, 18, 20-22)

It is apparent that at the very end of the world, unsaved men will finally realize the difference between true gold and fool's gold. They will recognize that they have been sold a bill of goods by "the god of this world" who is also "the father of lies" (2 Corinthians 4:4; John 8:44); and unfortunately, even church members can be deceived by this lying demon and seduced by the shimmer and twinkle of his fool's gold. Jesus rebukes such believers by saying:

> I know your deeds, that you are neither cold nor hot; I wish that you were cold or hot. So because you are lukewarm, and neither hot nor cold, I will spit you out of My mouth. Because you say, "I am rich, and have become wealthy, and have need of nothing," and you do not know that you are wretched and miserable and poor and blind and naked, I advise you to buy from Me gold refined by fire so that you may become rich, and white garments so that you may clothe yourself, and that the shame of your nakedness will not be revealed; and eye salve to anoint your eyes so that you may see. (Revelation 3:15-18)

In conclusion, the price of gold may be well over $1,000 an ounce today, but in the end, it is only fool's gold to all those who are not rich with the true gold of heaven; and all those who are rich in this world but not in the heavenly realm, will be eternally bankrupt from the devil's pyrite.

The Dead Cat Bounce

In the world of finance, a "dead cat bounce" is a small, brief recovery in the price of a declining stock or bond. The phrase was derived from the concept that even a dead cat will bounce if it falls from a great height and then hits the ground. Originating on Wall Street, it commonly applied to any case where a subject experiences a short resurgence during or following a severe decline.

It is fairly common knowledge that cats have an innate "righting reflex," enabling them to nearly always land on their feet and survive falls that would otherwise kill or seriously injure most other vertebrates. This is due to a cat's unusually flexible backbone, along with their keen eyesight and their inner ears' balancing ability.

There are also various myths and legends that promote the idea that cats have nine lives, which is, of course, anything but factual. Interestingly though, scientists have discovered that the purring of cats is actually a "natural healing mechanism" which has helped inspire the superstition that they essentially do have nine lives. Researchers have found that wounded or injured cats purr because it helps their bones and organs to heal and grow stronger after experiencing physical traumas that would often snuff out the lives of other four-legged creatures.

Well, cats may be unique in their ability to survive falls and to heal their injured bodies; however, after a cat is already dead, none of these fascinating capabilities can cushion their fall or bring them back to life. Instead, the only thing that can be expected from a deceased cat being dropped from a tall building is a slight bounce after impact.

When it comes to one's relationship with God, both individuals and nations can also manifest a dead cat bounce after experiencing a devastating fall or impacting ordeal. For example, when the twin towers in New York City were brought down by terrorists, there was both a surge of patriotism and a jump in church attendance. However, the increase in religious fervor and national pride was very short lived, especially when it came to the modest increase in religious participation and appearances at prayer gatherings.

The historical books of Judges, Kings, and Chronicles record example after example of the dead cat bounce regarding the nation of Israel. God would bring his rebellious people to their knees by judging them with droughts, disasters, and invading armies; and time and time again, the Jewish Nation would repent and turn back to God during their distress, only to once again forsake Him and His laws after being divinely delivered from their painful ordeals.

Perhaps the most classic dead cat bounce of all recorded in Scripture was when Jerusalem had been under siege by Babylon for many months and the city's inhabitants began to realize they were destined to eventually die of famine or disease or by the sword. In their desperation, they decided to renew their covenant with God by obeying His ordinances concerning slave ownership: "If you buy a Hebrew slave, he shall serve for six years; but on the seventh he shall go out as a free man without payment" (Exodus 21:2). In other words, if a Jew became greatly in debt, he could hire himself out as a servant in order to pay off his financial obligations (Leviticus 25:39-40); however, he was to be freed at the beginning of his seventh year of servitude, regardless of whether his financial obligations were completely paid off or not.

So the besieged people of Jerusalem held a solemn assembly and vowed to God that they would free the slaves which they had kept beyond the maximum six-year limit He had set. Their covenant with Him was made in the hopes that they would be rescued from their dire circumstances and that their prosperity would eventually be restored to them. God then tested the sincerity of their newfound religious fervor and their re-dedication to Him by having the surrounding Babylonian armies pull up stakes in order to fight against the advancing Egyptian forces (which Israel had hired to rescue them). As one may surmise, once Israel realized the threat of death and starvation was over, they immediately took back their newly freed slaves and subjected them once again to forced labor. The Scriptures tell us:

Although recently you had turned and done what is right in My sight, each man proclaiming release to his neighbor, and you had made a covenant before Me in the house which is called by My name. Yet you turned and profaned My name, and each man took back his male servant and each man his female servant whom you had set free according to their desire, and you brought them into subjection to be your male servants and female servants. ... You have not obeyed Me in proclaiming release each man to his brother and each man to his neighbor. Behold, I am proclaiming a release to you ... to the sword, to the pestilence and to the famine; and I will make you a terror to all the kingdoms of the earth. (Jeremiah 34:15-17)

Talk about a dead cat bounce! Isn't it truly amazing how fickle and undependable human nature is when it comes to obedience and commitment to the Lord?

People demonstrate the dead cat bounce in many of life's circumstances as well: There is the classic "jailhouse conversion" resulting in a sudden change of belief systems after being incarcerated, but a quick return to a prisoner's former lifestyle once he is released. Then there is the "foxhole conversion" where terrified soldiers cry out to God for their survival during battle, but soon forget their desperate bargains with the Almighty once the exploding shells and screaming bullets cease. Also, there is the "health conversion" where people diligently seek God after being diagnosed with a very serious or life-threatening disease, yet lose their newfound religious zeal after their medical condition improves. Lastly, there is always the "prosperity conversion" as men cry out to God during a financial crisis or after the loss of a job, only to turn around and "place Him on the back burner" once their monetary circumstances recover.

Let's be honest, short-lived faith during a time of crisis will never really be the kind of faith that perseveres under trial and presses on during prosperity. To remain alive in Christ during these times, faith must manifest righteous deeds, as James put it:

> Even so faith, if it has no works, is dead, being by itself. ... You believe that God is one. You do well; the demons also believe, and shudder. But are you willing to recognize, you foolish fellow, that faith without works is useless? ... For just as the body without the spirit is dead, so also faith without works is dead. (James 2:17, 19-20, 26)

"But the one who endures to the end, he will be saved" (Matthew 24:13). These words of Jesus imply the necessity of having a faith that endures all things in order to be saved. In the final analysis, it is only perseverance and obedience that will determine if one will spiritually land on one's feet; because without them, all other faith merely becomes a dead cat bounce.

The Big Cover-up

Each year, thousands of murders are committed in the United States, and approximately 35% of those murders go unsolved, or there is not enough evidence to convict those who are responsible for taking the life of another. Then, of course, there are hundreds of thousands of people who have gone missing without a trace in America's history, and many of these individuals are presumed dead, or legally declared deceased after seven years of being reported missing.[46]

Now multiply these figures the world over and throughout all of human history, and the number of unsolved murders increases exponentially. This is especially true where tyranny rules a country and where these murderous regimes bury their slain in mass graves, or when they attempt to dispose of them through incinerators, gas chambers, and torture rooms. On top of all these murders are the millions of aborted children whose annihilated bodies are viewed as too insignificant to even be considered human. Only God knows precisely how many are in the final count of this human carnage.

However, we do know of the very first murder and its accompanying very first cover-up. It was when Cain killed his brother Abel in a fit of rage and then buried him in order to cover up the evidence of his murderous deed. In Genesis 4:10-11, God says, "The voice of your brother's blood is crying to Me from the ground ... which has opened its mouth to receive your brother's blood from your hand." Cain concealed his brother's dead body by burying it in the ground, assuming that if it could not be found, then no one could prove he was guilty of killing him.

So when God interrogated Cain as to his brother's whereabouts, Cain insolently denied any knowledge of where Abel might be and arrogantly suggested that God was harassing him with his cross-examination! He deflected God's question with a question of his own: "Am I my brother's keeper?" Consequently, Cain was just the first in an endless parade of killers who deny any involvement in taking another person's life, and then suggest that the inquiring authorities are attempting to unjustly blame or convict them of crimes they supposedly didn't commit. Truly, God sees every murder and knows exactly who every murderer is, no matter how effective the cover-up may be. In God's economy, there is no such thing as "the perfect crime" or the "perfect murder." It is never a game of "whodunnit?" with God.

Even King David tried to cover up a premeditated murder by assigning a man by the name of Uriah to the front lines of a battle to ensure the opposing army would kill him; but in the end, God accused David through His prophet Nathan saying, "You are the man!" (2 Samuel 11; 12:7). Like Cain, David tried to cover up his killing; but unlike Cain, David confessed under God's accusation.

David even revealed that when he kept quiet about his murder of Uriah, his physical vitality began to waste away and he had absolutely no peace of mind (Psalm 38:1-8). It was only after he confessed his sin and pleaded to God (with a broken and contrite spirit) for forgiveness that he found peace and a restored fellowship with the God that he dearly loved, but deeply offended with his wickedness. All the same, David suffered the consequence of God's severe judgment for his sin, but God also graciously forgave him because of his truly repentant heart.

No longer did David try to cover up his crime with rationalizations and justifications, and therefore his sins were covered over and blotted out with the shed blood of an innocent substitute. This is the only "cover-up" that God wants to see in regards to any of man's crimes. All those who attempt to cover up their wicked deeds any other way will be found out and punished without mercy. As Isaiah the prophet predicts: "For behold, the Lord is about to come out from His place to punish the inhabitants of the earth for their iniquity, *and the earth will reveal her bloodshed and will no longer cover her slain*" (Isaiah 26:21). Also, Jesus said that "there is nothing covered up that will not be revealed, and hidden that will not be known. Accordingly, whatever you have said in the dark will be heard in the light, and what you have whispered in the inner rooms will be proclaimed upon the housetops" (Luke 12:2-3; see Matthew 10:26).

Certainly men in every age have devised all sorts of methods and justifications to try to cover up their murders—from baby killing to mercy killing, and from mass shootings to systematic genocide. When it's all said and done, however, only one cover-up will succeed in the eyes of an all-seeing God, and that is the covering over of one's sin with the sinless blood of the Lamb of God.

Ship of Fools

It has been well over 100 years since the ill-fated ocean liner that was christened as the Titanic came to rest on the bottom floor of the Atlantic Ocean. Her proud architects and skillful builders had boasted that their vessel was absolutely unsinkable; however, history records that the only thing the Titanic ever did was sink. She never even completed her maiden voyage as she collided with an iceberg at 11:40 that fateful night and sank around 2:20 in the morning on Monday, April 15, 1912.

On impact, its massive hull was ripped apart like a can of sardines. Its "airtight compartments" were quickly flooded with the icy waters of the rolling sea, and it sank beneath the black surface like an enormous millstone descending into a frozen grave. Although it was designed to be the pride of man's ingenuity, instead it became an ignominious coffin of rivets and steel. This much-hailed and glorious "ship of ships" became nothing more than an iron sepulcher entombing and dragging over 1,500 people to their final resting place.

It became a ship that was both constructed and operated by fools—fools that were absolutely positive it could never sink. They were so confident in their proud assumptions that they didn't even equip it with the necessary number of lifeboats that would be required for all passengers and crew in a time of crisis. Unfortunately, its ill-informed and gullible travelers believed in all the short-sighted hype concerning this "unsinkable" vessel and all got on board without ever questioning its lack of rescue provisions and emergency preparations.

In the end, however, the Titanic became nothing short of a titanic tragedy—a colossal tragedy that could have been avoided with a little common sense and sound judgment. Her captain, Edward Smith, ignored all the warning signals from other ships concerning the numerous icebergs that cluttered her route through the North Atlantic; and instead of slowing down and proceeding with extreme caution, he pressed on at full speed through the darkness with the intention of making record time from the port of

Southampton, England, to New York City's Grand Harbor. Well, the plummet of the Titanic is now history, and even though it has since been discovered 2½ miles beneath the ocean's surface (and there is even talk of raising it from its freezing resting place), it still lies as a mute testament to man's foolish pride.

What is also very interesting is that our planet has been referred to as a "ship" that is filled with passengers and crew. As a matter of fact, "Spaceship Earth" was a nickname coined in the 1960s by a cosmologist named R. Buckminster Fuller.[47] "Spaceship Earth" is functioning as a massive life support system for almost eight billion people and trillions of other living organisms and life forms. It is totally self-contained in the sense that it does not need to rely on any outside life sources for its survival, so they say.

However, the majority of today's passengers and crew have lost sight of the fact that our earthly vessel is desperately dependent upon the Source of all life, and the all-knowing Designer and Creator of our orbiting ship. Thus, we have truly become a ship of fools who ignore all of the warnings and guidelines of our Maker as our world leaders press full speed ahead in their reckless pride and selfish ambitions. They have become hell-bent on governing this planet without a divine compass or turning to the Almighty for guidance and direction.

As a result, our global ship has run headlong into a mountain of troubles that are ripping our world apart. Problems innumerable are flooding every nation on Earth as the hope of survival becomes dimmer and dimmer with each passing year. In addition to sinking lower and lower into insolvable dilemmas, its leaders simply play musical chairs on the deck. Their focus is concentrated on filling any seat of power they can grab, while totally neglecting to send out urgent distress signals to the Designer of their ship. Furthermore, most of its passengers have become too preoccupied with their entertainment, with their appetites, and with their economic pursuits to acknowledge their blight and to get into the only lifeboat that God has placed on board. The Lifeboat, of course, is none other than His Son Jesus

Christ, and He is the only one who can save this sinking ship and its hapless voyagers.

Regrettably, like Jonah of old, most people are simply defying God's commands, and instead, have escaped into the hull of the ship in order to enter a dream world of make-believe—a dream world where they assume they can actually ignore God without incurring His wrath or His judgments. Well, Jonah may have been God's prophet, but the pagan captain and crew of the ship on which Jonah was asleep clearly sensed that the hand of God was orchestrating their catastrophe. They perceived it was God that hurled the massive storm at their vessel, and it was the ship's captain who angrily aroused Jonah out of his slumbering stupor and commanded him to pray to his God for deliverance.

Jonah revealed the root cause of why God created the storm (for his rebellion against God), and urged the crew to throw him overboard in order to be spared God's judgment aimed at him. At Jonah's insistence, the reluctant crew finally threw Jonah into the raging waters, but only as a last resort (and only after they had suffered a great loss by throwing all of their precious cargo overboard in their vain attempt to stay afloat).

Clearly, the world is in the midst of a raging storm today—a storm that has long been predicted by the prophet Jeremiah:

> "'A clamor has come to the end of the earth, because the Lord has a controversy with the nations. He is entering into judgment with all flesh; as for the wicked, He has given them to the sword,' declares the Lord." Thus says the Lord of hosts, "Behold, evil is going forth from nation to nation, *and a great storm is being stirred up from the remotest parts of the earth.* Those slain by the Lord on that day will be from one end of the earth to the other." (Jeremiah 25:31-33)

Without question, today's world is being tossed to and fro by a great tempest. Everywhere we look we see killings, lootings, rioting, protesting, and mutiny while our shipwrecked planet steadily descends beneath the waves of economic collapse, moral upheaval, and natural disasters. Unfortunately, in the midst of all this distress, the ship's leaders have become drunk with power, its crew intoxicated with ambition, and its passengers inebriated with self-indulgence.

Our world has indeed become a ship of fools who refuse to seek the face of God and turn to Him in sincere repentance before all is lost. In short, no distress signal is being sent out to the King of kings. Instead, as with Jonah, we are descending like a stone in the belly of the beast; but unlike Jonah, the world would rather die in its rebellion than repent and be saved. Jonah confessed:

> I called out of my distress to the Lord, and He answered me. I cried for help from the depth of [the grave]; You heard my voice. For You had cast me into the deep, into the heart of the seas, and the current engulfed me. All Your breakers and billows passed over me. ... Water encompassed me to the point of death. The great deep engulfed me, weeds were wrapped around my head. I descended to the roots of the mountains [the ocean floor]. ... but You have brought up my life from the pit, O Lord my God. While I was fainting away, I remembered the Lord, and my prayer came to You, into Your holy temple. (Jonah 2:2-3, 5-7)

Jonah was a stubborn and foolish man, but he didn't die as a stubborn fool. He came to understand that God was his only hope of being rescued from his self-made disaster. Unfortunately, however, the vast majority of the world's inhabitants today will not humbly turn to God, regardless of how bad things get. Consequently, "Spaceship Earth" is doomed to a fate similar to that of the Titanic gravitating to a lifeless floor surrounded by deafening silence and crushing blackness.

In conclusion, only a fool would refuse to listen to God in the midst of a storm, and a boatload of fools is destined to be destroyed by their foolishness. As Solomon put it: "So they shall eat of the fruit of their own way and be satiated with their own devices. For the waywardness of the naïve will kill them, and the complacency of fools will destroy them. But he who listens to me shall live securely and will be at ease from the dread of evil" (Proverbs 1:31-33).

A Hole Ain't Nothin'

An old tobacco-chewing hillbilly once said, "A hole ain't nothin', but y'all sure as heck can break your neck in one!" These unrefined words uttered by such an uneducated hick may sound silly, but they actually reflect the profound wisdom of old King Solomon himself!

A hole is comprised of nothing and therefore its nothingness can be filled with or occupied by almost anything; and from the building blocks of atoms to the vastness of outer space, we see enormous voids of nothingness. However, as noted above, simply because a hole is empty space, it is anything but nothing; because falling into the deep hole of a well or a dirty hole of a mineshaft can quickly result in death or serious injury. As a matter of fact, even holes that can barely be seen with the naked eye can be very dangerous as well, because they can be the means of transporting severe illnesses or diseases. In other words, an accidental pinprick from a contaminated syringe can easily create a tiny hole that can become the tunnel of empty space which can then transfer deadly microbes to an otherwise healthy individual.

Depending upon the hole, it can be either deadly or life-saving. A small hole in the bottom of a boat can spell disaster and a massive sinkhole can result in tremendous loss of life and property; a breathing hole can sustain a life while a pothole can take a life; and a wormhole of bitterness can produce a hellhole in a relationship. Furthermore, a hole produced by something as small as a dislodged nail can have immense repercussions, as expressed in the following anonymous poem:

> For want of a nail, the shoe was lost;
> For want of a shoe, the horse was lost;
> For want of a horse, the rider was lost;
> For want of a rider, the message was lost;
> For want of a message, the strategy was lost;
> For want of a strategy, the battle was lost;
> For want of a battle, the war was lost.

A small nail missing from a horse's shoe left a miniature hole on the bottom of its hoof. That trivial hole loosened the animal's u-shaped iron plate until the remaining nails fell off, as well, resulting in the entire shoe being cast aside. The missing shoe caused the horse to stumble and throw its rider to the ground; and the rider's fall rendered him unconscious, thereby preventing him from delivering an urgent message. The critical (nondelivered) message was essential in order to win a strategic battle; and because an all-important battle was lost, the entire war ended in a catastrophic defeat for the army of the unfortunate rider (whose horse developed a small hole on the bottom of its foot). This cleverly portrays how even small holes can produce domino effects with far-reaching consequences.

On the other hand, men can find refuge or shelter, peace and quiet, and privacy in a hole in the side of a mountain (a cave). As such, a hole is where a man can find God, or where he can foolishly run from God; and a hole is where a person can save his soul, or where a person can lose his soul. God communicated with his prophet Elijah while he stood at the entrance of a cave, and He also protected 100 of His prophets in a cave (1 Kings 19:9-18; 18:4). Furthermore, Jesus resurrected Lazarus from a cave, and a cave is where the Lord safeguarded David and his household (John 11:38-44; 1 Samuel 22:1). We are also told that unrepentant sinners will try to escape from God at the second coming of Christ by hiding in holes or in caves and among the rocks of the mountains (see Revelation 6).

It is interesting to note that holes can possess enormous spiritual significance too, as demonstrated in Jesus' parable about the talents, where a servant who was entrusted with just one talent took what was given to him and dug a hole and buried his talent in it. When the master of that slave demanded an accounting from him, the unproductive worker dug up his master's money and returned it with a lame excuse of why he did nothing with it except to conceal it in a dirty hole (see Matthew 25:14-30). In telling the rest of the parable, Christ emphasized the dangerous consequences of burying our God-given talents into holes of slothfulness, holes of unfaithfulness, holes of selfishness, or holes of indifference. Such holes may appear insignificant to men, but in the eyes of God, holes can be very, very significant.

Another type of hole is a divine hole which God has placed in the heart of every human being that can only be filled by Him. Such a hole may not be visible to the naked eye, but it is truly the biggest and most potent hole of all. Massive black holes cannot be seen visibly, yet they have the power and the potential to swallow entire galaxies and to reduce them into nothingness. Consequently, if unseen black holes can be so powerful, how much more immense and powerful is the insatiable hole in man's heart that can only be filled by God? Therefore, when men attempt to fill this God-shaped hole within his heart with anything other than God, it is as foolish as trying to fill the ocean with sand. It is impossible, pointless, and insane!

Yes, a hole may appear to be nothin', but then again, a hollow space, void of substance, can be everything when it comes to life and death, both physically and spiritually.

Men Just Never Listen!

It's no secret that many women (especially married women) believe that "men just never listen" when they attempt to voice their thoughts or express their feelings to them. Communication studies, researchers, books, and seminars galore have expounded upon this male peculiarity, when the truth of the matter is that both men and women have difficulty listening for any number of reasons.

True, men are more inclined to tune out a woman's words, especially when she fails to get to the point or if she keeps interrupting him, or when he thinks she is nagging him, or he senses that she is accusing him of something. Also, there are times when a woman is simply expressing her feelings about a matter, hoping the man will listen with empathy and concern, but instead, he wants to fix the perceived problem and end the conversation. In any and all of these situations, there comes a point where most men will tune out what a woman is saying, and their eyes will glaze over, and the only thing their minds will hear is "blah, blah, blah, blah, blah."

However, women too can often be guilty of not listening to men if they believe that they are right and he is wrong, or if he becomes defensive, or if his reply gets too technical, or if he constantly repeats himself. Therefore, men can say or do a lot of things that can result in a disconnect where women simply stop listening, even when they may appear to be attentive.

Aside from other explanations, one primary and overriding reason for failing to effectively communicate with one another is because they each have separate agendas or they both have different expectations. This is true regardless of whether men are speaking to men or women are speaking to other women. Now, if we take this sad reality to the spiritual level, then failure to listen becomes a tragic fact of life. All throughout the Bible, we see numerous examples of where God clearly says what He means and means what He says about a particular subject, yet His words go in one ear and out the other or over our heads, for no other reason than people having their own agendas and personal expectations.

For example, on several occasions, Jesus told His disciples that He was going to be delivered up to the religious and political powers that be; and specifically, that He would be beaten, scourged, crucified, killed, and buried; and also that He would then rise on the third day, but they did not hear Him. Because they had assumed that Jesus was the Christ, He was therefore about to conquer the Roman authorities and they would in turn rule and reign with Him — so they had tuned out His words!

It appears the only one who listened to Jesus was a woman. It was Mary, the sister of Martha and Lazarus. While Mary sat at Jesus' feet and drank in every word He was saying, Martha ran around in a frenzy trying to prepare a meal and set the table. Martha was all wrapped up in her agenda of serving Christ; however, Mary was all wrapped up in listening to Christ. Consequently, Jesus then praised Mary for choosing the better part (see Luke 10:38-42). Due to the plain fact that she had intently listened to what Christ was saying, without having her own ambitions, this same Mary ended up anointing Jesus with a very costly perfume in order to prepare His body for burial, all while His own disciples were oblivious to His pending death (John 12:1-8).

It is also interesting to note how Christ's disciples remained deaf to His prediction that He would rise again on the third day. The only ones who seemed to have heard Him, were His enemies! The Pharisees said to Pilate:

> Sir, we remember that when He was still alive that deceiver said, "After three days I am to rise again." Therefore, give orders for the grave to be made secure until the third day, otherwise His disciples may come and steal Him away and say to the people, "He has risen from the dead," and the last deception will be worse than the first. (Matthew 27:63-64)

It truly is amazing how often people only hear what they want to hear, especially when it is God who is doing the talking. It is recorded eight times in the Gospels and eight times in the book of Revelation that Jesus said, "Let him who has an ear to hear, let him hear." God obviously puts much more importance upon a man's ability to hear than He does a man's ability to speak. James says that "everyone must be quick to hear" and "slow to speak" (James 1:19). Because when a man genuinely listens to God, then he understands what God is saying—even if it is not what he really wants to hear.

Nevertheless, people continue to be very selective in their hearing when God is speaking, and simply choose to hear what they desire to be told. For example, Jesus spoke of hell more than He did heaven, and He spoke of sin and the absolute need for individuals to repent of their evil deeds if they were going to be saved. He also warned of the dangers of greed, lying, hypocrisy, immorality, and hatred, and of the need to bear good fruit in keeping with one's repentance. He said He was the only way to heaven, the embodiment of truth, and the source of all life. Yet men constantly disregard these things, and choose to only focus in on what they want to hear—mainly that Jesus was loving, kind, compassionate, inclusive, accepting, and tolerant.

However, the apostle Paul cautioned about this kind of selective listening and how prevalent it would become in the last days, saying:

> I solemnly charge you in the presence of God and of Christ Jesus, who is to judge the living [the saved] and the dead [the damned], and by His appearing and His kingdom: preach the word; be ready in season and out of season; reprove, rebuke, exhort, with great patience and instruction. For the time will come when they will not endure sound doctrine; but *wanting to have their ears tickled, they will accumulate for themselves teachers in accordance to*

their own desires, and will turn away their ears from the truth and will turn aside to myths. (2 Timothy 4:1-4)

Paul also warns that because men refuse to listen to and obey God, He will then "send upon them a deluding influence," with all signs and wonders from Satan himself ... and they will be eternally judged for their failure to hear (2 Thessalonians 2:3-12). He cautioned that the devil could easily disguise himself as an angel of light and skillfully deceive men with "another Jesus," with "a different spirit" and "a different gospel," and that people would gladly accept his lies simply because his falsehoods are exactly what many people want to hear, rather than what they need to hear (2 Corinthians 11:2-15).

This is essentially what the demonic serpent did to the very first man and woman on the planet. Satan "tickled their ears" by telling them if they disobeyed God, they "surely will not die" but would become like God, possessing all wisdom and knowledge (Genesis 3:1-19). It's not that our first parents were hard of hearing, it's just that God's archenemy instilled doubt and managed to generate a spirit of discontent in the most contented place on Earth, causing them to turn their ears from the truth and to believe in a lie.

Now here we are, over 6,000 years later, and people still "just don't listen!" It's not simply men who don't listen, either; it's everyone who has ears to hear but who closes their ears when God tells them things they do not want to believe. From now on, therefore, whenever you overhear the exasperated lament of a woman declaring that "men just never listen," remember that both genders become notoriously bad listeners when what is being said does not fit their personal plans and aspirations, especially when the one speaking is none other than God!

The Cunning Serpent-fox

Satan has a lie for everyone, his shrewdness is truly beyond all cunning, and his deceitfulness surpasses all comprehension. Christ refers to Satan as "the father of lies," the apostle John labeled him as one "who deceives the whole world," and the great apostle Paul says that he "has blinded the minds of the unbelieving" (John 8:44; Revelation 12:9; 2 Corinthians 4:4). In the Garden of Eden, he managed to indwell a serpent, which was referred to as being "more crafty than any beast of the field which the Lord God had made" (Genesis 3:1).

Which "beast of the field" can even come close to manifesting the craftiness of a serpent? It would appear that only the proverbial sly fox can compete with the wiles of the serpent. Knowing this, Jesus referred to King Herod as being a "fox" when some of the Pharisees warned Christ that Herod was planning to kill him. Jesus then said to the religious leaders, "Go and tell that fox, 'Behold, I cast out demons and perform cures today and tomorrow, and the third day I reach My goal'" (Luke 13:31-32). When Jesus classified Herod as a fox, it was no accident or mere figure of speech. They are by far the most calculating, the most deceitful, the most elusive, and the most scheming of "all the beasts of the field."

In addition to their cleverness, they are one of the fastest animals in North America, with strides up to 20 feet and speeds up to 30 mph. Their sleek and slender bodies are designed for speed, and they seem to enjoy a good chase. They always draw upon a vast revenue of tricks to outwit and elude pursuing hounds. They are timid and cautious by nature, but can live up to 12 years by their ability to avoid predators. Foxes are also highly vocal animals; they have up to 46 different calls ranging from the nasal bark of a dog to the crying of a human baby. They can mimic the sound of screams, howls, shrills, barks, cries, yelps, vomiting, and whimpering. Lastly, they are opportunistic scavengers that take advantage of any situation in outsmarting its prey or any opponent.[48]

300

Wow! Do these characteristics not epitomize many modern-day politicians? And King Herod was truly the consummate politician of his day; no wonder Jesus referred to him as a fox! Yet even craftier than the fox are the serpents, also known as snakes, vipers, adders, and asps. From the rivers to the oceans, and from the deserts to the mountains, snakes are found on every continent except Antarctica. There are many varieties of species of serpents, a number of which may be harmless, and some that may even make good pets. For most people, however, snakes are creatures to be avoided at all costs.

Snakes can mature to be a few inches in length or grow to be 33 feet long. They can weigh only a few ounces or tip the scales at 500 pounds. Some snakes have been known to crush and eat animals as large as 130 pounds and suffocate a full-grown man to death. Some sea snakes have venom powerful enough to kill 1,000 men. There are also 5 different types of flying snakes that are not only poisonous but can glide up to distances longer than a football field (by flattening their ribcage and making side-to-side motions as they jump from tree to tree or from the trees to the ground below).

Like foxes, they are quick and agile, but unlike foxes, many species of snakes have highly toxic venom. One species of cobra can spit deadly poison at any threat that comes within striking distance. Furthermore, serpents are cold-blooded reptiles that can give birth to up to 150 snakes at a time. While some species are born alive, others are hatched from eggs; however, the mothers abandon their young at birth and leave them to fend for themselves (which says a lot about the resourcefulness and craftiness of even newborn serpents).[49]

In the Garden of Eden, God cursed the serpent by condemning it to crawl on its belly, suggesting that at one time, it had the ability to walk. God then doomed the serpent to eat dust all the days of its life. It is interesting to note, as well, that dust is essential for the life of most snakes, as they rely upon the constant flickering of their moist, forked tongue to collect tiny dust particles, which it then smells (with sensors in its mouth), giving the reptile a sense of direction, food, and danger. This is especially helpful because their eyesight is poor and they have almost no hearing ability.[50]

A fox may be sly and cunning, but a serpent can be dangerous and deadly; and an unsuspecting fox can be quickly brought low by a snake in the grass. As Solomon said, "If the serpent bites before being charmed, there is no profit for the charmer" (Ecclesiastes 10:11). Both John the Baptist and Jesus Himself referred to the religious leaders of their day as being a "brood of vipers." Christ also said to His disciples, "Behold, I send you out as sheep in the midst of wolves; so be shrewd as serpents and innocent as doves" (Matthew 3:7; 12:34; 10:16).

In addition to calling Herod a "fox," Jesus also called Judas a "devil," and the apostle Paul told Elymas the magician that he was a "son of the devil" (John 6:70; Acts 13:10). However, the ultimate viper, the ultimate fox, the ultimate "son of the devil" will be the coming political leader and false prophet who will rule the world with all the activity of Satan by manifesting complete power, signs, and wonders in order to damn as much of mankind as possible (2 Thessalonians 2:1-12; Revelation 13).

Moreover, this coming serpent-fox appears to be a descendant of Jacob, or Israel of old, who said of him, "Dan shall be a serpent in the way, a horned snake in the path, that bites the horse's heels, so that his rider falls backward" (Genesis 49:17). Because people refuse "to receive the love of the truth, so as to be saved," God will send them the deluding influence of a serpent-fox so that they will believe what is false, and be judged because they preferred a serpent's lie over God's unchanging truth.

In addition, this serpent-fox is never more cunning or danger-ous than when it disguises itself as a celestial messenger by quoting Scripture or by professing to believe in the God of heaven (see Galatians 1:1-9). Time and time again, the demons would loudly proclaim that Jesus Christ was the Son of God, and again and again, Jesus would command them to keep silent (see Mark 1:34; Luke 4:35; 4:41). There was even a time when an entire legion of demons called Him the "Son of the Most High God" (Mark 5:7; see Matthew 8:29); and although the exact size of a Roman legion depended upon one's historical time frame, a legion during Christ's day consisted of at least 6,000 men. Consequently, literally thousands of demons loudly proclaimed that Jesus Christ was the Son of God!

Furthermore, when Paul and Silas were evangelizing in the district of Macedonia, a demon-possessed slave girl followed them for many days crying out, "These men are bond-servants of the Most High God, who are proclaiming to you the way of salvation." Eventually, the apostle Paul turned to the woman possessed by an evil spirit and said, "I command you in the name of Jesus Christ to come out of her!" and immediately the demon was exorcised from her body (Acts 16:16-18).

The obvious question now arises as to why would evil spirits ever proclaim Jesus Christ as being the Son of God, when Satan and his demonic hordes do everything in their power to distort the truth about Jesus and His gospel? Simply put, it is because the serpent is craftier than all the beasts of the field, and the fox is the next craftiest beast in the field. When Satan is unable to hinder the good news of salvation, he will then do everything in his power to mix truth with error in order to convince men that it's all the same. It's all the same: witchcraft, divination, spiritism, Christianity, Hinduism, Buddhism, Islam, and even humanism--It's all the same! Plus, all paths lead to heaven, and all beliefs are equally valid. Satan often gets men to disobey God while at the same time getting them to proclaim God, thereby cleverly throwing everything into confusion and chaos.

Satan has a lie for everyone: stolen candy for the kiddies, illicit pleasures for the young, dishonest wealth for the middle aged, and corrupting power for the elders; but his greatest lies are aimed at those who are religious or political, by transforming his serpent features into angels of light. He manifests a different devil for every different level, but the serpent-fox, or man-devil, is the most dangerous deception of all; because "our struggle is not against flesh and blood, but against the rulers, against the powers, against the world forces of this darkness, against the spiritual forces of wickedness in the heavenly places" (Ephesians 6:12). Heavenly places can include high places in government, religion, as well as the spiritual realm.

However, the person who knows the truth about demons and about godless and cunning men will not be affected by their lies, any more than the apostle Paul was affected by the poisonous snake that bit him on the hand while he was gathering firewood (Acts 28:1-6). On the other hand, those who are in rebellion against God can be fatally poisoned by a serpent's bite just as surely as all those who were bitten by fiery serpents during the days of Moses (Numbers 21:6-9).

In short, a fox can be very clever and a snake can be very lethal, but a combination of the two brings their shrewdness to a whole new level. So it is really no accident when Christ mentioned both the fox and the demon in the same sentence when he said, "Go and tell Herod that *fox*, 'Behold, I cast out *demons. ...*'" Both the fox and the serpent epitomize deceitfulness and craftiness in ways that most people (including religious people) can never even begin to imagine.

The spiritual union of these two creatures cannot be outwitted except by the power and wisdom of God. Simply because a person proclaims Jesus as the Son of God, and the Bible as the Word of God, it means nothing if they are not committed to Christ and obedient to His Word. However, to those who are totally devoted to God's Son and faithful to His Word, the psalmist says, "[The] cobra, the young lion and the serpent you will trample down," and the apostle Paul says, "The God of peace will soon crush Satan under your feet" (Psalm 91:13; Romans 16:20). And when Christ returns and establishes His kingdom on Earth, Isaiah says: "The nursing child will play by the hole of the cobra, and the weaned child will put his hand on the viper's den. They will not hurt or destroy in all My holy mountain, for the earth will be full of the knowledge of the Lord as the waters cover the sea" (Isaiah 11:8-9).

The day is coming therefore, when both the deadly nature of the serpent and the cunning makeup of the fox will be divinely transformed into harmless and friendly creatures, like household pets. However, until that glorious day arrives, God's people (and everyone in general) should never underestimate the true nature of Satan and the coming antichrist. Because without divine wisdom, they are no match for the lethal cunning of the serpent-fox.

The Arrogant Fool and the Angry Bear

"Let a man meet a bear robbed of her cubs, rather than a fool in his folly" (Proverbs 17:12). This proverb is saying that it would be worse to be embroiled in a fool's actions than to confront an angry mother bear defending her cubs! Both literally and symbolically, the Bible references bears and fools. In Scripture, bears have profound spiritual significance as world powers and as instruments of divine judgment, as well as being creatures whose characteristics dramatically point to a number of penetrating spiritual realities.

Bears are unquestionably some of the most powerful animals on Earth. Hundreds of years ago (before lions were known in Europe) the bears were called the king of the beasts. Although they may appear to be slow-moving and lumbering animals, in actuality they have been known to reach speeds up to 35 mph for short distances (which is fast enough to outrun a thoroughbred race horse). Some polar bears amazingly have the stamina to swim nonstop for nearly 100 miles. Additionally, not all species of bears hibernate, but those that do—for as long as 4-6 months out of the year—their bodies virtually shut down while their metabolic activity provides for all their food needs. God has even given grizzly bears the instinct to wait until the onslaught of a blizzard before entering hibernation, in order to cover their tracks from any other creature knowing where it is hiding.[51]

Because bears are some of the most powerful and deadly creatures alive, the Bible manifests their unique characteristics when it comes to prophesy and judgment. As a matter of fact, the Scriptures describe God Himself as becoming like a raging bear when He stands up in judgment against His rebellious people and unrepentant mankind. Although a number of bears have been raised in captivity and even trained as circus performers and coached to be dancing entertainers, an angry bear is nothing short of terrifying and anything but amusing; and most definitely, neither is an angry God.

In chapters 9 and 13 of the book of Hosea, God said to His prophet:

> The days of punishment have come ... let Israel know this! The prophet is a fool, the inspired man is demented, because of the grossness of your iniquity, and because your hostility is so great. ... Even though they bear children. ... so I will be like a lion to them; like a leopard I will lie in wait by the wayside. I will encounter them like a bear robbed of her cubs, and I will tear open their chests; there I will also devour them like a lioness, as a wild beast would tear them. It is to your destruction, O Israel, that you are against Me, against your help. (9:7, 16; 13:7-9)

God told his prophet Amos that when He finally stands up in judgment against His defiant and rebellious people, there would be no escape from His divine justice. He said, "As when a man flees from a lion and a bear meets him, or goes home, leans his hand against the wall and a snake bites him. Will not the day of the Lord be darkness instead of light, even gloom with no brightness in it?" (Amos 5:19-20).

In addition, for 40 years the prophet Jeremiah warned God's people that if they did not repent of their sins, God would bring unimaginable destruction upon them; and even though Israel treated Jeremiah with utter contempt for all his warnings, the prophet nevertheless felt their anguish and affliction as if God had directed His anger at him personally: "I am the man who has seen affliction because of the rod of His wrath. ... He is to me like a bear lying in wait, like a lion in secret places. He has turned aside my ways and torn me to pieces; He has made me desolate" (Lamentations 3:1, 10-11).

Furthermore, when God's prophet Elisha had succeeded Elijah, a gang of young men began to ridicule Elisha with contempt. They knew that his godly companion had recently ascended to heaven in a whirlwind of fire, inside a chariot of fire, that was drawn by horses of fire, but instead of honoring and respecting God's remaining prophet, they insulted and mocked him, and in doing so they were insulting and mocking God as well. As a result, the Bible says, "[Elisha] cursed them in the name of the Lord. Then two female bears came out of the woods and tore up forty-two lads of their number" (2 Kings 2:23-24).

When Daniel had his prophetic vision of the future, he said he saw four beasts: a lion with wings (representing Babylon), a bear raised up on its side with rib bones in its mouth (symbolizing the armies of the Medes and the Persians), the leopard with four heads and the wings of a bird (denoting Alexander the Great and Greece), and then the coming fourth beast which will be even more "dreadful and terrifying and extremely strong" with "iron teeth," and (like a bear) will devour and crush and trample down its opponents with its feet (Daniel 7:5).

Lastly, the apostle John was given a similar vision of a composite beast, representing the coming global power, or world government: "And the beast which I saw was like a leopard, and his feet were like those of a bear, and his mouth like the mouth of a lion. And the dragon gave him his power and his throne and great authority" (Revelation 13:2).

People may view God as a meek and gentle lamb, but God uses the symbol of a bear when He stands up in judgment against a world that is absolutely at war with Him and His moral laws. Unfortunately, God's longsuffering and His merciful patience can be mistaken as a sign that He is indifferent to man's rebellion or He is asleep in regards to man's defiance towards Him. Well, a hibernating bear may appear to be harmless in its slumbering stupor, but if it is continually provoked from its resting place, its rage cannot be equaled. As Jeremiah predicts:

> The Lord will roar from on high and utter His voice from His holy habitation ... Against all the inhabitants of the earth. ... He is entering into judgment with all flesh; as for the wicked, He has

given them to the sword. ... Those slain by the Lord on that day will be from one end of the earth to the other. (Jeremiah 25:30-31, 33)

God may very well appear to be asleep in the heavens, but He is about to display the raw power of an angry bear when He arises to judge the world for all its wickedness. When Jesus Christ returns, His eyes are aflame with anger and burning with fiery indignation (see Revelation 19:1-16; Habakkuk 3:12; Isaiah 63:1-6). "The wrath of the Lamb" certainly appears to be more like a raging bear than a docile and adorable baby sheep, and it will be the fulfillment of Zechariah's warning when he wrote, "Be silent, all flesh, before the Lord; for He is aroused from His holy habitation" (Zechariah 2:13).

When foolish and arrogant men continue to provoke a forbearing and merciful God, they will truly discover what it means to "beware of the fury of a patient man." However, it is also interesting to know that when Christ does punish the world for its evil and "make[s] mortal man scarcer than pure gold," He will then rule and reign in peace and righteousness where "the wolf will dwell with the lamb. ... the cow and the bear will graze, their young will lie down together, and the lion will eat straw like the ox" (Isaiah 13:12; 11:6-7).

When Christ sets up His kingdom on Earth, even the fierce nature of bears will be changed into that of lambs, but not until the foolish rebellion of unrepentant sinners is eradicated by an angry God with the destructive force of an enraged bear.

The Glory Has Departed

For all our days have declined in [God's] fury; we have finished our years like a sigh. As for the days of our life, they contain seventy years, or if due to strength, eighty years, yet [the best of man's years] is but labor and sorrow; for soon it is gone and we fly away [or depart from this world]. (Psalm 90:9-10)

Perhaps the greatest figure in the Old Testament was the lawgiver, Moses. He wrote the first five books of the Bible and thereby laid the groundwork for both Judaism and Christianity. He also has become an important figure in Islam, Baha'ism, and a number of other faiths as well. He is mentioned almost 900 times in Scripture, and his writings have been studied by religious intellectuals for thousands of years. However, most people are not aware of the fact that his sacred text also includes the 90th psalm (at least that is what most scholars believe). It is within the verses of Psalm 90 that God's eternal state is contrasted by man's fleeting existence in this world. Moses emphasizes how men quickly flourish and then just as quickly, wither and fade away. Man not only returns back to dust, but his rapidly aging body begins to lose its glorious strength and appearance until, finally, the glory of youth has completely departed.

For centuries, mankind has searched in vain for the fountain of youth—that fabled spring whose waters were supposed to restore one's health and youthful vigor. It was sought in the Bahamas and in Florida by Ponce de León and Narváez, as well as De Soto and other explorers. The search goes on today in the form of researchers, scientists, doctors, and health gurus who continue to desperately seek out this elusive fountain of youth, but all of their efforts have proven to be in vain. Throughout the ages, quacks, charlatans, and con artists galore have tried to advertise and pedal fictitious snake oils and worthless remedies to gullible people desperately wanting to stay young or to retrieve their vigorous

310

youthfulness. However, neither science nor medicines, nor bogus nostrums nor scam artists can keep the glory of one's prime and the splendor of one's vitality from departing from their anatomy like a fleeting vapor.

There is a word which means "the glory has departed," and according to the Bible, that word is "Ichabod." It was the Hebrew name given by a woman dying in childbirth to her newborn son when she learned that Israel's enemies had stolen the ark of God, and that both her husband and her father-in-law died from God's judgment, and that the Philistines had defeated her people in battle. Consequently, her dying words were to name her infant son Ichabod, because she said the glory of Israel had departed (see 1 Samuel 4).

Perhaps this is why the fictional character and protagonist in Washington Irving's short story titled "The Legend of Sleepy Hollow" was named Ichabod. Irving's folklore was published in 1820, and the story took place during the American Revolutionary War. The horseman in Irving's legend was Hessian, an English artilleryman who was killed during the Battle of White Plains in 1776. He was decapitated by an American cannonball and the shattered remains of his head were left on the battlefield while his comrades hastily carried his body away and eventually buried it in the cemetery of the Old Dutch Churchyard of Sleepy Hollow in New York. Subsequently, every Halloween night, Hessian would rise from the grave as a vengeful ghost furiously seeking his lost head while riding on his hellish horse.

In Irving's narrative, Ichabod Crane is a schoolteacher from Connecticut who comes to Sleepy Hollow to make his living as a Schoolmaster. He falls in love with one of his students named Katrina, but his hapless affections for her are jinxed by a bullying prankster and rival named "Brom Bones" Van Brunt. Eventually, Ichabod is invited to Katrina's home for a Halloween party, but leaves dejected and crestfallen as Katrina disappoints him. He finds the path home dark and eerily quiet, and as he passes an alleged haunted tree, he sees a large dark figure with no head beginning to pursue him. Ichabod soon realizes the figure is carrying his own head in his lap, and Ichabod desperately tries to get his decrepit horse to run home as fast as it can, but he is not a skilled rider and his horse resists. Both Ichabod and the headless horseman end up by the church graveyard where Crane races on his horse to the bridge where the ghost is said to have disappeared, but not before hurling his detached head at him and knocking him off his horse.

Ichabod is never seen or heard from again, in spite of a search party finding hoof prints, Ichabod's hat, and a smashed pumpkin next to it. This leaves the townspeople to wonder if the headless horseman actually got the better of Ichabod Crane, or if Brom Bones actually pulled off one of the greatest pranks of all time.

Although this story is merely a fanciful tale, the ghost of the headless horseman lives on in the terrorizing rider of death. Likewise, mankind never seems to stop running from the ghostly specter of aging and from the cold-blooded Grim Reaper on his ashen colored horse of death and dying (Revelation 6:8). Every new wrinkle, gray hair, excess pound, ache and pain, and loss of memory and mobility are constant reminders of just how fast the Grim Reaper, or the rider of death, is pursuing us. With each passing day and week and month and year, it seems like the ghastly horseman is gaining on us; and once the years begin to turn into decades, the glory of youth truly begins to depart— leaving the elderly wondering, *"What has happened to me? Where did my life go? At what point did my appearance so radically change? How did I become so old and feeble? What happened to my beautiful hair, my pretty face, my slender body, my graceful walk, my shapely form, my charming smile, my dazzling teeth, my excellent hearing, my speed, my agility, my boundless energy? What? Where? When? How? Why?"* As Job said,

> Now my days are swifter than a runner; they flee away, they see no good. They slip by like reed boats, like an eagle that swoops on its prey. ... Man, who is born of woman, is short-lived and full of turmoil. Like a flower he comes forth and withers.

He also flees like a shadow and does not remain. ...
But man dies and lies prostrate. Man expires, and
where is he? ... he departs; You change his
appearance and send him away (Job 9:25-26; 14:1-2,
10, 20).

Psalm 103 says, "As for man, his days are like grass; as a flower
of the field, so he flourishes. When the wind has passed over it, it
is no more, and its place acknowledges it no longer (vv. 15-16). Furthermore, the prophet Isaiah said, "All flesh is grass, and all its
loveliness is like the flower of the field. The grass withers, the
flower fades, when the breath of the Lord blows upon it; surely the
people are grass" (Isaiah 40:6-7).

Let's face it, there is no fountain of youth or miraculous pill
that can stop the glory from departing or that can change the name
of Ichabod. However, Jesus Christ did unlock the secret of eternal
youth when He said of anyone who believes and obeys Him,

"My sheep hear My voice, and I know them, and
they follow Me; and I give eternal life to them, and
they will never perish; and no one [including death]
will snatch them out of My hand. ... I am the resurrection and the life; he who believes in Me will live
even if he dies, and everyone who lives and
believes in Me will never die" (John 10:27-28;
11:25-26).

Jesus also declared, "He who has found his life [or his glory in
this world] will lose it, and he who has lost his life for My sake will
find it" (Matthew 10:39).

The apostle Paul said that all those who put their trust in
Christ will someday be resurrected with immortal and
imperishable bodies. He concludes this glorious thought by
saying, "Therefore, my beloved brethren, be steadfast, immovable,
always abounding in the work of the Lord, knowing that your toil
is not in vain in the Lord" (1 Corinthians 15:58).

If we live long enough in this world, there will surely come a day when our reflection in the mirror will say to us, "The glory has departed," and we do not need to change our name to Ichabod to attest to it. However, neither the headless horseman nor the rider of death can overtake the glorious, immortal, and imperishable resurrected bodies of all those who have put their trust in the One who is life itself—the One whose glory will never depart and in whom the glory of all those who believe in Him will never fade or disappear.

References

A Tale Told by an Idiot
1. Lendrem, Ben Alexander Daniel, et al. "The Darwin Awards: Sex Differences in Idiotic Behaviour." *British Medical Journal* 349 (2014): g7094.

The Headless Wonder
2. "World Health Statistics 2016: Monitoring health for the SDGs Annex B: tables of health statistics by country, WHO region and globally". *World Health Organization.* 2016. Retrieved 27 June 2016.

"The Big One" Has Two Brothers
3. United States. US Department of the Interior. US Geological Survey. *Earthquake Information for the 1900's.* USGS Earthquake Hazards Program, 30 Sept. 2012. Web. 17 Aug. 2016.
4. Ibid.
5. Lindsey, Hal. *Apocalypse Code.* Palos Verdes, CA: Western Front, 1997. 296. Print.

Back to the Future
6. Jeffrey, Grant R. "Prophetic Time Indications." *Armageddon: Appointment with Destiny.* Toronto, Ont.: Frontier Research Publications, 1997. Print.
7. Toynbee, Arnold, and Jane Caplan. *A Study of History.* New York: Barnes & Noble, 1995. Print.

The Death of Time
8. Sagan, Carl. *Cosmos.* New York: Ballantine, 2013. 4. Print.
9. Sagan, Carl. *The Cosmic Connection.* New York: Anchor Press, 1973. 52. Print.
10. Sagan, Carl. *Cosmos.* New York: Ballantine, 2013. 27. Print.
11. Ibid., 282.
12. Oesch, P. A., et al. "A Remarkably Luminous Galaxy at z=11.1 Measured with Hubble Space Telescope Grism Spectroscopy." *The Astrophysical Journal* 819.2 (2016): 129.

The Sons of Pinocchio
13. Osmols, Dominika. "When Children Lie They Are Simply Reaching a Developmental Milestone." *EmaxHealth.* N.p., 09 Aug. 2011. Web. 17 Aug. 2016.

14. Feldman, Robert S. et al. "Self-Presentation and Verbal Deception: Do Self-Presenters Lie More?" *Journal of Basic and Applied Social Psychology*, Vol. 24, No. 2 (2002): 170

15. Komet, Allison. "The Truth About Lying." *Psychology Today*. N.p., 1 May 1997. Web. 17 Aug. 2016.

16. Harden, Seth. "Lying Statistics." *Statistic Brain*. N.p., 30 June 2015. Web. 17 Aug. 2016.

Cannibalism is Merely a Matter of Taste

17. Schaeffer, Francis. *How Shall We Then Live?* Old Tappan NJ: Fleming H Revell Company, 1976. 224. Print.

18. Courtois, Stéphane, and Mark Kramer. *The Black Book of Communism: Crimes, Terror, Repression*. Cambridge, MA: Harvard UP, 1999. 4. Print.

19. White, Matthew. "Aztec Human Sacrifice." *The Great Big Book of Horrible Things: The Definitive Chronicle of History's 100 Worst Atrocities*. New York: W.W. Norton, 2012. 157. Print.

20. Ibid.

21. Ibid.

22. Hoffman, Carl. "What Really Happened to Michael Rockefeller." *Smithsonian* Mar. 2014: 36. Print.

Witch Doctors and Snake Oil

23. Jacobs, AJ. "Modern Problems: "My Doctor Tells Me I Should Get a Colonoscopy. Is This Really Necessary?"" *Mental Floss*. N.p., 24 May 2014. Web. 18 Aug. 2016.

24. Ibid.

25. Ibid.

The Father of Despair

26. Frankl, Viktor E. Man's Search for Meaning. Boston: Beacon, 2006. 101. Print.

27. Keating, Dan, and Lenny Bernstein. "U.S. Suicide Rate Has Risen Sharply in the 21st Century." *Washington Post*. The Washington Post, 22 Apr. 2016. Web. 18 Aug. 2016.

28. Fox, Maggie. "Military Suicides: Most Attempts Come Before Soldiers Ever See Combat." *NBC News*. 25 May 2016. Web. 18 Aug. 2016.

29. "More Americans Committing Suicide than During the Great Depression."*Washingtons Blog*. N.p., 17 May 2013. Web. 18 Aug. 2016.

Legion of the Expendables

30. "How Quickly Do Different Cells in the Body Replace Themselves?" *Cell Biology by the Numbers Footer Comments*. N.p., n.d. Web. 18 Aug. 2016.

31. Bianconi, Eva, et al. "An Estimation of the Number of Cells in the Human Body." *Annals of Human Biology* 40.6 (2013): 463-71. Web.

The Curse of the God Gene

32. "Geneticist Claims to Have Found 'God Gene' in Humans." *Washington Times*. The Washington Times, 14 Nov. 2004. Web. 18 Aug. 2016.

The Godless Church

33. Neuhaus, Cable. "And Now Let Us Stray." *Saturday Evening Post* Jan.-Feb. 2015: 14. Print.

The Bigot Bomb

34. Mao, Zedong. "Problems of War and Strategy." *Selected Works of Mao Zedong*. Vol. 2. Peking: Foreign Languages, 1967. 224. Print.

Murder Has Changed Its Name

35. Orwell, George. *1984*. Milano: Mondadori, 1984. 14. Print.

The Ghosts of Winchester

36. Taylor, Troy. "The Winchester Mystery House." *Prairie Ghosts*. Apartment #42 Productions, 2013. Web. 20 Aug. 2016.

The Wheel Has Come Full Circle

37. "Baby Boomer Generation Fast Facts." *CNN*. Cable News Network, 24 Aug. 2015. Web. 20 Aug. 2016.

38. "Abortion Statistics US Data and Trends." *National Right to Life*. National Right to Life Education Foundation, 2014. Web.

The Lunar Lunacy Effect

39. Arkowitz, Hal, and Scott O. Lilienfeld. "Lunacy and the Full Moon." *Scientific American*. N.p., 1 Feb. 2009. Web. 20 Aug. 2016.

40. Ibid.

If it's Free, it's for Me!
41. Babrius, Caius Julius, Phèdre, and Ben Edwin Perry. *Babrius and Phaedrus: A Survey of Aesop's Fables*. London: W. Heinemann, 1965. Print.

The Collapse of a Star
42. Kazan, Casey. "Thirty Supernovas per Second in the Observable Universe! Is the Red Giant Betelgeuse Next?" *The Daily Galaxy*. 12 May 2011. Web. 20 Aug. 2016.

It's Déjà Vu All Over Again
43. "It's Déjà Vu All Over Again." Quote Investigator. N.p., 8 Oct. 2013. Web. 20 Aug. 2016.
44. Urban, Tim. "The Death Toll Comparison Breakdown." *Wait But Why*. 05 Aug. 2013. Web. 20 Aug. 2016.

Eaters of the Dead
45. Royte, Elizabeth. "Bloody Good." *National Geographic* Jan. 2016: 70-97. Print.

The Big Cover-up
46. "Getting Away with Murder." *The Economist*. The Economist Newspaper, 04 July 2015. Web. 20 Aug. 2016.

Ship of Fools
47. Fuller, R. Buckminster. *Operating Manual for Spaceship Earth*. Carbondale: Southern Illinois UP, 1969. Print.

The Cunning Serpent-fox
48. "Red Fox - Facts, Diet & Habitat Information." *Animal Corner*. 2003. Web. 20 Aug. 2016.
49. "Snakes: Facts." *(Science Trek: Idaho Public Television)*. N.p., n.d. Web. 20 Aug. 2016
50. "Snakes Do Eat Dust." *Creation Ex Nihilo* 10.4 (1988): Print.

The Arrogant Fool and the Angry Bear
51. Shormann, David. "The Grizzly Adventure Part 6." *Studying His Word and His Works*. 20 Mar. 2011. Web. 20 Aug. 2016.

Other published writings of John Hunt:

"Hopscotching to Hell, Sleepwalking to Heaven"
ISBN: 978-1-304-56814-4

NOTES

NOTES

NOTES